# What Others Say About Their Facebook Results

"Aw, the whole thing makes my head hurt. But other than puffery about 600-million customers, Perry's an honest man in a field rife with charlatans. If anybody can make practical sense of Facebook for marketers, it's Perry. He has his finger on its truth—as advertising media not social media. He also realizes there is a short window of time during which it offers the greatest opportunity. He identified this with Google Ads [formerly Google AdWords]. Now this book shows how to capitalize on ideal timing with this media. Finally, he is a well-disciplined direct-response practitioner who holds this accountable for ROI. I bestow my 'No B.S. blessing.'"

—Dan S. Kennedy, legendary direct marketing advisor and author of the NO B.S. book series, www.NoBSBooks.com

"*Ultimate Guide to Facebook Advertising* just might be your ultimate guide to earning a ton of money with this social media phenomenon. What you don't know about Facebook could hurt you and what you will learn about Facebook from this book definitely will help you. It's a fun and easy read and a surefire way to seriously increase your income."

—[The late] Jay Conrad Levinson, The Father of Guerrilla Marketing, author of *Guerrilla Marketing* series of books—over 21 million sold; now in 62 languages

"The coverage is comprehensive; if ever there were questions about whether 'Like' campaigns work, creating a solid offer, using video ads, targeting specific audiences, analyzing campaigns, or understanding the 'Facebook Pixel' (a piece of code), this outsized handbook has the answers. And if that isn't enough, Marshall offers free access to tools, videos, and case studies on his website. . . . Exhaustive in scope, expertly presented, and authoritatively written."

—Kirkus Reviews

"Bob Regnerus was challenged to find targeted customers for Bolder Bands and help us tell our story on Facebook. The results, quite frankly, are almost too good to be true. It was beyond our belief. With Bob's work over a short period, we achieved a level of sales that we could only dream of and now have an established fan base that quickly grew to 350K. With over 45,000 customers (and growing) we went from startup to a legit business inside of a year."

—Amy and JD Crouse, Bolder Bands


"I decided I had enough of trying to figure out Facebook, Google, and everything else besides trying to run my store during the hectic holiday rush. After hiring Bob Regnerus we saw increased sales by 16.3 percent over the previous holiday season spending the same amount on ads as before. Bob has proven to be much more than 'my Facebook guy.' He's provided me sage advice, sound critique, and expert opinions on many matters that affect the performance of my store and it's future."

—Sander Cohen, Dharmashop.com


"Bob Regnerus provides a level of wisdom and levelheadedness to any business owner's situation. Bob is able to calm the storm and deliver sound, grounded advice and direction. Think of a business owner who is in the throes of a violent storm—Bob is the voice on the radio guiding them to waters that makes the boat sail and not sink.

"Bob brings the experience of 'been there done that' in a very crowded market. What he brings is seasoning that is only gained through highs and lows of being an entrepreneur."

—Brandon Boyd, cofounder Feedstories.com


"I have known Bob Regnerus professionally for more than 15 years.

"Bob is a master consultant. He knows how to define the problem simply, he is 100 percent reliable, and he is a true professional in an industry that is filled with people who lack experience and professionalism. He makes everything easy and inspires confidence."

—Debbie Phillips Women on Fire

"I wholeheartedly recommend that you work with Bob Regnerus. If you want to dabble, you're gonna lose a lot of time and you're gonna lose a lot of money and you're gonna lose windows of opportunity. But if you want to get that unique combination of business insight as well as the videography then you can get really quick results."

—Les Cseh, President, Ally Financial Services

"I came to Bob for help injecting life into our Facebook Advertising Funnel. We had hit a plateau and response rates were dropping. I knew enough to be 'dangerous' and had tried a lot of things. Frankly, I needed to spend less time figuring this all out and more time focusing on my marketing and sales process. Having known Bob for years, I didn't hesitate to reach out and hand him the reigns. Within a week, we saw a huge surge in response after Bob tweaked our creative, honed our targeting, and implemented some innovative strategies to better connect with our prospects."

—Nate Hagerty, TaxProMarketer.com

"I was VERY skeptical about how well Facebook Ads would work for our food company. I approached Bob Regnerus with the challenge of finding these leads on Facebook. Our potential clients are located in select cities, and we limit our advertising to tightly selected ZIP codes. We also place restrictions on the type of leads we'll accept, so that made the challenge rather difficult.

"Through the seven years we've been working together, we're not only handing a record number of leads over to our sales teams, we're shattering sales records! All I can say is Bob delivers, and he works hard to both set a realistic expectation and deliver a result that makes us delighted."

—Mike Cohen, Blue Ribbon Foods

"With what I learned from Bob Regnerus, my client made another $10,000 today from my Facebook Ads. This is a new client, and in the first 26 days of working together I've helped him generate leads through Facebook that have turned into $25,000 with $4,000 in ad spend. Thanks Bob for helping me understand Deep Funnel Marketing on Facebook and how it helps clients make big-ticket sales!"

—Sam Bart, Online Agency Founder, Philadelphia Pennsylvania

"Perry Marshall has done more to de-mystify Google Ads [formerly Google AdWords] for business owners than any person on earth. With this book, he's done the same for Facebook. If you want to cut through the smoke quickly and make money advertising on Facebook, this is the book to read."

—Ken McCarthy, The System Seminar, Tivoli NY

"The irony of living in the Information Age is that good info has gotten harder to come by. The lame stuff still manages to clog the pipes, causing chaos and preventing you from discovering the legit specifics that can actually help you in your quest for business success and a bigger bottom line. Perry Marshall has been a first-stop, one-stop resource for the best possible advice on making Ads [formerly AdWords] work since Google unleashed it on the marketing community . . . and now, Perry's new tome on Facebook's astonishing (and yet-to-be-fully-tapped) power to reach gazillions of targeted, eager prospects (most of whom you'd never even know existed, otherwise) is the first and probably the only book you need to be one of those early adopters who score fastest. Perry's books are always essential. This one is perhaps more so than usual."

—John Carlton, the most respected and ripped-off
veteran copywriter on the web

"Perry Marshall led the pack with Google AdWords [now Google Ads] back in 2006. He's still leading the pack today with *Ultimate Guide to Facebook Advertising*. Perry, Bob Regnerus, Tom Meloche, and Mark Ingles combine insider knowledge of marketing on Facebook with proven marketing fundamentals for a powerful one-two punch that delivers results. Perry doesn't just theorize about how Facebook marketing works, he does it himself, and he's worked with thousands of others to hone his knowledge of this emerging landscape. If you're thinking of marketing on Facebook, or if you're already doing it, you'd be crazy to not get the *Ultimate Guide to Facebook Advertising*."

—Clate Mask, president, InfusionSoft

"Perry Marshall is a terrific writer who makes wonderful use of stories and analogies to illustrate a concept. He does this exceptionally well in the chapter on ad copy writing, 'The Power of Hidden Psychological Triggers.' That chapter alone is worth the price of this book.

"Many companies have tried Facebook ads and failed for one simple reason: they treated Facebook advertising like search advertising.

"Facebook is social advertising. Social advertising is about understanding and reaching the user. Not the user's behavior; but the actual person. This is where the book shines. It walks you through strategies of reaching your target audience based upon the person's social profile so that you aren't just accumulating 'Likes,' but actually gaining new customers.

"I'd recommend this book to anyone who is advertising, or wants to advertise, on Facebook. Social advertising is unique from most other types of advertising, and this book will teach you the concepts and how-tos you must understand so that your Facebook ads increase your overall profits."

—Brad Geddes, author of *Advanced Google AdWords*

"One of the things I love about Perry is that he always shoots from the hip. *Ultimate Guide to Facebook Advertising* is written with no holds barred, which means that all the 'juicy' tips that might get left out of other, similar books are all in this book. It's more than just a tactical 'how to.' It goes into the psychological aspects of ad writing specifically suited for Facebook and gives all kinds of practical advice for fan pages. So for anyone who really wants to get serious about Facebook advertising, this book is definitely a must read."

—Shelley Ellis, contextual advertising expert, www.ContentNetworkInsider.com

"Hands down, I have never seen a more comprehensive in-depth study of successful Facebook advertising than what you are holding in your hands. Perry and Bob have done it again, they've extracted the 'gold' within this amazing system of advertising that every astute marketer should devour and implement."

—Ari Galper, founder and CEO, Unlock The Game, www.UnlockTheGame.com

"Perry and Bob not only understand every nuance of the technical aspects of getting Facebook ads to work for your business, they also understand the psychology behind what works and what doesn't when it comes to advertising online. If you're looking for an über-effective way to master the art of driving traffic to your offers through paid advertising, get this book—it truly is the ultimate guide!"

—Mari Smith, co-author of *Facebook Marketing: An Hour a Day*

"Facebook advertising appears simple, but it's trickier than search engine marketing. In this book, Perry Marshall, Bob Regnerus, Tom Meloche, and Mark Ingles teach you the secret of 'Right Angle Marketing'—selling based on who people are and what they identify with. This is entirely different from Yahoo! or Google. They help you determine how to prioritize Facebook within your particular marketing mix. Then they take you by the hand and lead you through the minefield, showing you the tools, bidding techniques, and sales cycles of Facebook ads. Without their help, the odds are stacked against you. With their help, your chances of success are excellent."

—Alex Mandossian, Heritage House Publishing, author of *The Business Podcasting Bible*

"Perry Marshall is amazing! He reinvented himself from engineer to white paper expert to become the world's leading expert in Google Adwords [now Google Ads]. Now with his secret weapons, Bob Regnerus, Tom Meloche, and Mark Ingles, he's reinvented himself again, this time as the guru in Facebook advertising . . . through which, he points out, you can access 600 million customers in ten minutes."

—Bob Bly, author of over 60 books including *Complete Idiot's Guide to Direct Marketing*, *The Online Copywriter's Handbook*, and *Public Relations Kit for Dummies*

**Entrepreneur**
MAGAZINE'S

# ULTIMATE
# GUIDE TO

# facebook
## ADVERTISING
### Fourth Edition

- Access more than a billion potential customers in 10 minutes
- Leverage the latest game-changers to **pinpoint your most profitable audiences**
- Master strategies and techniques of successful Facebook advertisers

## PERRY MARSHALL  BOB REGNERUS  THOMAS MELOCHE
### WITH MARK INGLES

Entrepreneur Press®

Entrepreneur Press, Publisher
Cover Design: Andrew Welyczko
Production and Composition: Eliot House Productions

This publication is designed to provide accurate and authoritative information in regard to the
subject matter covered. It is sold with the understanding that the publisher is not engaged in
rendering legal, accounting, or other professional services. If legal advice or other expert assistance is
required, the services of a competent professional person should be sought.

Entrepreneur Press® is a registered trademark of Entrepreneur Media, Inc.

**Library of Congress Cataloging-in-Publication Data**

An application to register this book for cataloging has been submitted to the Library of Congress.

ISBN 978-1-59918-675-7 (paperback) | ISBN 978-1-61308-431-1 (ebook)

Printed in the United States of America

25  24  23  22  21                                                    10 9 8 7 6 5 4 3 2 1

# Contents

CHAPTER 24
## The Product Launch Formula and Facebook

CHAPTER 25
## Choosing the Best Facebook Funnel for You

CHAPTER 26
## Boosting Posts and Unicorns Guest Author Dennis Yu . . . . . . . . . . . . . . **335**

CHAPTER 27
## Keeping Track of Your Money and Results. . . . . . . . . . . . . . . . . . . . **343**

# Facebook Still Owns Planet Earth

People are walking down the street, banging into light poles because their faces are buried in Facebook. Therein lies your opportunity.

The most precious commodity in the world is attention. Everyone likes to be in the spotlight, and social media has given everyday people the opportunity to become "internet famous." Facebook is monopolizing it and chomping at it like a hungry beast. The average American spends five hours per day on their smartphone and over 60 minutes on Facebook, according to a study by Provision Living. Wherever you are right now, look up and someone around you is probably on Facebook.

This book is about how to get in front of those people, convince them to open their wallets, and then dominate markets because you're better at this game than all your competitors.

But be warned that Facebook Ads are a serious game. It's a blood sport—not something you just casually dabble in. If you get really good at it, it's a $1,000-per-hour skill. It gives you the ability to move mountains and nations. You can literally create cultures and movements at will.

But if you're just going to goof around with it and create some basic ads or try a few experiments—forget it. Go waste your money some other way because 90 percent of advertisers merely dabble with it and then their Facebook Ads amount to nothing more than an expensive tax write-off.

If you're going to take this game seriously, then you bought the right book. And you should also avail yourself of the online supplement at www.PerryMarshall.com/fbtools. Go there right now and download the goodies.

## IS FACEBOOK GOOD OR BAD?

I do not think it is a good thing that a billion people are spending this much time on Facebook. I didn't think it was a good thing when the same number of people were watching TV for five hours a day, either.

But nobody asked me. And they didn't ask you. That's just what people do.

If you're going to be successful as a marketer or entrepreneur, you must choose to live in the "is" world—not the "should be" world. In the "is" world, 95 percent of people float around in a miasma of mild hypnosis, looking forward to their next hit of "like" and "share" happy juice, or to extract their "pound of flesh" out of some stranger who disagrees with them about politics.

This book is all about how you get inside the minds of Facebook users and get them to do what **you** want them to do. Whether you're doing business as a church, a school, a winery, a life coach, a car manufacturer, or a seller of aluminum siding, you've got a job to do.

People are going to spend their time and money somewhere. If they spend their time and money with you, you succeed. If they spend it with someone else, you fail. The fact that people are in a state of partial hypnosis provides a platform where you can sell them your product or service. In this book, you'll learn how to harness that power.

### Working vs. Playing

Now, the very first thing you have to do is get real with yourself and realize that for you, playing around on social media is NOT the same as RUNNING social media or CONTROLLING social media—pulling the puppet strings of the world.

Millions of people quit their jobs to start a business. They're essentially being supported by their spouses. They go to work every day, and while they are changing bedpans at the hospital, they think their spouse is working when, in fact, they are just goofing off on Facebook all day. Doing stuff that sort of kind of looks like work.

And making zero money.

That person is like the chef who, instead of cooking, just stands in the kitchen and shovels food in their mouth all day.

Well, this is a book about making money on Facebook—not screwing around on Facebook. Facebook Ads is a serious endeavor. It's a profession. You will get nowhere with those bad habits. You either pull the strings of the Matrix from outside the Matrix, or you're in the Matrix being entertained by the Matrix. You can't do both.

I deleted the standard Facebook app from my phone. I hardly ever use Facebook. When I do use Facebook, I use the phone browser instead of the app. I never log into Facebook as a standard user until after 5:30 p.m. Most days I don't log in at all. But on the very same day, I may spend hours in the Facebook Interface and Facebook Advertising App being the chef and pulling the strings of the Matrix.

Never confuse activity with productivity. The two are not the same.

As a Facebook Advertiser, you are tasked with injecting creativity into the system, then measuring and tracking the results. You use your tracking tools—not checking out Facebook notifications every two seconds. Pay careful attention to what works and what doesn't. Notice trends, not stuff. Accept your job, which is to influence the hypnotized masses who are coming to Facebook for their entertainment addiction.

You are not the person who comes to the restaurant and feeds their face for five hours. You work in the restaurant. You serve up great dishes. You only sample enough of the soup to know whether it tastes good or bad; then you go on and create more great cuisine.

Sorry if this sounds preachy. But I have many customers and clients whose productivity, sales, profits, and income absolutely skyrocketed after they:

- deleted the Facebook app from their phone (along with Twitter, LinkedIn, and others).
- realized that the world is in an incessant, never-ending conspiracy to rob you of time, attention, creativity, and mental space.
- closed the Facebook tab in their browser.
- entirely stopped using Facebook in the usual fashion during work hours.
- blocked all email notifications from Facebook and other social media.
- halted ALL smartphone notifications from all social media apps—no banners on the screen, no little red numbers on your app icons, no distractions.

Go on. Do all of the above—now! If you don't, it will be devilishly difficult to master the key concepts in this book. Instead, Facebook will master you.

Facebook has taken over the world. It is the aquarium that lots of people live in. Facebook is your portal to influencing the world—their behavior, their opinions, their purchases, their relationships. You need to pull the levers without letting Facebook addiction take control of you. Facebook knows what its members look like, think, enjoy, and visit because it is the world's largest:

- Photo and video-sharing site
- Thought-sharing site
- Liking site
- Linking site
- Demographic and psychographic gathering engine

Even with Google's gargantuan lead, Facebook will possibly become the world's largest advertising site, especially as the internet continues its trajectory toward easy mobile device access.

## FACEBOOK HAS REDEFINED ADVERTISING FOR 21ST CENTURY USERS

The majority of internet users access it via smartphones and tablets. This is bad news for all the old-school internet companies, but it's good news for Facebook. Why?

Because Facebook was the FIRST company to put full-screen display ads in front of mobile phone users and get away with it on a daily basis. They have trained their users to accept this.

Nearly all other online ads are either in apps or tiny, inconsequential banner ads. Facebook puts display ads and videos right in the middle of the News Feed that are seen dozens of times every day. People actually share Facebook Ads (and good ads will get shared thousands of times)! Plus, in many situations, those ads don't really seem like ads. Above the ad, the post may say, "Suzy Smith likes ACME corporation" so the ad has an implied endorsement. This works on a massive scale.

You can upload your customer's phone numbers or email list to Facebook and Facebook will probably recognize about half of them. You can ask Facebook to target two million people who are in your target audience and Facebook can do that in an instant because of all the data it has already collected based on the users' patterns on the platform.

As exciting as all of this is, it is important for advertisers to remember that Facebook did not build the site for advertisers. They built it for regular users and for themselves.

The talented young college grads Facebook hires from the world's top universities don't say, "I want to work at Facebook to help them maximize ad revenue." Please know that even despite Facebook's massive gains in the ad department, the company doesn't exist simply to send you customers.

Regardless of why Zuckerberg built Facebook or what ideals his staffers may hold, the personal demographic information Facebook collects is tremendously valuable to advertisers.

Facebook is not stupid. It is more closely connected with its advertisers than any other platform on the planet. Facebook visionaries already have years' worth of additional ideas to implement. How do we know this? We see the ideas publicly volunteered every day on Facebook Pages by Facebook Advertisers.

Facebook knows more about you than your husband or wife. They know what sites you visit; they know a great deal of what you buy; and they have bought data from all kinds of other companies and appended it to their database so they know what you respond to. Facebook even has suicide prevention tools, and its A.I. (artificial intelligence) may detect depression way before doctors or parents. They know the one million other people in the world who are most like you, like the same things you like, and buy the same things you buy.

Adult supervision on Facebook is minimal, which is probably why it is so absolutely brilliant. The company aggressively hires fresh college graduates—the brightest college grads on the planet. These are the smart kids—smarter than you, smarter than us. Some have never had a "real" job outside of Facebook. They have never tried to live off revenue generated by an ad. They do not feel your pain.

Remember that. It is really important.

To use Facebook's paid advertising tools effectively, it is important to understand just how much its creators and designers are not really trying to help you. Fortunately, they do need cash, and we do need clicks, so we can get some great work done together. We focus on the clicks and they focus on connecting the world.

Facebook has the potential to be highly relevant for decades to come. Our rule of thumb is the founder's rule: When you have a dynamic and visionary founder running a business, better to bet on that business continuing to be a success for as long as you see that founder at the helm.

We suggest that as long as you see Mark Zuckerberg engaged at Facebook, you should plan on Facebook being a dynamic and growing, competitive place to advertise.

Oh, Mark was born in 1984.

He will probably be around for a long, long time.

1984? It turns out that *Little Brother* is the one who's watching you.

## One Tool to Rule Them All

*One Tool to rule them all,*
*One Tool to find them,*
*One Tool to bring them all,*
*And in the Facebook bind them.*

This poem should haunt Google (I do know for a fact that Google is scared to death of Facebook). We wrote it as a bit of a taunt in the first edition of this book back in 2011 because so many people were predicting Facebook's early demise. We predicted the opposite and were proved right. Facebook has indeed created one tool to bind the entire world together and Facebook, not Google, is in charge. Facebook currently reports that two billion people connect on the site every month. Two billion! Say that number a few times and let it sink in.

But wait, there's more!

Facebook acquired WhatsApp for $16 billion in 2014. WhatsApp now has over 1.6 billion monthly active users, making it the most popular messaging app of all time. Facebook also acquired Instagram, which now has 1 billion active monthly users. In addition, Facebook has communities on Messenger and Oculus. Facebook Advertising tools are your gateway to all of these communities and more.

Facebook isn't sitting still. If you look closely, you can see their hopes for the future. Facebook has acquired a whole series of smaller technical companies like these, acquiring technology for fitness tracking, speech and facial recognition, computer vision, augmented reality, video compression, and machine learning. And some people thought Snapchat had a chance!

The Facebook universe will continue to grow larger, more prevalent, and more powerful for years to come. One tool to rule them all, and in the Facebook bind them.

For example, smartphone Facebook users are usually continually logged in. As of the holiday season of 2019, Facebook reported mobile advertising was 93 percent of their total advertising revenue. This is no big surprise as mobile users are connected to Facebook nearly 24/7. Facebook on the phone is the only way to reach some of your customers. Plus, you can find customers you would never have imagined, such as visitors from another state currently traveling through your city within ten miles of your business. You reach them without even knowing it with a, "Come in for a special 30 percent discount!" ad.

Facebook users now check into your business when they visit you, without you even asking them to do so. No more pathetic "please like me" signs. Mobile makes it easy. When users check into your business, they automatically announce to their friends where they are and what they are doing. Friday nights in the big city need never be lonely again.

But wait, there's even more!

Facebook is supporting their community in big ways. They've made it simple to livestream video with Facebook Live, creating a whole new media form. Websites and apps can leverage Facebook's login. This is amazingly powerful now that so many users never log out of Facebook. Capture your customer's attention with live video, collect critical contact information, and get them to call you, register for events, and even donate to you fast and easy. Literally, it's all at the touch of a button.

One tool to rule them all, and in the Facebook bind them.

## YOUR MISSION, SHOULD YOU CHOOSE TO ACCEPT IT

So, what do you do with all of this information about Facebook? Simple. Your mission is to buy a click for $1, turn it into $2, and then make more profit than your competitors do from your $2. This is your mission and it has moved to Facebook. It is a new platform, but a very old mission.

The rest is just strategy and tactics. Many existing strategies and tactics that we have taught to over 100,000 Google advertisers work directly in Facebook. For more info see: *Ultimate Guide to Google Ads 6th Edition* (Entrepreneur Press, November 2020). For example, you need to understand your sales funnel, craft a compelling ad, have a focused goal for your landing page, and track and follow up with your leads and customers. More importantly, you want to do this *automatically*.

We will teach you the strategy and tactics required to fulfill your mission: to get those clicks and to turn them into customers and sales.

Some tactics, especially those built around audience targeting and bidding strategies, have changed dramatically for Facebook. Don't worry, we will show you the secrets we have found to be a successful advertiser on Facebook.

Facebook has dramatically simplified online advertising by making audience targeting and bidding quite easy. Your number-one job is creating ads and offers.

### Your Mission, a Penny at a Time

Those who like numbers will appreciate how powerful your fundamental mission is. Depending on the size of your market, your mission may also be stated as, "To buy a click for $1 and to reliably and repeatedly turn it into $.01 worth of pure profit."

This is how pro gamblers think. If they can find a game where betting a dollar nets them a penny, they are in heaven. They sit there for hours and hours playing round after round trying to bet as much as possible to earn that 1-percent net.

They even have a name for it. They call it "grinding." The best part about grinding when you're a digital marketer is that you do not have to actually sit at a table in a smoke-filled room. Digital grinding happens in that area of the web now called the "cloud," and clouds are much nicer than smoke-filled rooms.

Also, you do not have to live in Vegas. In the online world, the game comes to you.

Think about this for a moment: a 1-percent net ROI (return on investment) may be achieved within a matter of minutes from when the investment was made. What is the return on a dollar, on an annual basis, that can bring 1 percent every three minutes? The figure is so large it makes even Goldman Sachs blush. A penny, if enough clicks are available, is a fortune. Empires are built on a 1-percent net profit.

Don't despise making a penny, especially if you can make it reliably and repeatedly. Instead, focus on how to make a lot more pennies. Focus on how to get a lot more clicks.

Perhaps you can do that on Facebook?

For your sake, we hope so. Because advertising on Facebook is actually a lot of fun.

For some advertisers, using Facebook paid advertising to find new customers is also stunningly easy. Facebook Advertising may be a great fit that will cause new customers to fall into your lap. Facebook Advertising is almost always a perfect strategy to retarget and nurture traffic from any source.

My co-author, Bob Regnerus, is not only an expert in Facebook Advertising, he is also one of my longtime Roundtable members (my highest-level Mastermind). Bob co-founded a company called Feedstories (Feedstories.com) along with Brandon Boyd, which focuses on video creative and actually producing and promoting videos that sell. I am a client of Feedstories and I hire them to produce all of our promotional videos.

Most importantly, Bob is a friend and neighbor. He lives just seven miles from me, and we've grown up together in this business. I often ask Bob for advice, as does he of me. We trust each other. I am inviting you to trust him as he delivers powerful strategies and experience that will give any Facebook Advertiser a leg up on the competition.

—Perry Marshall

**TIP**

Get tools, video, and case studies with updates at www.PerryMarshall.com/fbtools.

## INTRODUCTION TO BOB REGNERUS

I am honored to be given the responsibility of writing this book and am very grateful to my friend Perry Marshall for asking me to take on this task.

When I signed on to write this book, I contemplated at length about what the real purpose of the book would be. It became clear to me that the mission is not merely to teach you the mechanics of Facebook Ads. It's to equip you with proven strategies that allow you to compete with large advertisers, level the playing field, and gain significant advantages over the competition by understanding how to stack the deck in your favor.

I've been in digital marketing since 1998 and paid advertising since 1999 with Overture, which was bought by Yahoo! in 2003. I moved to Google Adwords (now Google Ads) in 2003. I started with Facebook paid ads when right-hand-side ads gave them a viable PPC format in 2011 and when Facebook added promoted stories in January of 2012. This was the first time Facebook mixed in sponsored posts with friends' content.

The years 2012 to 2014 were the Gold Rush of Facebook Advertising. It was similar to Google Adwords a decade earlier. There were few advertisers and clicks were plentiful and cheap. The ads were new, and users actually loved them! Clicks were between five and ten cents and converted like crazy.

### From Zero to $7 Million

I was immersed in teaching myself Facebook Ads by playing in my own account, and after gaining confidence in my skills, I wanted to start taking on clients to let me learn even more and start to earn an income from this skill.

In September 2013, J.D. Crouse reached out to me along with his wife, Amy. They were just weeks into a new venture called Bolder Band Headbands and they thought they had something that people might want to buy. This was still a kitchen table business because they made headbands on their sewing machine at home and sold them mostly to friends and family.

J.D. and Amy wanted to see if people would buy their headbands online, and they wanted to know if I could help them find customers on Facebook. To me it was a great partnership—we were both trying to prove ourselves. I gladly accepted the challenge.

That little company, as of this writing, has generated eight figures in revenue and built a huge community of active customers who love their product. All of this was made possible by effective Facebook Ads and a lot of smart business decisions. In fact, the first year was so successful that Bolder Bands won the 2014 Build a Business Contest from Shopify!

I want to encourage you with this story. Maybe you won't win a contest or make eight figures, but I believe that Facebook is still an exceptional medium for both prospecting and nurturing potential customers no matter what your business goals are.

Think of me as your Facebook coach. The process I use to help my basketball players absorb new concepts and build confidence in their skills to be ready to perform at a high level is the same process I will use with you.

When we practice something new on the court, we first talk about why this skill is important to their overall game. Then we break down the skills into drills and we practice them over and over. Then, in real game situations where things matter, those skills are tested on the basketball court and we see how well we've done!

My desire is that you will use this book to practice those skills that help you dominate on the court we call Facebook Advertising. I want you to master these skills and fundamentals so that you achieve greatness and blow past your wildest dreams for your business!

—Bob Regnerus

# Read This First—How to Use the *Ultimate Guide to Facebook Advertising*

Fifteen years ago, very few people could have imagined an online media environment where anyone in the world could connect remotely and begin to share their life digitally.

Facebook's mission has always been "to give people the power to build community and bring the world closer together." Because of this connectedness and how online users all over the world have integrated it with their daily lives, Facebook has been and will continue to be one of the richest and most effective places to advertise your business.

Facebook is now a mature medium with much broader appeals to advertisers, and it is the best "person-to-person" advertising mass medium in existence. (*Person-to-person* means that we know more data points about our audience than traditional mass media). Facebook delivers what advertisers crave: a sizable audience and detailed targeting options.

Despite recent political interference and well-publicized privacy scandals, Facebook is still a platform people spend enormous amounts of time on. According to a recent Facebook shareholder report, roughly 2.36 billion people use the Facebook family of services (including Instagram, WhatsApp, and Messenger) every day, while around 2.99 billion people use at least one of these services each month. Statistics from multiple outlets have reported that the average Facebook user spends over 35 minutes a day on Facebook. With this type of factual information, it is a no-brainer that Facebook is a must-have platform for advertising campaigns.

Much of the information you will read here has changed since the first, second, and third editions of this book. We're going to tell you everything that's important to know as social media has evolved and grown over the years. In addition, we also want to stress that the strategies and fundamentals of Facebook Advertising have not changed and those principles have remained steadfast since this series was first published.

Here's an important part of this book to understand: We're not going to tell you how easy this all is. In fact, running successful Facebook Ad campaigns is a more arduous and challenging task than ever before. The playing field is now dominated by large companies with BILLIONS of ad dollars who have shifted a great deal of their budgets from traditional outlets into Facebook.

However, do not despair! This book series has always been about providing forward-thinking people an edge to help improve their businesses. By reading this book, you will have a distinct advantage over advertisers who accept defaults without question, don't stay on top of what works, and fail to measure how effective their campaigns are.

If you want to dominate on Facebook—if you want to learn what really works—if you want to develop a skill set that will be valuable to your current company and companies in the future, then this book is for you! This book will give you that dominance. It will provide you the information, tools, and strategies that have been proven to work and are largely ignored by bigger advertisers.

This book is for:

1. Beginners looking to learn the right way to approach Facebook Advertising from Day 1 to quickly get up to speed and generate results quickly.
2. Individuals currently running ads for their company or project. You will broaden your knowledge of Facebook Advertising and probably discover some strategies that are new and potentially huge for you.
3. Agency owners and employees who manage accounts for clients. This will increase your ability to generate positive results and stay on the cutting edge of strategies that are proven to work.
4. Businesses in all kinds of sectors such as: service, ecommerce, entertainment, non-for-profit, information/publishing, retail, institutions, and more.

You can consume this book in two ways. One is by reading from beginning to end, so you will gradually build your base knowledge and discover things you may have not considered before. Each chapter builds upon the next to give you more and more confidence as you progress.

More likely, you will want to treat this book as a reference guide and drop in on topics that you want to learn for the first time or brush up on. We wrote the book to help you quickly solve a problem or launch something you have developed on a tight schedule. Be sure to use the Table of Contents and Index to quickly locate where you need to go.

One note to consider: You will find it helpful to have your Facebook Ad Account opened as you study this book. You will learn best by simultaneously reading the book and practicing the concepts directly in your Ad Account.

Another important point is that Facebook will continually make changes to their ad platform and the Ad Manager interface. Types and sizes of ads will change. New placements will be introduced. Therefore, some of the details and screenshots we share in this book will either be out of date or different from what you currently see. Don't panic. You can always find updated specs and details in our Resources section at www.PerryMarshall.com/fbtools or on Facebook's Support Page. Our resources section will also give you deeper information into key concepts, useful tools, helpful videos, actual case studies, bonus chapters, and up-to-date strategies that will help you further distance yourself from the competition.

If you focus on the concepts of what you're learning, that is the most important thing.

No matter who you are, what level your Facebook Ad skills are, or how you intend to use Facebook, you're going to find immense value in this book. This will become your Facebook Ad bible that you'll want to share with all your friends because the advice here actually works to increase success quickly.

Thank you for investing in this book, and we look forward to teaching you!

# Chapter 1

# A Master Class
# in Fundamentals

I (Bob) coach high school basketball. In fact, I've coached youth basketball since I was 16 years old. That makes this next season my 35th year in coaching (do the math to reverse-engineer my age).

One thing that all players want to do at a practice is scrimmage. Scrimmages are practice games against teammates. Scrimmages are fun for players because they just get to play basketball. You'd think this was a good thing, but ask any coach about the LAST thing they ever consider doing at a practice—every experienced coach will answer, "scrimmage."

You can understand why the players just want to play (it's fun), but when you are just playing, you are ignoring the mandate to master the fundamentals like dribbling, footwork, passing, cutting, screening, and rebounding. Every movement and action on the basketball court is built on fundamentals. The best players that have ever played the game were masters of fundamentals and they worked on them constantly.

Players and teams that focus on mastering fundamentals excel on the basketball court.

The same goes for Facebook Advertisers. If you just jump in and start running an ad without knowing the fundamentals (or the rules), you're not only going to get embarrassed, but you're also going to lose a lot of money.

Rest assured, you will get your ads running as quickly as possible. In this chapter, you are going to learn three fundamental concepts. Like shooting, passing, and dribbling, these are three fundamentals you must understand to be a successful advertiser.

First, you'll learn about the concept of a marketing funnel and how prospects become customers. Second, you'll learn about five levels of awareness customers must go through in order to make a purchase. Lastly, you'll discover the three pillars of advertising success that make up every successful advertising campaign.

Let's get on the practice floor!

## MARKETING FUNNELS TRANSFORM STRANGERS INTO FRIENDS AND CUSTOMERS

Any modern discussion of digital marketing always talks about funnels. When most people say funnel, they are talking about the set of steps of moving someone from not knowing about you or your business to making a purchase. In other words, it's a sales process. A funnel is a great visual because sales is a process of elimination. It's widest at the top and can hold the most people. Then it gets smaller and smaller as people are disqualified until you get your eventual goal.

In basketball coaching, we start with all of the athletes who try out for the team. Then, we cut down to the members of the team. Finally, we get to the goal of five starters on the floor.

The goal of a funnel doesn't always have to be a purchase. It could be an email opt-in or registering for an event like a webinar. All funnels have an end goal. The rest of the steps are up to you. We show a typical funnel starting with a Facebook Ad in Figure 1–1 on page 3.

Notice how the numbers get drastically smaller with each step. That's why the visual of a funnel is accurate. It's a great visual concept for beginning sales and marketing process. Funnels will be a concept we revisit in a number of chapters, namely Chapters 21 through 25.

Another way of thinking about your funnel is by splitting it into three parts, as you can see in Figure 1–2 (page 3):

1. Top of the Funnel, or ToFu.
2. Middle of the Funnel, or MoFu.
3. Bottom of the Funnel, or BoFu.

Let's take a closer look at each part of this funnel:

**ToFu** has the widest audience that's the least ready to convert. They probably aren't aware of you or your business. Your goal here is to get some people in this

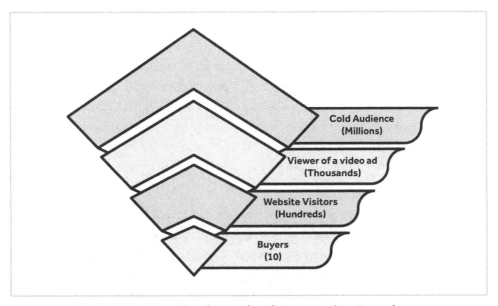

**FIGURE 1–1.** Simple Facebook Prospecting Funnel

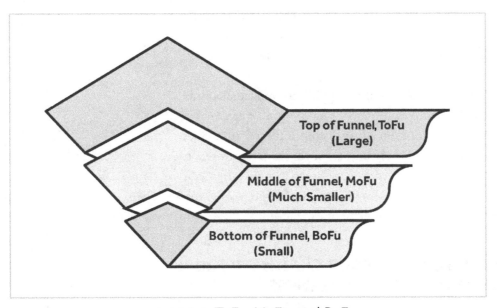

**FIGURE 1–2.** ToFu, MoFu, and BoFu

large group to raise their hand to indicate they are interested in you. You usually attract some of them with a content offer. The offer is usually content like a blog article, video, or even a small purchase. You're not trying to make a huge sale, but instead you're trying to attract attention. Once you have their attention, you move to MoFu.

**MoFu** has a targeted audience. It is usually a Retargeting (you'll learn more about Retargeting in Chapter 3) list and possibly an email list. In this stage, you have the interest of your prospects and they are considering your business. You can send to more specific blog pages, send more complicated ebooks, white papers, guides, or templates. All of these usually have a stronger call to action in them to make a larger purchase or connect to a salesperson and reach the BoFu.

**BoFu** holds your strongest conversion content. This could be webinars, pricing options, comparisons, demos, and live sales phone calls. People at this level are the most valuable to you, so you can spend the most ad budget on them per person. Since there are far fewer people at this level, your overall spending usually isn't as much as people at the higher levels.

Testimonials and customer success stories work at all levels of the funnel.

A small percentage of people will speed through your funnel all at one time. You should allow for this, but don't emphasize that path since so few people will use it.

There are plenty of incredibly complicated funnel examples you'll find online. Once you master the idea and implementation of one simple funnel to attract the attention of a cold audience, get them interested in your solution, and convert them to a buyer, then you can add more complicated steps. In Chapters 21 through 25 you'll see terrific examples of funnels you can implement on Facebook.

> **TIP**
>
> Retargeting is a technology that helps you keep in touch with users after they leave your website. For most websites, only 2 percent of web traffic takes any measurable action. Retargeting helps you reach the 98 percent of users who don't.

## HOW TO MOVE YOUR CUSTOMER FROM ZERO TO TOTAL AWARENESS

Do you remember when you first heard about the keto diet? You probably heard somebody say, "I'm doing the keto thing." You had no idea what they meant. Maybe it was a spice? Maybe it was a new workout program? Then, while chomping down bacon-wrapped beef like a grizzly bear just out of hibernation, they tell you it's a diet. "A diet?" you ask, trying not to stare at the grease running down their face onto their shirt.

Fast forward a few years and you not only know "keto" is a diet plan, but it's also a way of life. Just ten years ago there wasn't any recognition. Now, there are over 80,000 keto products for sale on Amazon.

When you first heard of keto, the sales plug "Buy One Get One Free Keto Cookies" wouldn't have made any sense to you. But as time went on, friends and coworkers told you it's a weight-loss diet. Then, they described the lack of carbs and showed quick weight loss. Now you know what problem it solves (weight loss). You know how it works (eliminating carbohydrates), and you know how to start the program (buy a book or read a few blog articles). Now when you see a keto cookie ad, it not only makes sense to you, but might also be worth checking out to see if they're new and don't taste like cardboard.

The customer buying cycle like the one described above is an interesting phenomenon. In Figure 1–3, you see a diagram of the typical buying cycle. It doesn't matter what

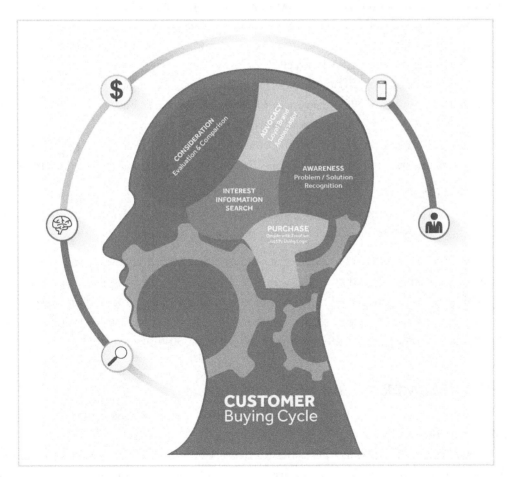

**FIGURE 1–3.** Customer Buying Cycle

you're buying—a new car, hairspray, or attorney services—there's a specific subconscious process we all follow. It's human nature.

Think about it. What was the last significant purchase you made?

If you're like most people, when you think back, it probably started with a problem you wanted solved.

Now, a problem doesn't have to be a major catastrophe; a problem can be some common everyday scenario like wanting to look good for an upcoming school reunion, generating more customers for your business, or where to take your special someone for your anniversary.

To be able to solve your problem, depending on your current level of market knowledge, you may need to do some research (e.g., you may already have a favorite romantic restaurant or maybe you haven't purchased a fashionable item of clothing in the last ten years). Research could entail visiting your local mall, performing a Google search, reading Amazon reviews, or asking your family or friends for recommendations.

After gathering information, the next step is to evaluate options—not necessarily from a logical perspective, but from an emotional one—such as asking yourself how this product or solution will make you feel.

When a solution feels right, all that's left is finding a great logical reason to go ahead and buy, but remember, "The mind will justify what the heart has already decided," as Roy H. Williams repeats over and over again in his many teachings.

After you've purchased your product or service, if you truly love it, you might become a raving fan and start telling other people about it. People do this for two main reasons:

1. To help others.
2. To further justify their buying decision. If their friends buy the same solution and love it, they'll feel better about their purchasing decision.

This last level is referred to as being a brand ambassador, and that's where you strive for all of your customers to end up.

This process of going from being completely unaware of a problem, then finding out about solutions and picking a solution is how everything works in advertising, even on Facebook. The idea of this timeline comes to us from a 50-plus-year-old book.

## THE CUSTOMER AWARENESS TIMELINE

In 1966, the late great Eugene Schwartz published the now-classic marketing book called *Breakthrough Advertising*.

Inside the book, Schwartz describes five levels of product awareness, as you can see in Figure 1–4 on page 7: the most aware, your solution aware, solution aware, problem aware, and unaware. Let's explore these a bit.

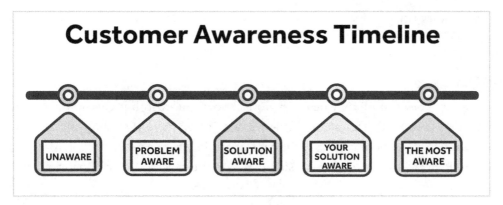

**FIGURE 1–4.** Customer Awareness Timeline

### The Most Aware

Prospects and customers who are *the most aware* know the benefits of your specific product or service. They could have already purchased it in the past. This is the easiest sale. Usually you can just put a discount or other offer out and people will purchase.

This is the most mechanical advertising. It's also where most advertisers start and stop on Facebook. This is the smallest group of people. They not only have to know that your product or service exists, but they already know *you* exist!

This is the Bottom of Funnel example you saw on page 3. It's the smallest part of the funnel with people who have already done most of the research in your market.

### Your Solution Aware

A prospect is *Your Solution Aware* when they know what you sell, but don't know everything it does. They might not be convinced how well your product or service works or might not know of its most recent improvements.

This stage of the Customer Awareness Timeline is where most advertising is done. According to Schwartz's timeless wisdom, your ad has to do one of six tasks for your specific sellable thing (let's use keto as an example):

1. Increase overall desire (keto's celebrity endorsements)
2. Clarify a specific desire (eat all you want)
3. Broaden existing desire, usually in time or location (eat out and don't ruin your diet)
4. Show new proof (another scientific study or another success story)
5. Show a new mechanism of how it works to make it better or remove prior problems (don't starve yourself on a diet)

6. Change the perception or mechanism to set it apart from competition (all other diets limit your eating)

### Solution Aware

A prospect is *Solution Aware* when they don't know you exist, but they know solutions exist. In this stage, you can name the desire or solution in your ad, but you don't want to have much about your company since it's unfamiliar to the prospect. You have to give proof to logically lead people to considering your brand versus the competition.

### Problem Aware

A prospect is *Problem Aware* when they have a need, but don't recognize it as a problem. You'll need to name the problem and/or possibly the solution in your ads. Your job is to intensify the problem and let prospects know there is a solution.

### Unaware

A prospect is *Unaware* when they don't know they have a need or problem (or they just won't admit it to themselves). Your ad has to make people aware of the problematic situation.

You can do this by identifying and declaring a problem to the market. Your ad usually isn't selling. It's trying to identify people who have this unknown need. Then your ad can intensify the problem to move prospects to problem aware.

Some old examples of this would be the "Ring Around the Collar" campaign from the laundry soap Wisk, or Wendy's "Where's the Beef?" ads.

Some more current examples would be 23andMe and others who created a market for people who suddenly need to know their ancestry and ethnic history, learn what genetic diseases they might be prone toward, or learn what type of diet they need to eat.

The keto example of this would be an ad that talks about "losing weight without counting calories." It calls out to people who want to lose weight but lets them know counting calories is a problem that can be solved. Unaware prospects are at the very top of the funnel. It's the largest group of people, but it takes the most work (and money) to turn these prospects into customers.

Each of these stages hold very different prospects. Each level of awareness has different needs and they need to be addressed differently. If you sell anything more complicated than an impulse buy (like a kitchen gadget or toy), it's very rare that you can do all of this with a single ad. As you'll see with the Deep Funnel Marketing topic in Chapter 21, there's a very specific process you can follow to effectively move people from Unaware to The Most Aware.

## THREE PILLARS OF ADVERTISING SUCCESS

When you keep the customer's level of awareness in mind, it helps you understand the Three Pillars of Advertising Success.

1. Right Audience
2. Right Creative
3. Right Offer

The Right Audience is a group of people who have the same level of awareness.

The Right Creative needs to speak to a single audience and move them forward along the Customer Awareness Timeline and further down your funnel.

The Right Offer converts or moves prospects into "buying action."

No matter what type of advertising you are doing, you can always diagnose problems with your campaign by focusing on each of these three areas one at a time.

This also provides you a baseline to IMPROVE your campaigns by testing these areas to increase response.

Can you test your offer and creative to a new audience?

Can you try a twist on your creative to the same audience?

Can you change up your offer to cater to a different need or emotion of the same audience?

Experienced advertisers develop a sense for where to begin a diagnostic when an ad isn't performing well. They will know how to tweak these dials to improve an already successful campaign.

We have a phrase in basketball, "If this was easy, everyone would be doing this!" So, while getting started with Facebook Advertising is easy, it's difficult to master. As with any skills you develop in your life, you'll start to instinctively know how to properly set things up to avoid mistakes, and where to look when things go wrong. Facebook Advertising is no different. Learn everything you can, correct your mistakes, and you will slowly develop mastery.

# Chapter 2

# Creating Your Business Page And Setting Up Business Manager

Before you can advertise on Facebook, you have to have a Facebook Business Page and an Ad Account inside Facebook Business Manager. Business Manager is where a company manages their Facebook Page and Ad Account, assigns permissions to every person authorized to work on that business inside of Facebook, organizes all of their assets, manages audiences, and accesses all the reporting features.

In this chapter, you'll discover how to use Business Manager to set up your Business Page on Facebook and create an Ad Account to enable you to run your first ad.

## CREATING YOUR BUSINESS PAGE

To create your Business Page on Facebook, start with your personal account. From your personal Facebook account, click on Pages, then click the Create Page button at the top. Choose your Page category as either a Business or Brand or a Community or Public Figure.

Name your Page the same as your business. Add a category. As you start typing, it will provide matched categories. See Figure 2–1 on page 12.

Now that your Page is created, it's time to personalize it. You'll need two images: one for the profile photo and another for the cover photo.

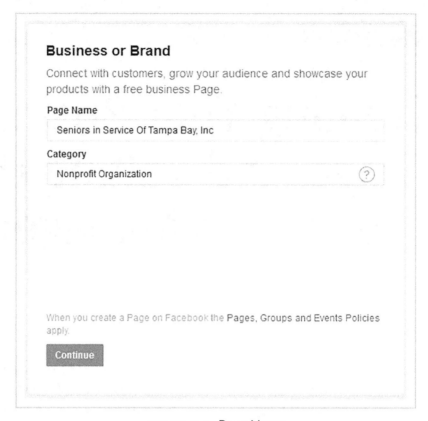

**FIGURE 2–1.** Page Name

Your Page's profile photo appears square in some listings and round in all of your posts, ads, and comments. Once you upload it, be sure it still looks good when it's cropped into a circle. It should be 170x170 pixels in size.

Your cover photo is at the top of your Page and should be 851 pixels wide by 315 pixels tall. You can even use a video as your cover photo. Sites like Canva.com have free templates to help you get these the right size. See Figure 2–2 for sample photo sizes.

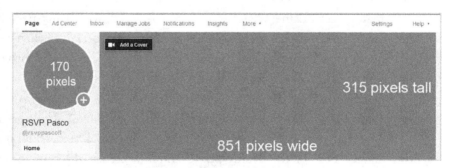

**FIGURE 2–2.** Photo Sizes

Once you have the photos customized, the next step is to fill in as many details as you can about your Page. Click the Edit Page Info button below your cover photo. Once you've filled that out, choose About in the left-hand column and fill in as much as you can of those details. While you're filling out the details, remember that you're filling them out for a prospective client to read. After you complete your Business Page, you'll move on to creating a Business Manager account.

## CREATING YOUR BUSINESS MANAGER ACCOUNT

Business Manager is where you'll organize and manage your business-related activity on Facebook. It will hold your Facebook Business Pages and Ad Accounts, and allow you to add marketing partners to help manage your business. Even if you already have an Ad Account, you still should create a Business Manager. It is separate from your personal Facebook account so you don't have to worry about mixing business and pleasure.

That said, you'll need a personal Facebook account to create a Business Manager account just like you did for your Business Page. It's part of Facebook's security policy to confirm the identity of anyone running ads.

To create a Business Manager account, go to https://business.facebook.com and click Create Account.

After entering your name and business email address, fill out your address information and your Business Manager account will be created.

### Create an Ad Account

Once it is created, you'll be able to add your Page and add or create your Ad Account. An Ad Account is what enables you to create and run ads on the Facebook platform. Click Add Page to add a Page you already own. Then click Add Ad Account to either move an Ad Account you already own to your new Business Manager or create a new Ad Account if you don't have one, as seen in Figure 2–3 on page 14.

If you're not sure if you have an Ad Account, you can go to Facebook Ads Manager at https://www.facebook.com/adsmanager/manage and see if any accounts show up. If any accounts show up in the drop-down of accounts, click on them and copy the ID out of the address bar. It will be the part after the act=##### in the address. As an example, the account ID is 37889474699799195 in this link: https://business. facebook.com/adsmanager/manage/campaigns?act=37889474699799195&business_ id=255539969999811.

If you need to create a new Ad Account, you'll need to name it. Usually the name of your business or Page makes the most sense. Then choose your time zone and payment

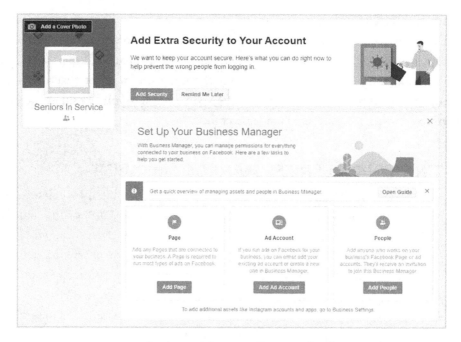

**FIGURE 2–3.** Business Manager Page and Ad Account

currency. Be sure the prefilled versions are correct. Once they're set, there is no changing them.

Choose if you'll use the Ad Account just for yourself or if you're creating it for another business. It's very important to choose the right option because if you choose another business, you can gain access to their Audience Manager, an important tool to effectively choose who to show ads to. You'll learn about that in Chapter 5.

You can add people to your Business Manager account only after adding your Page and Ad Account. You should add anyone you'd like to have access to your Page or Ad Account here. When someone is added to the Business Manager account, they are defaulted to lowest-level access called, Employee Access. This will only allow them to work on assigned accounts and tools. You can also add finance roles to see or edit billing info. This is usually for a bookkeeper or accountant. It's always good to have an additional admin on your account in case you get locked out. Just make sure it's someone you trust. See Figure 2–4 on page 15 for the levels of access.

If you choose a non-admin user, you have to choose what access they have. Grant them access to part of both your Page and your Ad Account, as seen in Figure 2–5 on page 16.

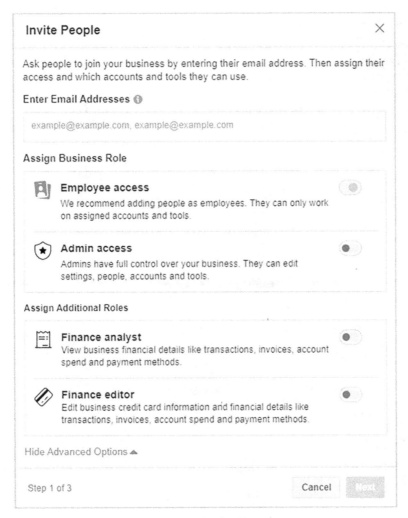

**FIGURE 2–4.** Invite People

## Business Settings

Once you have your Page and Ad Account set up, the next thing to do is to update your business settings by clicking on the button that says Business Settings or the gear symbol in the top right corner. There are two things you should set up here. The first is linking your Instagram account if you have one, as seen in Figure 2–6 on page 16. This allows you to run ads on both Facebook and Instagram from a single platform.

Under Accounts on the left, choose Instagram Accounts, then:

1. Login to Instagram

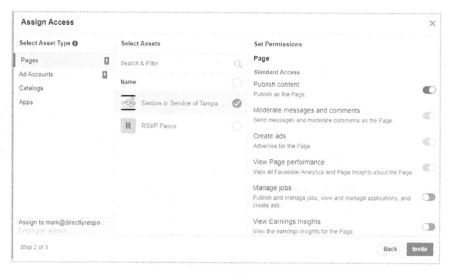

**FIGURE 2–5.** Assign Access

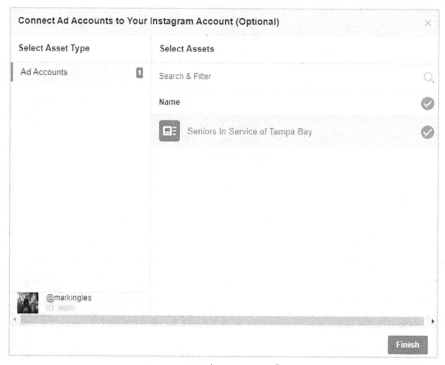

**FIGURE 2–6.** Instagram Setup

2. Choose Your Ad Account

3. Click Finish

Choose Payments on the left and add a credit card.

Finally, click on Business Info near the bottom of the list and verify all the settings are correct. At the bottom of the list is a Setup Guide that will walk you through any important steps if you get distracted and don't finish all of the setup in one sitting.

Now that your Page and Ad Account are set up in your new Business Manager, you're ready to run ads!

# Chapter 3

# Retargeting Technology to Convert More Prospects Into Customers

Could you imagine how excited a clothing retailer would be if they could place a tracking device on every person that walked into their store? Furthermore, what if that tracking device could also report to the shop owner every product the person stopped to look at, touch, and try on?

Not only does this technology exist on the internet, it's considered normal. Any business that does not use this will fall hopelessly behind and probably be out of business in short order.

The technology, of course, is general Retargeting, which we've all seen work. You visit a product page on an ecommerce website and then almost instantly you see that product plastered all over your News Feed for the next few days.

This truth is well known: The bulk of your website's visitors leave without ever engaging with you. They don't fill out opt-in forms or buy anything.

A study by Marketo found that 98 percent of visitors to your website, on average, are anonymous; you don't have any information about them at all. You won't be able to reach them if they leave. That's why Retargeting is important—so you *can* reach them, even if they leave.

In this chapter you are going to discover what Facebook Retargeting is and how you can leverage this technology in ways to enhance the profitability of every campaign you run on Facebook. In addition, you'll learn how to set this up and use this technology in all of your campaigns.

## THE POWER OF RETARGETING

Retargeting is one of the most important advancements in marketing in the last 150 years. It's right up there with classified ads in newspapers and commercials on television.

This technology has removed the pressure from advertisers to "get that sale now." In version 1.0 of web marketing, we used to agonize over the wasted opportunity of paying for a website visitor and having them leave without buying—or at least leaving us their email address.

It forced advertisers to painstakingly tune ads and web pages to "get responses now." The smartest of marketers learned to split test ads, offers, and landing pages to get to the most optimal combination and maximize their response rate.

All of this activity was good, and it forced advertisers to be very efficient, but it did a disservice to the visitor (and quite frankly the advertiser) because it removed the element of time from the equation.

It also perpetuated a mindset that there was an elusive "perfect" ad, offer, or landing page. Practically, you know that one-size-fits-all doesn't fit your customer base. You have people that buy from you for all kinds of reasons because they are wired differently.

It's a fool's game trying to squeeze every customer through a single portal. In reality, you need to have many doors for which to invite customers to walk through and begin a conversation with.

Retargeting technology gives you the gift of time and conversation. You now have time to relax and converse with your website visitors versus pushing them to an action.

Anyone that knows me (Bob) well (or has stepped into my office) knows I love sports. After being a high school basketball coach for over 30 years, my approaches to business and coaching bleed together, so much so that I will use business analogies with my players and sports analogies with my clients.

Retargeting is analogous with basketball. One of the mantras we have on my team is "next shot." There has never been a player with any significant playing who has made every shot in a season. Most players have multiple opportunities in a game to make a shot, but even the best miss about 55 percent during a game.

Retargeting is the ultimate "next shot." When you miss a shot, you get a chance to attempt another, perhaps even in the same possession, same half, same game, or the same season. Same goes with your visitors. You might miss a shot to make that sale on their first visit to your site, but you might make your shot on the next visit that day, or perhaps on a visit the next day, next week, or next month.

You know how this works because you've seen it in action. You'll visit a web page and then ads for the product you just looked at will follow you around the web for days and weeks. For example, if you're on the keto diet, would you rather see ads for steak or cookies? A steak ad would feel natural to you while a cookie ad would feel out of place.

A good way to tell if your Facebook Retargeting campaigns are creepy and annoying or if they're acceptable is to ask yourself how they would work in real life. Let's say you walked into a store in a mall. You pick up a cell phone case, look at the price, and set it down. If a salesperson came over and gave you a little more info about the case's manufacturing in the U.S. and that it has a two-year guarantee, you would probably think that was helpful and wouldn't mind. But if the salesperson then follows you around the store shouting, "You forgot to buy the case!" you'd be annoyed. The same is true of Facebook Retargeting ads. There's a balance.

Have you ever thrown a rock into a lake? What happens when a rock penetrates the water? It makes a splash and you see ripples rolling outward from the point of entry. The ripples near the middle are the biggest, and as they extend outward, they get less and less noticeable until they eventually disappear.

Retargeting is like that. When a visitor hits your website, it's like a rock hitting the surface of the water. The ripples extending outward represent time and interest toward your ad.

Therefore, time is important. Recency in relation to their visit is very important in Retargeting. When you build audiences to retarget, you define the amount of days from the visit you want Facebook to include.

As it goes, you understand that someone who visits today is more valuable than those who visit tomorrow, or next week, or next month. Just like the ripples in the lake, the further out from the last visit, the less likely that visitor will notice you.

While you can define Retargeting Audiences from 1 to 180 days in Facebook, we generally recommend you set your standard audience durations to 7, 14, and 30 days.

When creating Retargeting campaigns, ask yourself, "What's the next step I'd like a visitor to do?" It's not always to purchase. In your first Retargeting campaign, one strategy is to provide more information.

## RETARGETING TURNS LOSING CAMPAIGNS INTO WINNERS

Without Retargeting, the economics of advertising are working against you. We have a client where the Return on Ad Spend (ROAS) for initial traffic is negative.

### RETURN ON AD SPEND

Return on Ad Spend (ROAS) is a marketing metric in advertising to help you evaluate its effectiveness.

Here's the formula:

$$Revenue \ / \ Cost = ROAS$$

A ROAS greater than 1 indicates a profit; a ROAS less than 1 indicates a loss.

Check out Figure 3–1 to see some numbers. For prospecting, this client is losing money. The ROAS is 0.261.

Another way to look at this is to understand how much it takes to make $1.00. On a losing campaign, you divide the Amount Spent by Revenue. Here you get 3.83. So, he is paying $3.83 to make $1.00.

However, with a Retargeting campaign (Nurturing), his ROAS is 3.696. Quite a solid return. Since this is a positive ROAS, that means he's *making* $3.70 for every $1 he spends.

For the entire campaign then, he's profitable with an ROAS of 2.667 ($53k/$20k) or making $2.67 for every $1 he spends as shown in Figure 3–1.

| Campaign Name | Delivery | Amount Spent | Link Clicks | Adds to Cart | Website Purchases | Website Purchases Conversion |
|---|---|---|---|---|---|---|
| Nurturing (FS) | ⊙ Active | $14,087.37 | 6,532 | 848 | 511 | $52,072.32 |
| Prospecting (FS) | ⊙ Active | $6,024.85 | 13,573 | 44 | 16 | $1,572.62 |
| ⟩ Results from 2 campaigns ❶ | | $20,112.22 Total Spent | 20,105 Total | 892 Total | 527 Total | $53,644.94 Total |

**FIGURE 3–1.** Effect of Retargeting on ROAS

It's also interesting to note that he is actually spending almost 2.5 times more on Nurturing (Retargeting) than he is on Prospecting because the return is so much greater.

The economics of this campaign are quite good. Although not shown, he is getting a first-time visitor to his site for around 45 cents, which is cheap. He knows that just a fraction of the 13K visitors will buy on their first visit because they don't know him yet.

He knows that within 14 days, he can get a significant portion of those visitors to buy and he's willing to invest more of his ad dollars to get these customers to convert.

The bottom line is that Retargeting makes Facebook Advertising profitable for this client. Without it, he'd go broke!

## CREATING A SUCCESSFUL RETARGETING CAMPAIGN

Clearly, Retargeting is necessary and good for advertisers. Yet, we've all seen examples of *bad and lazy* Retargeting. Almost everyone has a story of how they bought a vacuum cleaner and then saw ads for more vacuum cleaners for the next month. That vacuum should last years if not decades! That company is clearly not suppressing their buyers, so is wasting precious ad dollars on a customer who has already bought!

How about those "zombie ads" that just won't die? You visit a site and you see the same ad multiple times on every website you visit or in your News Feed for months! This is a lazy and poor Retargeting strategy.

Good Retargeting isn't really remembered: it's simply clicked on.

We're going to show you how to do good Facebook Retargeting!

Retargeting is accomplished by two main technologies: cookies and pixels.

*Cookies* are little bits of info that are stored in your browser to uniquely yet anonymously identify your browser. Cookies are how Facebook knows you were looking at a particular page and then can allow an advertiser to show ads related to your visit to that site.

*Pixels* are little bits of code on the websites you visit that set a cookie to uniquely tag you. Large companies like Facebook and Google (as well as many other specialized companies) use these pixels to "cookie" you. These major players can associate your cookie with your identity because you're logged into their system. The big players don't share your personal info with the end advertiser, so you remain anonymous to them.

Cookies are not something you have to worry about. The pixel is something you will need to install on your website. More on that shortly.

There are a few best practices to help you think about how to create your Facebook Retargeting strategy.

## RETARGETING PRINCIPLES FOR OPTIMAL PERFORMANCE

Retargeting is very powerful for profitable advertising campaigns, but you want to be sure you follow a few principles to make it perform in an optimal way. As with any tool or technology, there's a basic way to use it, but we want you to gain an edge over other advertisers, so we're going to teach you what the experts know.

### Segment Your Visitors

People visiting your site can almost always be segmented into buyers and non-buyers. The more you can segment them, the more targeted your ad will be to them.

If you have a blog, each topic or category could become a segment. As you'll learn in Chapter 5, you can also segment by time spent on your site. If you can't segment based on buyers or non-buyers, or topics or product lines, you can still segment by time on your site.

You'll learn more about segmenting shortly.

### Timing Is Everything

Do you remember what you had for dinner last night? Do you remember what you had for dinner two Tuesdays ago? The answer is you'd have to think about it to remember.

That's how visitors to your website are. Within 24 to 48 hours, people have forgotten a lot about you. No offense; they're human. They are distracted.

As it goes, the more recently someone visited your site, the more interested they are in your business. This is called *recency*.

Facebook uses this idea of recency in everything they do. You'll see when you create a Website Visitor Audience, you'll have to tell it how many days people are to stay in the Audience after visiting your website.

We generally recommend you use Audiences of people that have visited your site in the last 1, 7, 14, and 30 days, but you can create as many as you like or need depending on your sales cycle.

If you have a long sales cycle, using an Audience that's three times as long as your average sale will keep everyone engaged. So, if your average sale takes 30 days, you should use an Audience of 90 days to ensure you include every potential buyer.

Everything about Audiences is covered in Chapter 5.

### Stop Repeating Yourself

Most advertisers' first attempt at remarketing fails because they only have one ad that says, "Buy Now." If someone didn't buy on the first attempt, there are many, many possible reasons. You have to address those and give the visitor a good reason to come back. That reason could be more content or it could simply be a better deal if the price was the issue.

You'll discover several strategies for keeping people engaged and moving along the Customer Awareness Timeline toward doing business with you later on.

### *Retargeting Is Not Just for Non-Buyers*

There are many strategies where Retargeting can be used other than convincing non-buyers to buy.

For example, you can use Retargeting to reach recent buyers and offer them an additional product or service (cross sell or upsell). Buyers are usually the most likely to buy again. Often this is very counterintuitive, because you might assume they don't "need" more. So, try and increase your profit margin by asking them what every good fast food restaurant asks, "Do you want fries with that?"

You can also retarget people to engage them in a series of videos or articles over a span of time. As you'll learn, you can mimic an email marketing sequence in the Facebook News Feed without needing to capture their email address. We've referred to this in the past as an "invisible autoresponder."

You can also use Retargeting to get people to take other actions such as liking your Facebook Page, visiting your YouTube page, opting into a special report series, or inviting them to an exclusive event.

Facebook has the ability to track users for up to 180 days, so you have the ability to stay connected with them for six months, which is an eternity in internet time.

## THE FACEBOOK PIXEL IS THE NEW WAY TO BUILD A LIST

I sat down with a business owner last week and he was talking about how he installed "that pixel thing" on his site and now he was waiting for all the traffic to show up from Facebook. He was absolutely correct in his desire to get his pixel installed, but obviously uninformed about how it worked!

Installing your Facebook Pixel is the first thing you do after setting up an Ad Account. It's the cornerstone of Facebook Advertising.

It used to be that advertisers were obsessed with building up Facebook followers with Page likes. If you had a lot of likes, you could reach those people fairly easily.

However, likes are no longer necessary. What advertisers should be obsessed with instead is pixeling visitors to track and react to a person's behavior. There's no need to create a robust Facebook Fan Page because it is much better to connect with people right in the News Feed than through content and ads.

The Facebook Pixel (we will also refer to this simply as "the pixel" in the book) is a little bit of code you put on your webpages to send data to Facebook about all of your visitors that Facebook matches to its users. This allows you to connect visitors on your website to your advertising on Facebook, allowing you to do two main things:

1. Build Retargeting Audiences
2. Measure the Results of Your Ads

## BUILDING RETARGETING AUDIENCES

The Facebook Pixel allows you to build a Retargeting Audience based on people who visited a page or multiple pages on your website.

A very basic Retargeting Audience is simply one made up of everyone who visited your website. A more advanced approach is to segment your website visitors into multiple audiences based on specific pages they visit on your site. This could be individual product pages, blog posts, checkout pages, etc.

For example, someone who has added products to their shopping cart is much more likely to buy than someone who visited a landing page for five seconds and then left. So, the audience of people who added products to their cart or even started the checkout process are more valuable than someone who simply landed on the product detail page.

Facebook helps you create these segments based on pages or events. In the scenario above, the event is called Add To Cart. Segmenting your audience by pages and event gives you time to tell a story and lead people through your sales process at their own pace based on their actions on your website.

## INSTALLING THE FACEBOOK PIXEL

**Stop what you're doing and install the Facebook Pixel right now**. Seriously. It's the first thing we check for a new client, and it's the first thing you need to do after setting up an Ad Account. The first step is to install the pixel's base code, which is in your Ads Manager, then go to Events Manager. Click Add New Data Source and then Facebook Pixel, as seen in Figure 3–2.

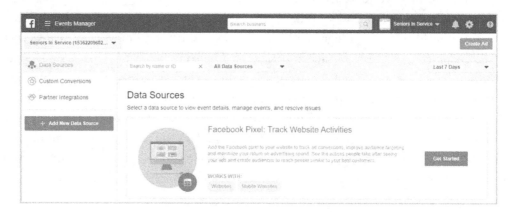

**FIGURE 3–2.** Initial Pixel Setup

Put in your website URL and Facebook will suggest a partner integration if you use one of the 30 or so most popular website platforms like WordPress or Shopify. This is the easiest way to install the pixel if it applies. If you're not using one of the partner platforms, you'll install the pixel code manually.

Follow Facebook's instructions to get your pixel installed. One of the questions it will ask is if you want to enable Advanced Matching. YES, you should enable Advanced Matching. This is a technology Facebook uses in their algorithm to make cross-device conversions much easier to track. For example, many people discover a product first on their mobile device, then buy it later on their desktop. This feature helps Facebook know who these people are.

## SETTING UP EVENTS

Once the base pixel code is installed, you can set up events. An *event* is simply an action a visitor takes on your website. It might be filling out a form with their email address, adding to your shopping cart, or completing a purchase. Facebook has the ability to optimize for any event you set up. The easiest way to set up an event is to use a partner integration. They include the most common events that advertisers need to track or optimize for.

To set up events yourself, go into your pixel and choose Set Up New Events from the Setup menu in the top right corner and choose Use Facebook's Event Setup Tool. The tool will allow you to set up events without modifying any code. See Figure 3–3.

**FIGURE 3–3.** Set Up New Events

Next, add a URL to a page you'd like to track events. It could be a landing or product page. Then you'll see your page with a Facebook Event Setup Tool on top of the page, as seen in Figure 3–4 on page 28.

Choose any buttons or links you'd like to track and they'll be added to your event list. Any events you add here will be available to build a Retargeting Audience and optimize your ads.

**FIGURE 3–4.** Facebook Event Setup Tool

If you have a catalog website like Shopify or WooCommerce, you can connect it here. That will allow you to automatically show ads for products your visitor looked at but might not have purchased or even cross sells or upsells for buyers.

## CREATING CUSTOM CONVERSIONS

Facebook has standard conversion events that they automatically measure for you in their standard reporting (PageView, Lead, Purchase). Often, it's necessary to further define a conversion when you have multiple events happening within your account. Perhaps you have multiple lead forms being promoted at one time, or individual order forms for various products and services. A Custom Conversion allows you to report and optimize on those specific conversion events. An example would be if you are running prospecting ads and you have two ways to generate a lead: by registering for a webinar or by registering for a phone consult. The pixel automatically tracks leads for you, but how can you know how many webinar registrations and phone consults the ad produced? By using a Custom Conversion.

To create a Custom Conversion, choose Custom Conversions from the Events Manager section of your Business Manager. Then click Create Custom Conversion at the top. Find the URL of the thank-you or confirmation page of the event you'd like to track.

In the Website Event box, you can choose All URL Traffic if you're not sure, but if you're already tracking it as a standard event (like a Contact, Lead, Purchase, etc.), choose that standard event name.

Paste in the URL of the thank-you or confirmation page in the URL box and potentially shorten it to the unique part. Name your Custom Conversion and assign it a value. If your Custom Conversion is not a purchase, you can assign it the value of a penny so the value is actually a count of the number of results.

In the example for the webinar, you'd paste in the URL of the thank-you page of the webinar registration and name that Webinar Registrant. Then you'd create a second Custom Conversion using the URL from the thank-you page of the phone consult form and call that Phone Appointments. See Figure 3–5 for a Custom Conversion setup.

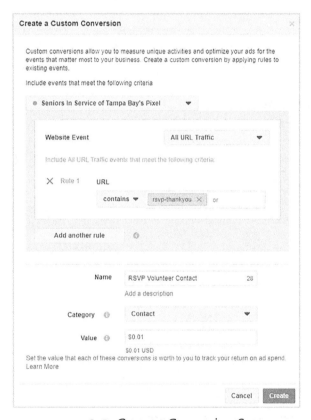

**FIGURE 3–5.** Custom Conversion Setup

Now you can both optimize for each of these events and see the results of the ad by adding these columns to your View and Reports. You'll learn how to do that in Chapter 27. For now, just get any Custom Conversions setup that you might want to track.

## VERIFYING YOUR PIXEL SETUP

About 20 minutes after your pixel is installed, you should start seeing activity on it. You should see the PageView event and possibly other events. If you don't see any activity, the easiest way to troubleshoot your pixel is using the Facebook Pixel Helper Chrome Extension from Facebook (as seen in Figure 3–6). It will allow you to see if your pixel is set up correctly. You can find it in the Chrome Store. It will not only verify your pixel, but it will show you what data is sent to Facebook. It will even allow you to set up custom events and link to analytics about your visitors. It's something you should install to help you understand the power of your pixel.

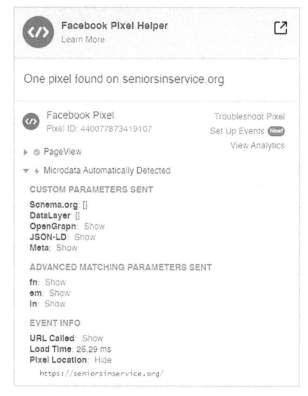

**FIGURE 3–6.** Pixel Helper Chrome Extension

## MEASURING THE RESULTS OF YOUR ADS

By connecting your website to Facebook and Retargeting, you close the loop between spending money on Facebook Ads and making money on your website. This is the only way to truly know which ads are working. Let's walk through a few ways you can measure your ad results.

## Tracking Conversions

A conversion can be any activity on your website. It might be someone giving you an email address or purchasing a product. It might be as simple as watching a video or clicking a button. The conversion information is passed back to Facebook so you can see which ads are working.

For Facebook to really optimize for a conversion, it should have over 50 conversions per week. If you don't have that many conversions, choose an event that's higher up the funnel. For example, if you don't get 50 sales a week, rather than optimize for a sale, optimize for an Add To Cart. Or if you only get 50 leads a week, optimize for a Page View until you get up to 50 leads per week.

## Optimize Targeting

Once Facebook knows which people convert after clicking your ad, it can start showing your ad to similar people to the converters rather than just the ad clickers if you're optimizing for an event.

## Gain Insights About Your Website Visitors

You can learn things about your visitors like their demographics: age, location, language, gender, lifestyle, education, relationship status, job role and household size. You'll get the top few pages people like. You'll learn about how often they log into Facebook and about their past purchase behavior.

Through the course of this book, you'll understand and appreciate all that Facebook will do for you. You'll tap into its power over time.

# Chapter 4

# Story: Separating the Amateurs from the Pros

You might be tempted to skim or skip this chapter. DON'T!

Have you ever been to a party or networking event and there was one person in the corner of the room with a growing audience surrounding them? Odds are that person is a storyteller. Some people are naturals, while some have to work at it. I'm one who has to work at it, but here's a story that might help you understand me better:

They say success is never a straight line. Ask any entrepreneur with a few gray hairs and they may vigorously shake their head in agreement.

I thought it was important for you to know one of the authors of this book (Bob) isn't perfect. (I can't speak for my co-authors, however.) In fact, I want to show you my scars so that you know that not only have I accomplished enough to be qualified to teach you, I have the street cred of a fighter who has survived to tell you all about it. I've collected amazing victories and suffered some devastating defeats.

I've always been a bit underestimated in my life. I was a skinny asthmatic who was the youngest in his class. I entered high school 5'1" and 90 pounds wet. I'm a bit of a late bloomer I suppose because I left high school 6'1" and 150 pounds.

I don't come from money, but I do come from a line of hard-working people. I've carried on that trait by working my way through high school as a janitor on weekends and working my way through college as a computer operator.

After college, I cut my teeth and navigated through the corporate world. After working 12-hour days for six years, I was motivated to start my own business. I was able to land a programmer-for-hire gig at a credit reporting bureau. I was able to work my own hours, start my high school coaching career, and have time to dive into emerging technologies and study Direct Marketing.

From 1999 to 2009, I built a highly successful marketing agency. In that time, I also wrote three books and spoke on stages all over the country. I charged high fees and was in high demand. It was hard, but satisfying work that not only gave my family a nice income, it also provided incomes for dozens of people that worked for me.

However, in 2008–2009 the economy tanked. Unfortunately for my agency, many of our clients who had been making money for years suddenly saw their businesses dry up, which in turn caused our revenue to stop like a car careening into a concrete barrier.

At age 39, I reached what could only be described as a personal and business crisis. I suffered my first anxiety attack and spent a night in the hospital wondering if I was dying. There's nothing like not knowing where money will come from to make payroll and pay creditors to send you into a tailspin.

To keep the lights on and people fed, I borrowed money and racked up credit card debt thinking we'd be able to market and sell our way out of a hole. Finally, in early 2009, I had to lay off my entire staff, which included friends, family members, and my current business partner, Brandon.

The only way I knew to survive was to hustle. I took on coding projects, did marketing consults, and serviced small Google Adwords clients to service my debt and pay the bills.

This time was humbling for me, but it also was a time for me to go back to "school." I wrote my fourth book. I helped others write books too. I started a radio show with my friend Mark Imperial on 560-WIND in Chicago. Although I didn't realize it at the time, those things not only kept me above the surface of the water, they taught me a great deal that is so much a part of my life now.

It was about 2012 that I started to pay attention to Facebook Advertising. I actually got to meet Tom Meloche, one of our co-authors, because I invited him on my radio show for an interview.

I remember after that interview I began to study Facebook more intently. I invested in a $97 course and began to learn everything I could. As my confidence steadied, I sent out an email to my old crusty mailing list and asked who wanted help with Facebook Ads.

That email produced JD and Amy Crouse of Bolder Band Headbands (I tell their story in this book). It produced Sander of Dharmashop.com. It produced Mike of Blue Ribbon Foods.

From those clients and several more, I quickly grew my income and within 12 months paid off my six-figure debt and started a 401(k) for my retirement and a 529 plan for my daughters' college education.

It led me to Facebook headquarters in 2016. It led me back to my friend Brandon Boyd who I laid off seven years before that, and we started Feedstories together.

Today we're a growing video and Facebook agency. I'm writing this, my fifth book, getting new speaking opportunities, reconnecting with old friends and clients, and finding new opportunities to serve and impact people's lives.

I tell you this not to brag, but to encourage you.

Many of you are on the path like I am. You may be experiencing the highest of highs or suffering through the lowest lows.

My best advice and words to you are to stay with it. Keep fighting! Success may be one meeting, one project, or one opportunity away.

Entrepreneurship will have its highs and lows. It's not a path many will choose to follow. I tell my basketball players, "If it was easy, everyone would be playing this game." I say the same to you. If entrepreneurship were easy, everyone would own a business.

That's my story. See how it helps build a foundation for my own business? Story helps you succeed.

In this chapter, you'll read several case studies and a set of questions to ask yourself to help you bring out *your* story. Almost all of the businesses we work with believe they're boring, but then in the next breath say their business is different. Developing your story helps visitors see you're not boring and believe that your business is different.

## STAND OUT WITH STORY

You have two choices to get more sales with your advertising. You can spend more money, or you can add more depth to your brand's story to stand out.

When you share slices of life with your audience, you will get more people following you and make it super simple for you to connect with your audience. People love to be connected to people who share the same slices of life with them and will go out of their way to support someone they believe in.

Following are examples of how stories have driven my client's businesses over the years.

### From Kitchen Table Startup to Shopify's Retailer of the Year

J.D. and Amy from Colorado reached out to me in 2013 in response to an email I sent out looking to pick up new Facebook clients.

Amy had created a new type of headband from her kitchen table. She told me that she had hated how headbands she bought would always slip off her head during workouts and they were ineffective at soaking up the sweat and keeping it out of her eyes. After a tireless search for something that worked, she decided to make one herself.

After finding the right combination of material and design, she found something that worked and began wearing it to the gym. Her friends took notice and asked her to make some headbands for them as well.

After her friends used the headbands and raved about them, Amy went to her husband J.D. and said that they might have a little business on their hands. She made a small batch of these headbands and sold them to other women at her gym.

It was then that J.D. (a marketing consultant) knew they had something that they could market. It was kismet that the very next morning my email arrived and J.D. immediately reached out and set up a call for the three of us to chat.

After getting validation that people would actually pay for these bands, J.D. and Amy knew the next test would be to sell these online to complete strangers and see if they really had something.

However, they had legitimate concerns. They were worried about making a product in their home that had no proprietary materials or technology that would make it patentable. An enterprising company could catch on and they could easily knock them off.

I remember that call as if it were yesterday. I said, "Amy, I know this is just a headband and I know that there's nothing inherently special about the material or way you make them. However, I believe that you can have a successful business because we're going to connect your product to you. We're going to tell your story and we're going to build a following of women who are just like you, and they will be loyal to your product and you and become champions for what you're doing. They may try and knock off your product, but the only thing they cannot knock off is your story. No one can replicate your story and how this product came to light. That's how we're going to make this successful!"

Now, you have to understand that Amy did not intend to launch a personality-based business. She certainly didn't think that creating a headband at her kitchen table could actually become a significant business. She did not feel special. She did not think that people would be "inspired" by her.

But in order to make this work, I knew she would have to be the face of the company. I challenged her to be herself and that this product would attract customers who were just like her. Facebook is the ideal medium for this kind of strategy.

Amy is a humble, middle-aged Christian mom and wife with three kids, who loves CrossFit and running. She is as comfortable dressing up for a night with friends as she is dressing up in workout clothes and working up a sweat. She and her husband have a passion for business and blessing their hometown. Just count the "slices of life" Amy shares with her audience!

I said, "There are tens of thousands of women just like you and all we need to do is tell your story."

One of the fundamentals of story is the more you connect with people, the more they will buy your product. In this case, we already knew the product was good based on the feedback from their first customers. Now, all we had to do was tell the story and find more people like that on Facebook.

We started with a video of Amy telling her story of how she created the headbands.

I have included a link on the resource page to a 30 second and two-minute version of our early videos available at www.PerryMarshall.com/fbtools. You should watch them. It's cool to see how the video has evolved. This video isn't the highest quality but note the most important thing: We just had her tell her story. Then we included clips of her working out and put in still shots of her friends wearing the headbands. We put a simple happy music track under it and away we went. That's how it all started.

In the second year of business, Bolder Bands won Shopify's Build-A-Business Fashion & Apparel Retailer of the Year Award in 2014 amongst thousands of companies.

Seven years later, Bolder Bands is still in business. Millions in sales and hundreds of thousands of fans and counting, all built upon a really good product from a really good person who told a really good story.

## WHY STORIES AND FACEBOOK MAKE SUCH A GREAT PAIR

Stories make you immune to competition. People are going to knock off your product, but they can't knock off your story.

The Facebook News Feed is simply a scroll of stories from people and brands you choose to follow. Facebook is the only medium to truly connect your business with new people who are very similar to you and will enjoy hearing your stories and seeing your pictures and video.

Twitter is very short. Instagram is very visual. TV and radio don't have any real-time feedback (comments section) and besides, are too expensive for most of us.

Facebook is the perfect platform where you can develop an entire lifestyle or personal brand and truly build a following. Yes, it's harder in 2020 than it was in 2014, but people are doing it every day. Who you are, why you do what you do, and why you created the product is really important.

The people that we've seen the most success with have been the ones willing to be vulnerable and go deep, the ones who skip past the superficial stuff. They've got something of value to offer the marketplace. They open up personally and tell real stories about themselves and their products and why a product is special.

Even for simple things like headbands, jewelry, and checks, there's a story to be told.

It's your job as an advertiser to discover the story of the product, the company, and the customers and weave that into your marketing to take advantage of Facebook's strengths.

We spend the MOST time with our own clients diving into their story. Not nailing your story will give you poor results. When you find the unique story angle to connect your business to the product to the marketplace, you have set yourself up for success.

## THE RIGHT TIME TO DELIVER YOUR STORY

The time to tell your whole story is not when you first meet your future customer. If you had a chance to watch the 30-second video of Amy for Bolder Bands, you notice we carefully chose to do a five-second intro of who Amy was. Then we dove into the part of her story that most resonates with her customers.

We see her working out and she talks about WHY she created Bolder Bands. She both identified with her core audience and she identified the problem her product solved: It stays on her head. It leads right into their slogan: "Bolder Bands stay put so you don't have to."

We purposely did not choose models; we hired (actually we didn't even hire) Amy's friends. They were happy to be in her video. People can watch that video and identify with the other women in the video.

It doesn't make sense to lead with your backstory or core beliefs. You start with the part of the story that's important to your customers. They don't care about you just yet, but that time will come.

So, first, within your story, identify hooks to your product and service to get the viewer's attention. Then, once you have their attention and pique their interest, you have a platform to go into more detail with your story to keep them interested.

## PRODUCT ALWAYS FOLLOWS STORY

One of the misunderstood fundamentals of advertising is that many people think:

*I have this great product, and all I have to do is put out an ad and everyone is going to buy it.*

People fall in love so much with their product they forget actual people have to buy it. Yes, there are a few products that stand out on their own, which people will buy without a story. However, a majority of products and services can't stand alone without a story angle.

Too many ads are superficial. They trot out features. They detail things that are EXPECTED of a product, but nothing that attaches an emotion to the product so people understand WHY they need it.

When storyboarding an ad, you get someone to talk about their back story, core beliefs, and why they do what they do because it starts to get their mind focused on the reason that a product or service exists. It gets them into the mindset of how the product or service benefits the marketplace and their users, not just utility.

## PEOPLE DON'T LIKE TO BE SOLD TO, BUT ENJOY BUYING FROM PEOPLE THEY LIKE

Most businesses don't understand human behavior. Most businesses think advertising is transactional.

We have an orthodontist in town who dominates the entire marketplace and draws people from different cities. He lives in the same town just 1.5 miles from his office.

He coaches local sports teams. His kids go to the local school.

His office is built like a home.

His social media isn't full of boring orthodontist articles. He fills it with pictures like "removals of the month" with pictures of teenagers smiling brightly now that have their braces off.

There's a kids-only waiting room with video games and TVs for the kids and comfy chairs, workstations, wifi, and coffee for the adults.

The staff wears themed T-shirts each month and posts pictures of themselves so people get to know them, too.

People enjoy going there and spending thousands of dollars with him!

He has an outstanding practice and uses Facebook to amplify that. Facebook is a great way to force multiply and leverage your business. People stop and look at things that are fun and interesting and like, comment, and share those ads.

Smart business owners will take charge of the conversation and be the one people want to do business with. Everyone else will be complaining about the lack of business and never realize the true reason why they fail.

## "I'M NOT A STORYTELLER!"

This is an objection we hear all the time. Business owners use this excuse to cop out of doing the harder work of digging deep into finding their own story.

Don't fall for this trap!

Listen, if you feel you're too boring, find excited customers who will talk about your product. Allow them to tell their story about how your product changed their life and you'll begin to see common threads. The experience they have with your company will spur your inner storyteller.

You don't have to be great at holding an audience like Jimmy Fallon. You just have to be *you*. Get the help of someone like Feedstories to help you find your story, but don't go out without having a story to tell.

Here are a few more of our clients from diverse businesses that at first glance you might find difficult to find a story to tell. Perhaps they can get your creativity flowing.

### How Do You Fill a Yoga School with Future Yoga Teachers?

Another client has a mission to make yoga therapy a part of the United States healthcare system. He also wants to train up passionate yoga teachers to step up from part-time gigs to a full-time career.

How does he connect with medical administrators, insurance execs, and part-time yoga teachers at the same time?

We asked him once on camera, "Why did you get into yoga?" He told us about his mom who suffered a back injury and they quickly determined surgery was the only option. Unfortunately, the doctor botched the surgery. She couldn't walk for 10 years and her quality of life was diminished for the rest of her life.

Our client had been into yoga for years, but that event got him to go deep into yoga and yoga therapy, and he soon realized: Had he known then what he knows now, he could have saved his mom from surgery and she might have had a better life.

If you would tell that story to a part-time yoga teacher, I bet they too have a story about someone they love who benefited (or could have benefited) from yoga. That story inspires new people to take up yoga. Using this story in our Facebook Ads that targeted yoga teachers is far more powerful than running an ad that had just a simple money benefit like, "Get 200 Hours of Yoga Training and Work Full-Time."

Also, outside of Facebook, this same story was used to gain inroads with hospitals and insurance execs who are afraid of malpractice and are beginning to embrace other therapies that cost less money and offer less risk.

### How Do You Sell Artisan Jewelry at Premium Prices?

One of my favorite clients is Sander, who owns a business called Dharmashop.com.

They sell ethically sourced, artisan, hand-crafted jewelry and prayer items from Nepal. Dharmashop buys these items from these artisans at a fair price (not from sweat shops or factories) and imports them to the U.S. Then, they donate a portion of the profits back to orphanages and missions for refugees.

The products are beautiful, and we used stunning product imagery of their bestselling pieces to capture the attention of customers with Facebook Prospecting Ads. Then, we retargeted them with videos that tell the story of the company.

Since Sander travels back to Nepal one or two times per year to visit the artisans, he took along a camera crew and filmed the artisans and the products being made. This compelling story connects to people who value ethically sourced items, those who love the style and function of the products, and those that do business with socially conscious companies that share profits with charities and good causes.

This allows Dharmashop to avoid heavy discounting and sell their items for a higher price. People understand the quality of the items. They understand they are hand-crafted. People love that portions of the profits go to support the artisans *and* charity.

Are any of these aspects applicable to your company?

### How Do You Sell Commoditized Items in a Shrinking Market with Many Competitors?

Another client of ours sells checks.

Checks are pieces of paper your parents and grandparents used to buy groceries and pay the gas bill.

Check use is shrinking and margins are tight. Competitors sell using deep discounts. Only a few select markets still use checks as their primary means of paying vendors.

So, how do you survive in a market like that?

We chose to put the owner on camera to tell his story. We added personal connection to his business. No other check company was doing that. He was able to talk about the "elephant in the room" where the same checks you buy from your bank are ten times the price he sells them for. "Banks are ripping you off; there's a better way."

We started running his video ad on Facebook four years ago, and the same ad is still running today.

We not only target potential customers; we have an extensive Retargeting strategy to tell this story to folks who Google his business and come in via organic and paid campaigns.

This client is thriving on Facebook, getting between 4:1 and 10:1 return on his ad spend in any given month, and it's been that way for years.

It works because he is selling differently from other check companies, and 80 percent of his revenue is from small businesses. These business owners buy from him because they want to back a fellow small-business owner. They don't buy it because he's the cheapest. They buy because he's the most personable.

## GETTING YOUR STORY FROM INSIDE YOUR HEAD INTO YOUR ADS

We hope this chapter gets you inspired to connect more deeply with your customers not only to help your bottom line, but also to enrich the Facebook News Feed with actual good content instead of the lazy ads more advertisers choose to push in front of us.

Story makes your ads better and raises the stakes for every other advertiser.

In Feedstories we use why, what, and who questions to both prepare someone for a video session but also to produce ads for Facebook. We've provided you a few of the questions that you can ask yourself, or better yet, have someone ask you.

We like to encourage people to answer these questions out loud and record. Then, you can transcribe the audio and turn your answers into advertising copy!

### *"Why" Questions to Answer*

- Why do I do what I do?
- Why did I get into this business? (There's always a triggering event.)
- Why do customers love doing business with me?
- Why can our products and services change lives?

### *"What" Questions to Answer*

- What's my background?
- What is my superpower? Most people don't know their own superpower. They take it for granted. If you don't know this, send an email to five to ten of your closest friends and ask, "What are my biggest strengths?" Or for a deeper study check out the "Definitive Selling Proposition" course—link the is available on the Resource page at www.PerryMarshall.com/fbtools.
- What's the story behind my product or service?
- What problem does my product and service really solve?
- What does it do better than any other product?

### *"Who" Questions to Answer*

- Who is my customer—what are their burning needs and desires?
- Who has had success or transformation because of my products or services?
- Who can give me testimonials and reviews to establish my credibility?
- Who has published stories about me in print or online I can talk about or reference?

# Chapter 5

# Targeting Your Customers with Facebook Audiences

I (Bob) am entering my 35th year of coaching basketball. I've taught boys and girls from 5 years old up to 18. I'm currently coaching the Sophomore boys' team at my alma mater.

I've coached boys for 23 years and girls for 12.

If you know Perry, he's not a "team sports" guy, but he often asks me how my season is going. One day over coffee, he asked me what the difference was between coaching girls and boys.

I told Perry that girls are fun to coach because they appreciate the fundamentals. They listen to my coaching and need very little outside motivation to work hard.

Girls are motivated by encouragement and positive feedback. In the most general sense, they respond to being led or pulled.

Boys on the other hand are also fun to coach, but more difficult. Especially 16-year-old boys who are turning into men and have an attitude of "I know everything."

When I went back to coaching boys the second time around, I was 12 solid years into coaching girls using a quieter voice with lots of nurturing and "pulling" them along.

Unfortunately, that doesn't work well with teenage boys. I quickly had to build back up my voice. I needed to have a more powerful voice of authority. Boys need to be motivated by pushing them.

I found they respond much better to healthy criticism mixed with positive encouragement.

Boys need to be pushed. Girls need to be pulled.

I don't know if those gender norms carry into business, but I will ask you, "What motivates you?" Are you the type that needs to be pulled in the right direction or someone that needs to be pushed?

When shopping for coaches and mentors, know which style motivates you the most and align with someone who has the qualities you need.

Your customers will act in the same way. As you begin this chapter talking about Audiences, it's helpful to know that there are customers that prefer to be pushed, and some that prefer to be pulled. A good advertiser will understand their audience so well that their ads perfectly align with how their customers desire to be led.

If you recall from Chapter 1, choosing the right audience is the first pillar in the three pillars of advertising success. In this chapter you're going to learn how to strategically choose the right people to target your ads toward. By choosing the right target, you will increase conversions and decrease acquisition costs. This improves your Return on Ad Spend and therefore improves profitability.

## SMART ADVERTISERS KNOW "EVERYONE" ISN'T THEIR CUSTOMER

Companies love their product, and the most ambitious (but delirious) business owners have significant issues nailing down their target market. The inability to do this is one of the costliest indecisions an advertiser can make.

For instance, we know that 99.99 percent of the readers of this book do not have the advertising budget of Coca-Cola or Ford. Therefore, we're writing this book based on the assumption that none of you has multimillions, or even ANY money to spend on branding.

To be a successful Facebook Advertiser, you need to identify the MOST likely prospects for your product or service because your budget has limits. You must understand WHO is the perfect person to buy from you.

This is often referred to as your customer *avatar*. This simply means that you can define very unique characteristics about the perfect buyer for your business. Some people even give their avatars a name. You can also call this your target market.

For example, a client of mine sells high-end skin-care products. Their avatar is a professional woman, married, with a four-year college degree, and who is between the ages of 28 and 39. They also have a secondary list of characteristics, but notice for this example that they are intentionally ignoring millions of people.

This limits their spending and gives them a much narrower target for their ad creative. They only need to speak to the needs of these women. They don't talk about things that concern younger women or older women. As you can imagine, this increases their ability to convert traffic into customers, and gives them a chance to be more profitable than their competition and have greater success advertising on Facebook.

## FACEBOOK'S FOUR TYPES OF AUDIENCE TARGETING

Facebook defines target markets as Audiences, and Audiences are groups of people you choose to target to see your ads. There are four types of audience targeting:

1. Custom Audiences that are created by a user's activity both on and off Facebook
2. Demographics including age, gender, language, and location
3. Detailed targeting using additional Facebook demographics, interests, and behaviors
4. Connections of people who like your Page, event, or app and their friends

A mistake almost all new advertisers will make is to jump right to targeting cold audiences using detailed targeting. That's going to be a costly and frustrating mistake.

You will have a competitive advantage regarding the right way to approach Audiences. If you can develop campaigns using Audiences in the following order, you will find multiple successes over those trying to compete with you.

Here is a targeting hierarchy (or priority) for using Audiences:

1. Customers using a Custom Audience
2. Unconverted Leads/Prospects using a Custom Audience
3. Engagements using a Custom Audience
4. Compiled lists using a Custom Audience
5. Lookalikes
6. Interest or Detailed Targeting

Notice where Interest and Detailed Targeting is placed: dead last. That is because it's the costliest and least-converting audience you can build.

The first four are all Custom Audiences, and that's where you'll spend the most time in this chapter.

## CUSTOM AUDIENCES

Custom Audiences are groups of people from sources both on and off Facebook. Custom Audiences are created by going to your Asset Library, then Audiences in your Business Manager account. It's linked in the top navigation.

There are ten sources to create Custom Audiences. The first four are derived from your sources:

1. An uploaded list of customers or prospects called a Customer File
2. Website traffic using the Facebook Pixel
3. Activity from Mobile Apps that use Facebook's Plugin (called the SDK)
4. An Uploaded List of Offline Activity

These Audiences can come from your website, shopping cart, customer relations management (CRM) software, app, or even other businesses. When you upload your list, Facebook will attempt to match the people in your list to its users and allow you to advertise to them.

The other six are Custom Audience Sources derived from Facebook:

1. Video Engagement
2. Lead Forms
3. Instant Experiences
4. Your Facebook Events
5. Your Facebook Page
6. Your Instagram Business Profile

Other than the Customer File and Uploaded List of Offline Activity, all of these Audiences are dynamic. That means people will be automatically added when they perform an action and removed from the audience after a timeframe you specify. Let's dive into all ten.

## BUILDING CUSTOM AUDIENCES FROM CUSTOMER LISTS

Audiences based on an uploaded list of customers or prospects are called a Customer File Custom Audience. This is one of the most powerful Audiences you can create.

You can either use an automatic integration from someone like Mail Chimp or Constant Contact, or you'll upload a file with your existing customers or prospects in it. Even though Facebook calls this a Customer File Audience, it is not limited to just customers. It can be your prospects or even people who haven't heard of you.

For security, Facebook takes your data and hashes it before uploading it. That means Facebook doesn't have access to your actual customer list. Facebook will know who they matched, but it won't have any personal information about the non-matches.

There are three reasons to create a Customer File audience:

1. You can use this list to serve ads directly to your customers. Since your existing customers are the most likely people to buy from you again, therefore the very

best strategy when starting to advertise on Facebook is to advertise to your existing customers.

2. It's a good practice to keep an updated list of your customers on Facebook as a way to suppress prospecting ads. You don't want to spend advertising dollars on prospecting ads to existing customers. It not only drives up your ad costs, it also prevents customers from having to say, "I already have this." It also keeps customers from potentially seeing discounts and other prospecting strategies that don't apply to them.

3. Lookalike Audiences are lists of people Facebook builds for you that look like a model list you provide them. You will use Lookalike Audiences for targeting cold traffic. Logically, it makes sense to give Facebook a list of your customers so they go find more people that are just like them. This audience almost always outperforms any manual targeting you can do for prospecting.

When you upload your customer file, you can select whether the file contains Customer Lifetime Value (LTV) data in it. If you include this column of data, it helps Facebook get you more customers like the big spenders. If you don't include this column, it treats all customers equally.

If you can get LTV exported out of your CRM or shopping cart, great. If not, don't spend much time trying to calculate it. The benefit of having LTV is it helps Facebook segment your customers into big spenders and small spenders and will try to get more people like the big spenders when you create Lookalike Audiences. This will be covered later in the chapter.

When you create a Customer File Custom Audience, you can download a file template and use that to help format your exported file. You'll notice the example data has multiple rows named "email" and "phone." That's a big benefit if you have multiple contacts for a customer. If you have business and cell numbers or home and work email addresses, include all of them. The more info you can give Facebook, the more likely it will match your list to its users.

The 15 possible identifiers are: Email, Phone Number, Mobile Advertiser ID, First Name, Last Name, ZIP/Postal Code, City, State/Province, Country, Date of Birth, Year of Birth, Gender, Age, Facebook App User ID, Facebook Page User ID. The most common ones are First Name, Last Name, Phone, and Email.

If your file has full names in one column, you can either split them into First and Last or ignore them. When you include phone numbers, be sure to include the country code, even in the U.S. A correct U.S. number would be 1-800-555-1212. Always include the two-letter country code as well even if everyone is from the same country for the country field.

Again, it's highly recommended to download the file template, then copy and paste your data into the template.

### Create a Customer File Custom Audience

Here is how you create a Customer File Custom Audience:

1. Choose Custom Audience from the Create Audience Box at the top of Audience Manager.
2. Choose Customer File under Use Your Sources.
3. Choose if you have Customer Lifetime Value (LTV) in your file.
4. Once you are ready to upload your file, you will have to tell Facebook the source of the data. Usually, it's sourced "Directly From Customers" since it came from your CRM or shopping cart. If you acquired the data some other way like renting, trading, or purchasing it from a broker, you should choose the Partner option. Choose the Original Data Source as shown in Figure 5–1.
5. Download the file template CSV.

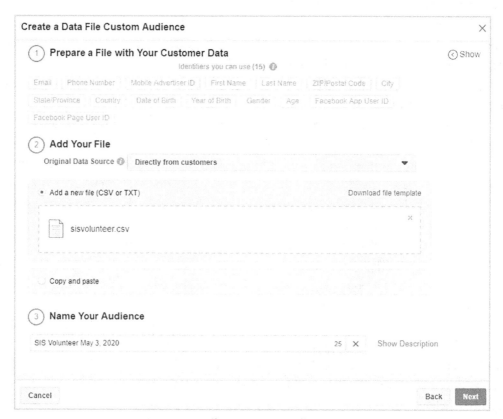

**FIGURE 5–1.** Customer File Custom Audience Creation Step 1

6. Copy and paste your data into the template.

7. Save the template. The name you use doesn't matter.

8. If you're using desktop software like Microsoft Excel, exit the software.

9. Click Upload File or drag and drop the CSV file you created.

10. Name your Audience. The source of the list is usually enough. For example, "Customer List Export Dec 25, 2020" or "Prospects From Trade Show." It will show the date of upload so you could skip that part in the name.

11. Click Next.

12. Now you're on the Preview and Map Your Data screen as seen in Figure 5–2. If you followed the template, everything should be mapped properly. Facebook shows you the column headers and a few lines of sample data so you can choose what fields to map.

13. Click Upload & Create to finish.

14. After your list is uploaded, Facebook will match it to its users in the background. This takes as few as five minutes and up to a few hours. You don't have to wait to use it. Facebook won't match everyone on your list to its users, but it usually matches 20 percent to 80 percent of your list. If it matches over about 2,000 people, you'll see a number of matches. If it's smaller than 2,000, you'll just get an estimate or it will say it's not available because it's too small to display. It will still be large enough to use.

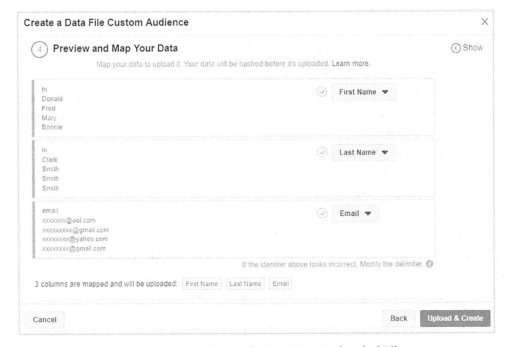

**FIGURE 5–2.** Preview and Map Your Uploaded File

### Adding or Removing Members from a Customer File Audience

You can add or remove members from your uploaded customer lists by selecting the list and choosing Edit. This allows you to upload a new file with the members you want to add or remove. The most common use of this is to add recent sales transactions and new buyers to a list of customers. You want to add to the existing list rather than create a new list of buyers because it will be used for ad targeting in your previously created Ad Sets and you would have to change the Custom Audience everywhere you use it. Adding and removing saves a ton of work.

### The 80/20 of Your Customer List–Recency, Frequency, and Monetary Value (RFM)

There's a simple, yet advanced strategy that will significantly increase the accuracy and performance of your customer list and any Lookalike Audiences you create from it.

This strategy is to create a list of your existing customers and pull out the valuable people from it. The process you will use to select these customers is based on Recency, Frequency, and Money Value (RFM for short).

In the very next chapter, our guest author Brian Kurtz will go into the details of RFM and why it's such a critical strategy for advertisers.

RFM was first used in the 1930s by mail-order catalog merchants to target offers to people most likely to buy again. It costs a lot of money to mail advertisements, so they needed a way to know which customers would have the highest chance of responding when testing and mailing their new offers. This method reduced wasted ad costs and increased conversions.

*Recency* refers to how long ago someone purchased from you. The theory is that customers who most recently bought from will most likely buy again. Recency also refers to the number of days since someone took an action. Facebook puts Recency right into their Audience creation using the term "in the past ___ days". You'll see this setting for all of the Custom Audiences you build with the exception of a customer list.

*Frequency* refers to how often someone buys from you. The most frequent buyers are the second most likely to buy again after recent buyers. Someone that buys from you two, three, five, or ten times is much more valuable and more likely to buy again than someone who buys just once.

*Monetary Value* refers to the total amount of money someone has spent with you. Lifetime sales is the value you can append to your customer file (referred to as LTV). A customer that spends more money with you over time is someone that you want to sell more to (because they prove they buy more). It's also a great person to model when building a Lookalike Audience.

You won't be surprised as you build this list that your absolute best customers will be in the top 20 percent of more than one category.

RFM not only applies to customers. It can also apply to visitors, app usage, or Facebook engagements.

For example:

How RECENTLY did a person visit your website? Those who have visited more recently will be more likely to convert than those who visited a while ago.

How FREQUENTLY did a person visit your website? A person who visits more than one time is more likely to buy than someone who visits once.

How MUCH TIME (time equals money) did a person spend on your website? A person who spends more time on your site is more likely to buy than someone who spent less time.

You'll see how to do each of these in the Audience setups later in this chapter.

## BUILDING WEBSITE TRAFFIC CUSTOM AUDIENCES

Audiences built from visitors to your website are called Website Traffic Custom Audiences. You must already have Facebook's Tracking Pixel installed to be able to use this Audience type. You can advertise to everyone who has been on your website in the last 180 days. Because there is constant traffic on your website, this Audience constantly changes.

The simplest Website Traffic Custom Audience is All Website Visitors (see Figure 5–3). This Audience is made up of anyone who visited your website within your given time frame.

While All Website Visitors is a good starting place, you will want to create smaller, more targeted Audiences based on specific key pages of your website. In the Seniors In

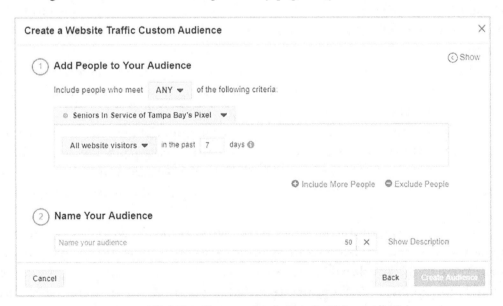

**FIGURE 5–3.** Website Custom Audience Creation: All Visitors

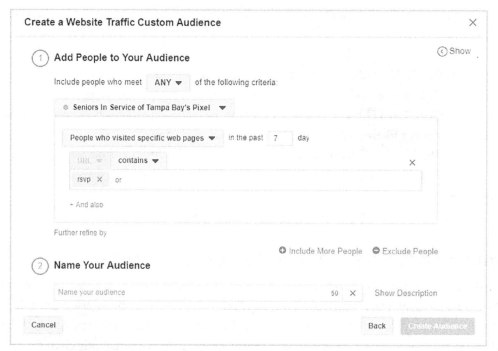

**FIGURE 5–4.** Website Custom Audience Creation: Specific Pages

Service example, we created an Audience of anyone who visited any pages containing the word "RSVP," indicating a person was getting more information about one of their RSVP volunteer programs. See Figure 5-4.

You can also segment the Audience based on any custom events you have defined or more likely standard events like Add To Cart or those who filled out a contact form. These events are especially useful if your pages and URLs don't lend themselves to creating an Audience (like a one-page site with many sections).

If you want to create more events since you set up your pixel in Chapter 3, go to your Asset Library —> Events Manager. Then, choose your pixel, click Settings, then finally choose the Event Setup Tool. See Figure 5-5 on page 53.

Facebook allows you to target people who have spent the most time on a page or across all the pages on your site. Instead of choosing a duration in minutes, you choose the top 5 percent, 10 percent, or 25 percent of time spent. This lets you target the biggest time spent without having to figure out what the time thresholds are. See Figure 5-6 on page 53.

When you create an Audience based on events or specific pages, you can further refine your Audience by choosing the frequency or device. You can use the frequency of visits to only target people who have been to your website more than once, or by device. Your device choices are desktop, mobile (including tablet), iOS, and Android. These are useful if you are promoting an app that only runs on iOS or Android.

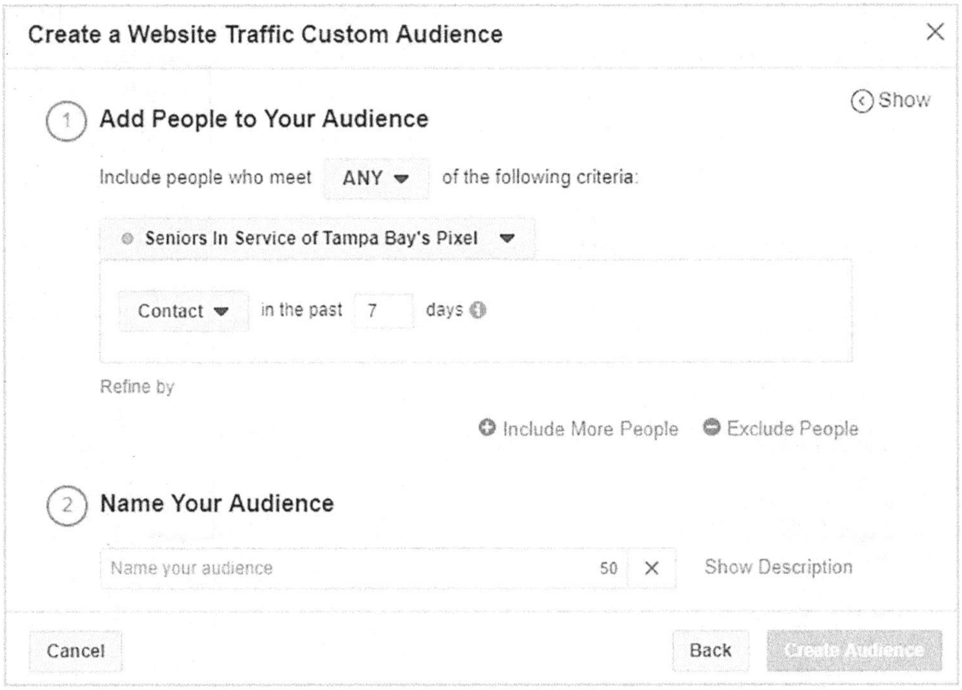

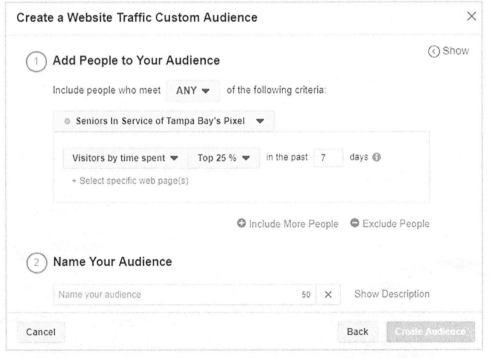

**FIGURE 5-5.** Website Custom Audience Creation: Events

**FIGURE 5-6.** Website Custom Audience Creation: Top Time Spent

Just like you can add people, you can also exclude people when setting up your Audience. When you click on Exclude People, you'll get the same options as you would if you included them. One of the best uses of this is to exclude people who have taken the next step. Figure 5–7 shows the Seniors In Service Audience for all visitors who haven't given their contact information.

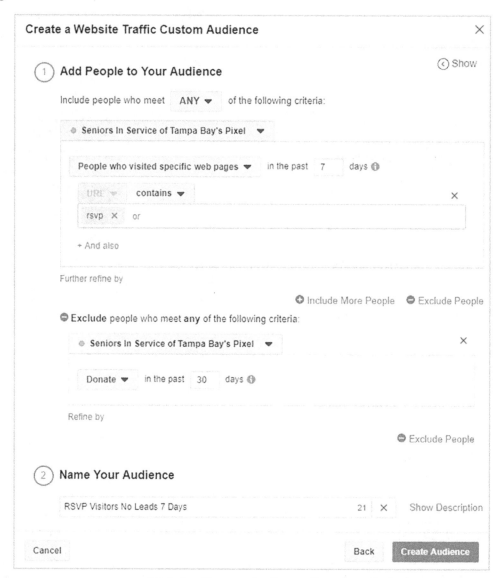

**FIGURE 5–7.** Website Custom Audience Creation: Exclusion

As you have seen, you can create a very simple Audience all the way to a very complex one. One warning: Be careful when setting up too many criteria for your Website Custom Audience because your Audience may be too small for Facebook to target people.

## BUILDING CUSTOM AUDIENCES FROM MOBILE APP ACTIVITY

Building Custom Audiences of people that engage with your app is very useful if you want to run an ad to your users to promote something like a new feature. You might also want to create a Model Audience of people who purchase things from your app so you can target cold traffic using a Lookalike Audience of purchasers.

You must have the Facebook SDK installed in your app to track any events inside your app. This functions the same way as a website pixel in that you can use common events like app installs, percentage of active users, or even in-app purchasers.

## BUILDING CUSTOM AUDIENCES FROM OFFLINE EVENTS

You can define any events that happen offline like phone calls or in-store purchases. The most common application is to upload sales transaction data from your point of sale system. You can also upload a list of people that attended an event or leads you collected at a trade show.

In order to make sense of these audiences, you will have to define these events in your Event Manager section of your Business Manager. Once that's done, you can create these Audiences and run ads to them.

## BUILDING CUSTOM AUDIENCES FROM FACEBOOK SOURCES

Your next source of Custom Audiences comes from activity that happens on Facebook and Instagram. You can easily create audiences from interaction with your videos, Lead Forms, instant experiences, events, Facebook Page, and Instagram profile.

### Video Engagement Audiences

You can create an Audience based on a user's video consumption. This is tracked by video so you can be very specific.

How much of a video people watch is a good indicator of how interested they were in the content. You can create Audiences based on either time watched or percentage watched.

The time elements you can build Audiences with are 3, 10, and 15 seconds (which Facebook defines as ThruPlay). You can also create audiences of people that watch 25 percent, 50 percent, 75 percent, and 95 percent of selected videos. Anyone who watched 75 percent or more of a video is really engaged with the content and found it interesting enough to stay tuned. This will be important when we discuss specific Retargeting strategies in Chapters 21 to 23. Note that Facebook will allow you to be charged on ThruPlays or Impressions.

However, if you consider your own activity on Facebook, you may scroll by most posts with videos while some you will watch for longer.

The best practice is to create two types of Video Engagement Audiences. Those who watch three seconds or more will make up one Audience that you suppress from seeing the same prospecting ad twice in a time period. The other will be an Audience of 75 or 95 percent or more watchers who indicate they are interested in what you're presenting and indicate they are becoming warmer and more aware of the business.

Again, note that this has nothing to do with your pixel. They never leave Facebook in this instance so there is no pixel activity. This is all done on Facebook, and you can use these Audiences to nurture an ongoing conversation over a time period with a prospect.

Here's how to create a Video Engagement Custom Audience:

1. Choose Custom Audience from the Create Audience Box at the top of Audience Manager.
2. Choose Video under Use Facebook Sources.
3. In the Engagement box (as seen in Figure 5–8), choose how long you want the person to have engaged with your video. Your choices are at least 3, 10, or 15 seconds viewed, or at least 25 to 95 percent watched.
4. Click Choose Videos to pick which video or videos you want people to have watched to be in the Audience.

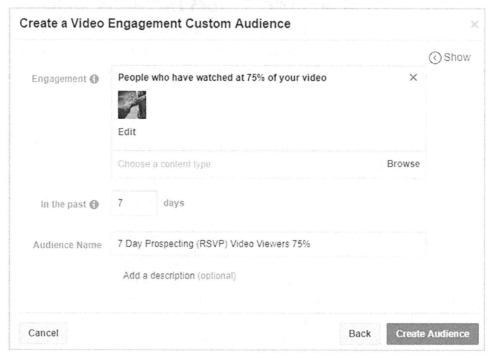

**FIGURE 5–8.** Video Engagement Custom Audience Creation

5. Fill in how many days you'd like people to stay in the Audience using the In The Past box.

6. Name your Audience. We recommend a format of <time frame> <video content or titles> Video Viewers <engagement amount>. For example: 7 Day Prospecting (RSVP) Video Viewers 75 percent.

7. Optionally, you can add a longer description to help you know who is included in the Audience.

## Lead Form Audiences

You can segment people who have completed a Lead Form Ad you advertised, and also target those who viewed it but didn't complete it. An obvious strategy for those incomplete forms will be to run a new ad inviting them again to fill out your Lead Form as shown in Figure 5–9.

You can target people that completed the form as well, and you might want to invite them to something like a webinar online or invite them to an event in your office or place of business.

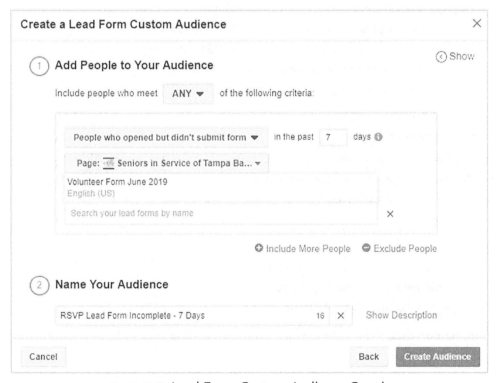

**FIGURE 5–9.** Lead Form Custom Audience Creation

### Instant Experience Custom Audiences

You can create an Audience based on someone opening or clicking inside one of your Instant Experiences (which you will learn about in Chapter 12). You can target people who have interacted as long as a year ago.

### Facebook Event Custom Audiences

If you're promoting an event on Facebook, this Audience is segmented by people who have engaged with your event in a number of ways. This includes:

- People who had the intention of purchasing
- People who have engaged with tickets
- People who have engaged
- People who have purchased tickets
- People who have responded *Going*
- People who have responded *Interested*
- People who have visited the event Page
- People who responded *Going* or *Interested*

You can come up with all kinds of ideas on how you can run different ads to folks who engaged with your event.

You can post updates to the event and run an ad (to be sure people see it) by targeting the ticket purchasers and those that RSVP'd *Going*. You could target people that landed on the Page and didn't respond and also those that responded *Interested*. Run an ad to remind them of a sign-up deadline.

### Facebook Page Audiences

People who engage with your Page is another source for Audiences. Although, you will find this is no longer as useful as other Audience types. You can target people who have viewed or interacted with your Page or posts in five different ways:

1. Anyone who visited your Page
2. People who engaged with any post or ad
3. People who clicked any call-to-action button
4. People who sent a message to your Page
5. People who saved your Page or any post

If you don't have any website traffic but you do have over 100 fans, this might be a good first Audience.

### Instagram Business Profile Audiences

Similar to Facebook Pages, creating people that engage with your Instagram Profile isn't as often used. However, if you see a need, you can target people in five ways that have interacted with you on Instagram:

1. Everyone who engaged with your business.
2. Anyone who visited your business profile.
3. People who engaged with any post or ad.
4. People who sent a message to your business profile.
5. People who saved any post or ad.

## USING FACEBOOK'S ARTIFICIAL INTELLIGENCE TO BUILD SIMILAR AUDIENCES

Facebook has the ability to "model" any Custom Audience you create on their system. This is called a *Lookalike Audience.*

When you create a Lookalike Audience, it engages Facebook's Artificial Intelligence (AI) to help you find people similar to your model audience. Facebook calls this a Lookalike Source Audience. Lookalike Audiences are the preferred Audience to use for prospecting on Facebook. Simply put, a Lookalike Audience is a collection of Facebook users that the AI determines is most like your model audience.

Your Model Audience should contain somewhere between 500 to 5,000 people. If you give it less than 500 users, there aren't enough data points for the AI to see what is unique about those users. When you start to get above 5,000, the AI gets overwhelmed with too many data points and your Lookalike Audience will not be very targeted.

The smallest Lookalike Audience you can create is 1 percent of a country's Facebook users. In the U.S., it's about 2.2 million people. In Canada, it's about 250,000. The largest you can create is 10 percent.

One percent and 2 percent Audiences are usually enough for most businesses.

Most businesses are advertising to drive sales, so it makes sense to model your customer list when creating Lookalikes.

However, if your goal is inexpensive traffic, you might choose recent website visitors as your model.

If you want people to download your app, you can create a Lookalike Audience from recent App installs.

## *How to Create the Best Lookalike Audiences*

When most new advertisers think about Lookalike Audiences, they think the best Model Audience is their existing customer list. While this seems like a good idea, with one small extra step you can make a Lookalike Model that's made up of your very best customers and find more like them. If you upload your entire customer list, you're telling Facebook that your best customer who might have spent thousands or tens of thousands of dollars is equally as valuable as someone who has only spent $10 and then asked for a refund! Using the segment of your customer list that represents only your best customers is a better way to create a model. While you probably know who some of your best customers are by name, the way you create a "best customer" model is through the RFM process described earlier in this chapter.

Here is a way to approximate your best buyers using RFM segmentation:

1. Recency: Export a list of your orders and keep the newest 20 percent. Don't go back more than about 18 months.
2. Frequency: Sort and count by customer. Take the top 20 percent of the most frequent customers.
3. Monetary: Export a list of customers with their total spending and take the top 20 percent.
4. Combine the lists and you'll see that many customers will overlap. The total number of customers on the list should be between 500 and 5,000 to build a good model. If you have more than that, use the top 10 percent or 15 percent rather than 20 percent.
5. Upload this list as a Customer File Audience and call it Customer RFM Model or Best Customers.

If you have trouble creating a list using RFM, there is a video on the Resources page that shows you how to do it at www.PerryMarshall.com/fbtools.

You could also choose to model a file of prospects or any other outside file of people. Just remember, it should have about 500 to 5,000 members to be the optimum size for modeling.

To start, choose the customer file you want to model. Then choose Actions —> Create Lookalike.

You'll be presented with an option of Value-Based Sources or Other Sources as shown in Figure 5-10 on page 61. Value-Based Sources include sources with sales transaction data like a Website Visitor (on the checkout page) or Customer File Upload (with an LTV column of data), and they are used if you are prospecting for more customers. Under Other Sources, you'll see the rest of your Audiences.

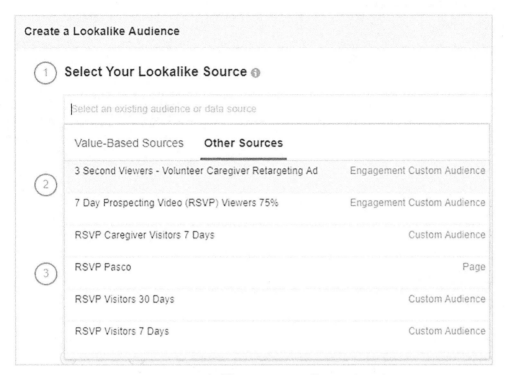

**FIGURE 5–10.** Lookalike Source Audience Creation

Once you've chosen your Lookalike Source Audience, choose the country you want to advertise to. Then, create one Lookalike Audience at 1 percent size. In the U.S., it will give you an Audience of a little over 2 million people as you can see in Figure 5–11 on page 62.

Some larger advertisers with larger budgets exceeding $1,000 per day choose 2 percent as their Audience these days and get good results. This gives them about 4.4 million people in the U.S. while giving the Optimizer more data points to choose from.

Your Lookalike Audience will be fully populated in 15 minutes to several hours.

One feature of these audiences is that they are dynamic. The Facebook AI is constantly working and this Audience will refresh with new users at a rate of about 30 percent a month.

Lookalike Audiences are very powerful. Back in Austin, Facebook stressed their ability to find the right target for our ads.

After hundreds of tests, we have found that to be true. At least 85 percent of the time, in our estimation, a Lookalike Audience will achieve lower costs and better cost-per-action than an Audience we try to build using Interest or Detailed Targeting.

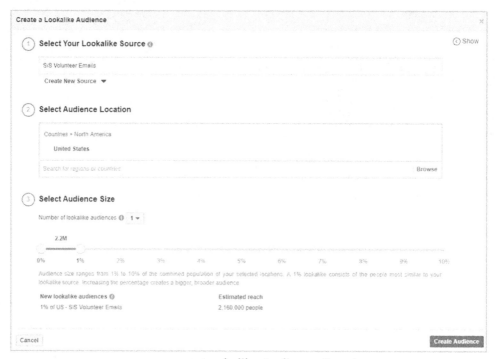

**FIGURE 5–11.** Lookalike Audience Creation

This innovation has made life better for advertisers. By essentially using powerful AI technology to automate the bidding process and select the very best audiences for you, all your time can be spent on the thing they haven't figured out how to automate yet, Creative. Creative is covered extensively in Chapters 12 through 17.

## USING DETAILED TARGETING TO NARROW YOUR AUDIENCE

Oftentimes, Lookalikes on their own aren't quite enough for you to build a perfect target audience. You need to be able to narrow down your audience by age, gender, location, or language.

You still have some ability to target people based on the categories and interests of Facebook users, but since the privacy scandal, many of the most useful categories and criteria have been removed. Many of the remaining options are much too broad to be effective for targeting the right audiences.

You will learn about this in Chapters 9 to 11 where everything about Ad Sets is covered.

# Chapter 6

# Using RFM to Sell to Customers Most Likely to Buy

### Guest Author Brian Kurtz

W hen I was asked to write a chapter for this book (which really is an ultimate guide to Facebook), I was excited . . . especially because it was on the topic of "RFM."

If you don't know what RFM is (and it has nothing to do with how fast your car engine is running), this chapter will be illuminating; and if you do know what RFM is, it will reinforce much of what you have learned already in this book (and other marketing books) and I believe you will gain some new insights as well.

One thing though: RFM is not simply a marketing tactic, technique... or even a strategy.

It is a fundamental way to assess human behavior based on how human beings transact with each other.

And that hasn't changed since the beginning of time.

Once you deeply understand the principles in this chapter, you will be ready to play a much more sophisticated game on Facebook...and in any other medium you may use in the future.

Analyzing the RFM data on your customer database might be the most critical, high-leverage thing you can do with your list.

RFM is a pretty simple concept, accessible to anyone, and much of it can be done by observation and "tallying" (or tagging) your prospects and customers.

But many people aren't using this method, even when they could be getting huge gains from it.

That said, RFM can be both simple and sophisticated. We used it on multimillion-name databases, and you may need a statistician to help calculate RFM formulas and models for you if you have a huge list.

But even on a small list, you can use these principles to explode your results.

I have done it on both.

I've gone from working with a nine-million-name database when I was at the iconic direct marketer/publisher Boardroom Inc. (where I had to hire a PhD doing all of my modeling through RFM); to my role at Titans Marketing, with a "database" of around 9,000 names (which I don't use a PhD to help me . . . just a BA in English, which is me).

If I can do it, so can you.

Regardless, understanding this bedrock concept should get you thinking in different ways about the markets you promote to and the people who are already in your internal database (i.e., your list).

## R IS FOR "RECENCY"

"Recency" says that a prospect or customer who has interacted with you recently is more responsive (and immediately more valuable) than someone who responded less recently.

When I started in the business, I remember that this didn't make sense to me. I thought that if someone just bought from you, they would have less money to buy something else right away. That seemed like a logical line of thought, but actually humans behave very differently.

When someone is in buying mode, don't get in their way. In that moment, they are looking for help with something, and you can present a sequence of high-quality solutions that can solve their problem. Make the appropriate offers early and often. The best online marketers today understand this concept of recency and striking while the iron is hot.

Some do get a bit overzealous (e.g., popup after popup once you buy something)—and, like anything else, selling should be done strategically and thoughtfully.

It's not about selling them everything under the sun immediately because they just made a purchase.

When you start understanding the data on when people buy, how they buy, and why they buy, you can start segmenting names and predicting the best times to make them offers—and the best sequence for those offers. And the products don't all have to be yours. If you don't have anything else to offer, sell affiliate products.

Fortunately, most marketers know the importance and value of recency. When you buy something online today, it can be a surprise when you don't get a cross-sell or upsell immediately after your purchase. If you cross-sell and upsell aggressively, right after the new customer just bought something, you already understand recency quite well.

In direct mail the segments of recent buyers are called hotlines, and list owners still charge a premium for those names. Over a few decades of mailing millions of names and almost always selecting hotlines from lists, I can tell you with certainty that choosing this segment is usually the make-or-break factor on whether a list pays out.

But marketers cannot live on recency alone.

## F IS FOR "FREQUENCY"

"Frequency" pushes us to combine the most recent buyers with the most frequent buyers. These customers, called multi-buyers, are always among the most valuable people on any list.

But they don't have to buy frequently to be super valuable—they can also inquire or respond frequently and still be valuable.

For example, if someone on my list buys a direct marketing book and then buys a second direct marketing book, they become a VIP based on their purchase frequency. I'm confident they'll buy a third and fourth book sometime in the future.

But I also had someone correspond with me—without buying anything—to ask very sophisticated questions based on information I had provided in blog posts. That frequency of communication led him to join one of my high-level mastermind groups. Because we had this frequent contact, he became hugely valuable in the long run. Frequency comes in all shapes and sizes. It's easy to recognize the value of frequent buyers; frequent contacts require you to pay more attention.

In the world of Facebook and other online media where you are not making a sale immediately, others have coined a new term in addition to "RFM": "RFT," where the "T" means "time spent with y"—which is a data point that needs to be added. More on that in the "M" section below.

Recency and frequency give you a one-two punch that will enable you to segment any list, no matter what size, in order to focus on the people who will be your best customers for subsequent products or offerings. Now, if you're an experienced marketer, this might sound basic to you.

Of course, someone who bought from you multiple times is a better customer than someone who bought from you once (or never), right?

But let me add creative and copy into the mix here: Are you communicating with your multi-buyers (or your "multi-queries") using tailored language, creative, and offers, based on their purchasing and interaction history with you? Or are you sending the same message to the multi-buyer who bought their third product from you today as you are to the one-time buyer from six months ago?

The first group is "family" while the second group are "guests." And to keep multi-buyers coming back, you need to target each group differently. (The same is true of frequent contacts too.)

There are even cases where frequency trumps recency.

Let's say you had a customer who bought multiple products and then disappeared six months ago. If you don't contact them again with messaging that speaks to them like family ("We want you back!") rather than messaging that speaks to them as a guest (like any other new prospect), you could be missing a huge opportunity to reengage them with your offers.

And based on the direct marketing rule of thumb that previous buyers are your most valuable prospects, this would still apply if they stopped buying a year ago or even more.

I remember mailing to expired subscribers, many of whom subscribed multiple times to a newsletter—but these actions were five to ten years old. We were able to revive many of them with the right offer and messaging.

And there is a further lesson for those of you who work exclusively online: Keeping track of as many previous buyers as possible with an accurate email address could be money in the bank for a very long time.

You might know this instinctively, but I have consulted with too many marketers and heard too many horror stories from folks who use one-size-fits-all copy to all segments of their audience. Something as simple as "we want you back" to a segment of frequent former customers (who may not be recent) can increase your response rate significantly.

And there are all the tactics to get folks to open an email or click on an ad that are not my specialty, but I make it my business to know all of those and many are in this comprehensive book.

Frequency analysis is critical and should be done on any list of any size. The more frequently someone has bought from you in the past, the more frequently they are likely to buy from you in the future.

If you can get someone who has bought multiple products, and they also exist within a hotline of recent buyers, now you've got the cream of the crop. And if the frequency has led to them spending a large amount of money with you, knowing that information could enable you to spend more on reselling that frequent buyer than others who have not spent as much.

That's why there is a third leg to the RFM stool that we need to be aware of, since the more your customer spends with you, the more you can invest in them for even more sales in the future.

## M IS FOR "MONETARY"

We round out this RFM formula by making sure you know the total amount of money every person on your list has spent with you.

Creating tiers based on different spending levels will give you far more information about how much customers might spend with you in the future. However, the amount of money spent by each customer in isolation can be deceptive. Combining it with recency and frequency is the most powerful way to segment your list.

In my previous world of $39 newsletters, for example, monetary value was the least important element of the RFM selection criteria, except when the customer had also bought recently and frequently. That is, one $39 purchase alone is not very powerful, but the customer becomes more valuable as they buy more over time.

If you are selling a high-ticket item, one purchase could be a lot more significant in determining the future buying behavior of that customer. If a buyer has spent a high dollar amount in the past, they're likely to do so again in the future.

As with recency and frequency, how we talk to people who have spent a lot of money with us, as opposed to people who have spent less money with us, can once again make our messaging more powerful to each segment.

And don't forget about where "T" (Time) replaces "M" when you are warming up a list online to get them into an ascension program, for example.

The amount of money they have spent with you might be totally irrelevant as you communicate with your prospects with free content, useful reports and white papers or just solid information.

And their first purchase may be a $2,000 product (if you are doing a launch of a course for example) . . . but the first product could also be a stepping stone to the high ticket item, so you need to combine the "M" with the "T" . . . and the recency and frequency of their spending and communication.

No one lives on the R, F, M (or T) alone . . . your instinct about knowing your best customers before you do RFM analysis comes into play as well.

Isn't that why marketing is so much fun? And especially direct response marketing, where even when you use your instinct, you don't have to guess once you have measurable results.

## RFM IS AS IMPORTANT ONLINE AS IT IS OFFLINE

RFM is a universal language for all marketers, and it is a cornerstone for list selection and segmentation.

It is still the best way to analyze past behavior and how that past behavior will dictate future behavior.

Again and again, over decades of use across multiple industries, it's obvious that these factors are worth paying extra for in the external lists we select, and it should guide how we communicate and market to the lists we own as well.

When you're working online, it's even more important to be slicing and dicing your list through an RFM formula according to how people are buying and behaving. Remember, make sure you don't have one-size-fits-all promotions. Talk to your customers based on their relationship with you, calculated through RFM. This approach can be a game changer and can turn up some unexpected results. Let me share a quick story to bring this home.

I have a friend and client who has something like 18 different related products, and she does a great job of cross-selling and upselling those products to existing customers who have bought some (but not all) of them.

But when I saw a breakdown of her buyer list, the majority of buyers had only bought one product, and most of the others had bought two or three at most. It seemed that with some RFM segmenting tweaks, there would be huge potential to get more of those one- to three-time buyers to buy much more, given all the related offerings available. She immediately got on board with this when I noted that there was one person on the list who had bought all 18 products (and no, it was not a relative!) . . . and I asked the question, "When was the last time you invited this 18-time buyer to dinner?"

Of course, I was being a little sarcastic . . . but I was also trying to make an important point. It's easy to forget that lists are people too. We can lose sight of that when we spend all day sitting behind our computers and spreadsheets.

What would my client have discovered if she had in fact taken that customer out for a meal? Imagine all the insight she would have gleaned—the buying motivation, the questions and doubts they had overcome, the language they used to describe the incredible value they were obviously getting from her products.

So, from that question, we started surveying the most recent, frequent, and high-dollar-spending customers, finding out why they bought multiple products and also in what order they bought the products, looking for trends in buying behavior. That led to a logical (and much more successful) contact strategy.

We started offering products to previous buyers in a sequence that made more sense based on what the multi-buyers had told us about their purchasing motivation and also by tracking their buying behavior over time rather than simply making random offerings.

It was all based on RFM. We paired this with fresh copy and creative that spoke to why their recent purchase led perfectly to the next purchase, customizing the copy to different segments.

I have used this concept of contact strategy in the past too. I recall the exercise of going through the highest-value customers, figuring out the next best product to offer them, and creating a logical path for new subscribers and buyers. We looked at the transaction data on every customer we'd ever had, and after we tracked the purchase history on many of them, we would map out the most appropriate pathways.

The path forward was based on how they initially got on the list and on what promotions made them buy most often a second time. And then we would try to determine what the second, third, and fourth purchases would most likely be, based on each unique entry point to our funnel (though we weren't calling it a funnel back then).

We were trying to predict what their next purchase would be, and we would then automatically send them an inexpensive promotion for it.

A simple and obvious example was when we discovered that the buyers of a health book were most inclined to subscribe to a health newsletter as their next purchase. Once we knew that, rather than wait until the next promotion went out for the health newsletter, we implemented a new contact strategy where every time a new customer bought a health book, we would send them a low-cost piece of direct mail offering them a free trial to the newsletter.

The original book was sold as a bill-me-later offer, so when we received payment for the book, it would automatically trigger the bill-me-later offer for the newsletter, since the customer had proven they were interested and creditworthy.

They became paid subscribers to the newsletter at a very high rate with a much lower promotion cost. Having been recent book buyers—specifically, creditworthy book buyers who were intensely interested in health—made them more likely to be frequent buyers.

## FACEBOOK DIDN'T INVENT EVERYTHING

I can't go into a discussion of regression modeling in this chapter—which is the technique I used at Boardroom to model that huge database of millions of names, with that aforementioned PhD—which was all based on RFM (transaction data, not necessarily demographic data and psychographic data).

There are too many intricacies to do this topic justice and my time is almost up contributing this chapter.

But I want to share an interesting story that will give you some perspective of "then" and "now."

I did a podcast some time ago talking about my new book, *Overdeliver* (Hay House, 2019).

The host of the podcast, while I was talking about RFM, took me down a rabbit hole I didn't expect to go down—that is, how we used RFM at Boardroom to model up to nine million names (with many details of the technique and why it is so powerful).

I was happy when he moved on to another subject . . . although in a way, this was one of the most important things I did in my 34 years at Boardroom.

However, I felt the audience wouldn't connect with it, so I thought it was a waste of time for the podcast.

Some weeks later, the host released the podcast on Facebook, and I got some nice feedback, which was a relief since as stated above, I thought I had gotten too much in the weeds when I discussed regression modeling.

And my favorite comment came from a young marketer, which made my day:

"This interview with Brian Kurtz was amazing. I always thought Facebook invented lookalike models! Mind blown!"

Well, I wasn't talking about "lookalike models" (something that a new generation of marketers are learning about, especially with Facebook)—regression modeling is a lot more detailed and precise, and it creates more predictable results.

And Facebook didn't invent lookalike models or regression models.

It occurred to me after reading this from a somewhat sophisticated marketer, marketers should look to the "original source" on every technique they use (which is an entire chapter in my book).

They should do this not for nostalgic reasons, or to talk about "the good old days of direct marketing," but for the fundamentals that led to everything that is state-of-the-art in marketing today.

And I believe they could be so much better at their work if they knew this information.

I guess it's about finding out where babies really came from (not the stork) . . . and one of those most important babies is RFM.

Brian Kurtz has had two careers. The first spanned 34 years as a force behind Boardroom Inc., an iconic publisher and direct marketer. His second is the founder of Titans Marketing—a direct marketing educational and coaching company. His most recent book is *Overdeliver: Build a Business for a Lifetime Playing the Long Game in Direct Response Marketing*. Learn more at BrianKurtz.net.

# Chapter 7

# The First Building Blocks of Your Facebook Advertising Campaign

I once did a coaching session with a client who had a bunch of Facebook traffic coming in at a very good price, but their cost per lead was really poor.

I checked their landing page. The page was loading quickly and was functioning properly. There was nothing mechanically wrong. The page had an opt-in box that was placed in a prominent position. It didn't seem like visitors were lost or confused.

Looking past the mechanics and into the offer, they were offering a special report that seemed very reasonable and attractive to their audience. They did a decent job of promoting the fact they wanted the visitors to opt-in.

I turned back to the Facebook campaign and quickly noticed something there.

They had set up the campaign incorrectly. They chose a Traffic Campaign and not a Conversion Campaign, and as you will learn, that makes all the difference in the world. You have to choose the right campaign objective from the start.

In this chapter you will learn about the choices you have for setting up Facebook campaigns, what each type is used for, and how to select the one that is best for your situation.

## A SEMINAL VISIT TO FACEBOOK HEADQUARTERS

In a visit to Facebook's Advertising Headquarters in 2016, I (Bob) had the chance to meet with the head engineer for the Ad platform. Throughout our conversation, he repeated this one phrase five different times:

*We are very good at giving you what you want, so be sure to select the right objective for your campaign.*

Here's what he meant. If you choose Engagement as an objective, Facebook will find people who LOVE to engage with posts and show your ads to those folks so you will get the best cost-per-engagement possible.

If you choose Traffic as an objective, Facebook will find people who LOVE to click on ads and visit websites so you will get the best cost-per-link click possible.

If you choose Conversion as an objective, Facebook will find people who are most likely to convert, whether it's leads, sales, events, etc., so you will get the best cost-per-action possible.

There are millions of data points and artificial intelligence coded into Facebook's algorithm known as the Optimizer. Simply put, Facebook knows a great deal about its users and it knows a great deal about how they behave. The Optimizer is scary good about finding the right people to match up to your Campaign Objective.

After discovering this issue with my client, they created a new campaign with a Conversion Objective and optimized it for leads. They soon cut their cost per lead from $9.53 to $3.79 cents after about one week!

## THE FACEBOOK CAMPAIGN STRUCTURE

Facebook helps keep you organized with a three-level campaign structure. Creating and managing ads are broken down into three parts:

1. *Campaigns.* Where you set up your budget and optimization method
2. *Ad Sets.* Where you define your audience (who can see your ads) and placement (what part of the Facebook platform to show your ads on)
3. *Ads.* Where you produce your creative

Campaigns set the objective for the Facebook Ad Campaign. You can also say this is how you set your advertising goals. In this chapter, Campaigns will be covered in detail and you will be directed on to how choose the best objective for your circumstances. Note that Ad Sets and Ads are covered in Chapters 9 to 12.

When you set up a new Facebook Campaign, you will need to define two key variables: Campaign Objective and Campaign Budget.

Facebook used to have very few options for Campaign Objectives. As the medium has matured, advertisers have been asking for more choices that are aligned with their marketing goals.

As of mid-2020, there are 13 main campaign objectives you can choose from.

For the beginner, it's a bit overwhelming at first. When you understand the marketing goals for your campaign, it makes it quite easy to select the best campaign objective for you. Facebook has done a good job categorizing these to help you decide which one is best for your situation, as you can see in Figure 7–1.

When you start a new campaign, you are presented with a number of choices, as seen in Figure 7–2 on page 74.

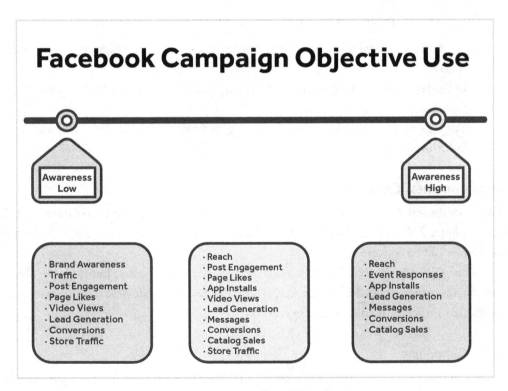

**FIGURE 7–1.** Campaign Objective Use

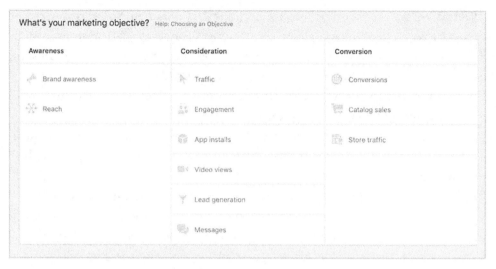

**FIGURE 7–2.** Campaign Objectives Using Guided Creation Method

## CHOOSING THE PERFECT CAMPAIGN OBJECTIVE

In the next few sections, you will learn about each of the Objectives in order of increasing awareness of your brand.

The guidelines below will help you start to choose the correct campaign type:

- Awareness Campaigns are for targeting prospects who are Unaware and Problem Aware.
- Consideration Campaigns are for targeting prospects who are Problem and Solution Aware.
- Conversion Campaigns are for targeting prospects who are Solution and Your Solution Aware.

### Brand Awareness Campaigns

Brand Awareness Campaigns are for advertisers who want people to remember their brand. Figure 7–3 on page 75 shows a very basic Brand Awareness ad. Notice the lack of an offer or call to action.

There will be little need for most advertisers to use this objective because you always want to allocate your ad dollars for ACTIONABLE EVENTS. However, if it is used, it is most often targeted to cold, unaware traffic.

### Reach Campaigns

Reach Campaigns are for advertisers who want to maximize the number of people who see their ads and how often they see them.

**FIGURE 7–3.** Default Brand Awareness Ad with No Headline or URL

Later, you will learn how to strategically use this campaign type for Retargeting because you can use it effectively to reach audiences where total number of people seeing the ad is more important than Facebook being selective who sees it.

For instance, if you have an audience of 1,000 people, using a Reach Campaign will signal to Facebook that you wish for them to attempt to show your ads to as many people in this audience as possible without bias.

Other Campaign Objectives (as you will soon see) direct Facebook's Optimizer to utilize more intelligence to determine who sees your ads. They will purposefully "ignore" a portion of your audience to get you better performance.

The Reach Objective is most often used for audiences that are warm and aware of your business versus cold, unaware traffic.

## Traffic Campaigns

Traffic Campaigns show ads to users with the intent of moving them away from Facebook to your website, app in the App store, Facebook Messenger, or WhatsApp.

Typically, you are attracting cold, unaware traffic when utilizing a Traffic Campaign.

These campaigns are best suited for situations where you want to maximize the number of people visiting your website at the lowest cost-per-visit. Most often you do not require this traffic to take any other action on your web page.

This type of campaign is heavily used by websites that derive revenue by showing ads on their website. The amount of revenue they collect is based on the number of people who view pages on their website where they show ads. To make their numbers work, they need the most visitors possible for the least amount of money.

You might see this used by a company like Buzzfeed or Huffington Post who value website visits more than generating leads or sales. Each of those visits are important to them and they need to buy as much cheap traffic as possible.

### Post Engagement Campaigns

The Post Engagement Campaign objective will show your ad to people most likely to Like, Comment, and Share your ad. The only time you will use this objective is to give an ad social proof. There is an advanced strategy in Chapter 23 involving using a Page Engagement Campaign for an ad to begin with, and then using that same ad with all that social proof in Traffic, Reach, or Conversion Campaign.

You can run Post Engagement Campaigns to both cold and warm traffic.

### Page Likes Campaigns

A Page Likes Campaign optimizes ads for people that are most likely to like your Page. The only reason you might run this type of campaign is that you have a new Page on Facebook and you want to grow the Page Likes quickly. We typically tell clients that you'll want to get 100 Page likes to signal to people that you're a real business.

You'll most often run this campaign to cold, unaware traffic. However, we've also run this campaign to people that are aware of a business to get them started Liking a new page.

Businesses have spent a lot of money in the past to build up their Facebook Page Followers and these days there's not much advantage to do so. We don't recommend you run this type of campaign at all except for building up the Likes on a brand-new page.

### Event Responses Campaigns

Event Responses Campaigns are to get people to respond (by saying they are Going or Interested) to events created on Facebook. In order to create this campaign, your event must be active and tickets must be sold online.

You will only run this campaign typically to warm, aware traffic for events that happen in a local or regional area.

We have seen entertainers post their gigs on Facebook as an event, and then they will run an Event Responses Campaign to let their fans in a specific regional area know when and where the gig is and get them to RSVP.

In fact, I have personally seen these ads for Billy Joel and Zac Brown (now you know my taste in music) when they were in town to let me know about ticket sales and even special pre-show events.

## App Installs Campaigns

The App Installs Objective will be used to advertise your Apple or Android app on mobile devices. Facebook gives you the ability to drive users right from your ad to the Google Play or App Store and optimize for Install actions or Purchase actions.

The great thing for advertisers is that you can allow Facebook to track everything in your app so you can track many user events and actions.

When you set up your ad, you can specify not just what platform to advertise on, but also what versions of iOS or Android as well as the type of device like iPads vs iPhones.

Before you can create an ad for an app install, you'll have to register your app in the App Dashboard on the Facebook Developers' site. Although it's not required, you should also integrate the Facebook SDK into your app so you can track events like Installs or Purchases and optimize your ads for those.

App Install Campaigns are suitable for both cold and warm traffic depending on the marketing goals you have.

## Video Views Campaigns

Many of the strategies we introduce to you in this book will rely heavily on using Video Views Campaigns. One reason is that you can use this campaign type to sort and sift cold traffic and identify people who might be interested in what you're selling without requiring them to leave Facebook.

For instance, one of the most inexpensive ways to prospect is using a video ad and casting a wide net to a cold audience because video views are quite cheap in the Facebook universe.

Facebook tracks the stats of every video played on its platform. They know how long an individual user watched your video. In Chapter 5, you learned how to build an audience of people based on how many seconds (or what percentage of a video) they viewed and how you can re-engage them with another ad.

### Lead Generation Campaigns

Lead Generation Campaigns are a unique way to collect leads for your business without having to build a form on a web page. In fact, this objective allows you to collect a great deal of information from a prospect without them ever having to leave the Facebook platform!

When a user clicks on your ad, Facebook will show that user a form. The form is usually pre-filled with any info Facebook already knows about a user. For example, if you want to collect a person's name and email address, that information will be prefilled on the form and the user simply has to click a Next and Submit button. They won't have to type anything!

This is a low-friction way to collect leads. You avoid disrupting the person's user experience by keeping them on Facebook instead of switching to your website and back again. They usually don't have to type their contact info because it's prefilled. They also never have to check their email or spam folder for a confirmation. Especially on mobile devices, it's a simple and elegant way to collect leads.

You will typically use Lead Generation Campaigns for cold, unaware traffic. However, you can generate leads from warm traffic if you are promoting a new product, service, or event to people already connected to your business.

A couple caveats. In order to collect leads, you'll need to have a Privacy Policy. Even though you'll collect leads directly on Facebook, you'll still have to have this Privacy Policy on your website. If you don't have a Privacy Policy, just Google "privacy policy generator" and use a tool to generate one for your site.

The other caveat is that you will need to retrieve these leads from your Facebook Page. There are many ways to easily do this, including automatically connecting your form to your CRM so everything happens automatically.

You'll learn exactly how to set up and use Lead Generation Forms in Chapter 18.

### Message Campaigns

Messages Campaigns allow you an opportunity to run an ad that will initiate a conversation with a Facebook user through Facebook Messenger or WhatsApp. You can also show ads called Sponsored Messages inside existing Messenger conversations that users already have with your page.

There are a number of creative ways to use this type of campaign. We've personally used this objective to connect with our most ready prospects by asking them a question and inviting them to a conversation. Many prospects often just need to get a simple question answered before they buy, making this a great solution to do that.

This campaign can work on cold, unaware traffic. However, it's more likely you will use this with warm traffic.

## Conversion Campaigns

Conversion Campaigns allow you to optimize for an event on your website. It could be as simple as visiting a page or as complicated as completing a purchase.

These campaigns truly tap into the power of the Optimizer and it's one of the main reasons you will want to have the Facebook Pixel installed on every page of your website.

Here are just some of the events you can optimize for:

- PageViews
- Content Views
- Button Clicks
- Leads
- Add to Cart
- Initiate Checkout
- Purchase

You can even define Custom Conversion types and have your campaign optimized on those events.

Many new advertisers are tempted to optimize for a Purchase Event right away. However, purchases are the rarest event on a website. Facebook says you should choose an event that has at least 50 conversion events a week or the Optimizer will have trouble choosing the best people to show your ads to.

In Chapter 10, you will learn how to choose the right event to optimize for and how your conversion window and optimization method affects it.

You can use a Conversion Campaign for both cold and warm audiences. You can use events both at the top of the funnel like a Page View and at the bottom of the funnel like a purchase.

Since the Optimizer does a better job with more events, create your first Conversion Campaigns near the top of the funnel. Choose events like View Content of Key Pages, then create Add To Cart or Lead event Ad Sets, then finally create Purchase Event Ad Sets. Even though purchases are the most valuable, they have the least number of events to give the Optimizer enough data to work efficiently.

## Catalog Sales Campaigns

Catalog Sales Campaigns are for ecommerce stores with many products. If you use one of the major ecommerce platforms like Shopify, WooCommerce, BigCommerce, or

Magento, there's a Facebook Feed Plugin that will connect your store to Facebook. If you use another platform, you can still use Catalog Sales Campaigns. However, you'll have to manually export your products, format them for Facebook, and upload them.

The main reason for using a Catalog Sales Campaign is that you can utilize Dynamic Ads. These ads use an ad template that automatically pulls in images and details from your product catalog. Once the template is created, the ads are created on the fly when needed and allow you to have ads for every product on your site by simply creating one ad.

Smart advertisers will use these ads to retarget non-buyers. You've undoubtedly seen this before. You viewed a product on an ecommerce site, and then the next time you were on Facebook you saw an ad for the exact product with the same image. This is a smart use of Catalog Sales Objective.

This simple, no-sale Retargeting is built right into the Facebook Ad platform. You can target people who have Viewed or Added to Cart But Not Purchased for a given number of days (up to 180). You can also upsell or cross sell specific products after purchase of a certain set of products.

### Store Traffic Campaigns

Store Traffic Campaigns are used by stores that have multiple locations (like franchises). Store Traffic Campaigns reach people within a certain distance of each location and help a Facebook user to find or contact the store that's closest to them. It's meant to increase foot traffic in your stores.

We will not discuss Store Traffic Campaigns beyond this as this objective is beyond the scope of what most of the readers will be looking for right now.

To get more information on these campaigns, see the Resources page of this book at www.PerryMarshall.com/fbtools.

# Chapter 8

# Budgets and Bidding Strategies for Optimizing Your Facebook Campaigns

Perry once received an email from a Google advertiser named William B. Doyle

*I read the webpages about your Google AdWords [now Google Ads] and received the five-part email series.*

*But I didn't buy it. Now I regret it.*

*Being a total newbie to the Google AdWords scene, I tried it and was impressed with the beginning of actual sales!*

*Not much. Two or three ebooks a day for a week.*

*Then my first weekly Google bill (I didn't know they automatically charged your credit card EVERY week!). $128. Hmm. That's not too bad but it severely cut into those $25 ebook sales commissions!*

*Then I thought I would save money by tweaking down all the numbers, not knowing what I was doing.*

*Second week: same sales rate, a couple hundred dollars profit.*

*Second Google bill: $2,600+!!!!!!*

*OMG! That's more than I make in a month in my day job!*

*All campaigns I immediately put on "pause" and promptly emailed Google: "WTF?"*

*I have no idea how or when I'll be able to pay them.*

*I should have bought, read and followed your book.*
*Argh!*
*As soon as I am able to do so, I AM BUYING YOUR BOOK!*
*Yes, you can use this as an unsolicited testimonial.*
*Thanks for being there.*
*Bill*

The Lesson: Once Facebook (or Google or any other platform) has your money . . . you're not getting it back. Your budget and bid strategy are crucial, especially if you can't afford to make expensive mistakes.

Setting your budget is a crucial step to protect your hard-earned dollar! Budgets and Bid Methods establish your Advertising Economics. Your budget defines how much you are willing to spend on the ads inside a Facebook Campaign over a period of time.

In this chapter, you'll learn how the Facebook Ad Auction works. You'll also learn about bidding strategies to help you achieve your advertising goals. Since budgeting is one of the most common questions we answer from advertisers, we will de-mystify this topic and you'll know how to set it up like a pro does!

## DAILY VS. LIFETIME BUDGETS

In early 2020, Campaign Budget Optimization (CBO) was scheduled to be a default setting. As of this writing, it is not mandated nor a default setting. You can choose to allocate money for your campaigns at the campaign level by turning this feature on. If you need more control over your budgets by audiences or ads, then it's better to manage budgets at the Ad Set Level.

You have two choices for your budget timeframe. The first is a Daily Budget where you specify an amount to spend each day. The other option is a Lifetime Budget where you specify how much you'll spend in total over a span of time as shown in Figure 8–1 on page 83.

A very good rule of thumb is that you can use Daily Budgets for campaigns you intend to run for an extended time and want to have a set amount spent each day. Use Lifetime Budgets for campaigns that will run for a specific, shorter periods of time.

One factor to consider is using the Conversion Objective. Remember the Optimizer is working to fulfill your objective. When you choose Daily, Facebook knows it only has 24 hours to achieve your Objective. As long as you give it enough Budget, it will work faster to fulfill your Objective. The trade-off will be that your results may not be as optimized as possible and thereby not as cost efficient.

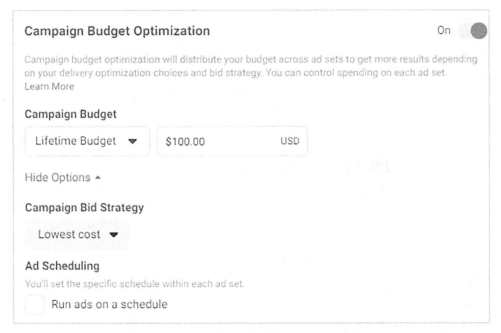

**FIGURE 8–1.** Campaign Budget Options

With a Lifetime Budget, the Optimizer has more time to fulfill your Objective and will take longer to optimize. However, the results will tend to be more cost efficient and accurate.

## CHOOSING DELIVERY TYPE

For Delivery Type, if you choose the Standard Method, you should expect to see your budget spent equitably over a 24-hour period. If you choose Accelerated, Facebook will spend your budget as quickly as possible, and that might cause your ad to stop running well before the day is over. There are very few reasons to accelerate your ads, so you will likely always choose standard.

Note that setting a Daily Budget is an average. Some days Facebook will spend a little more and other days they'll spend a little less. Ultimately, it will average out to your Daily Budget over time.

With a Lifetime Budget, you have an opportunity at the Ad Set level to place parameters on your ad to determine when your ad will run (called Ad Scheduling). You can set a start date/time and end date/time. You can also choose various times of the day that it runs, as well as select days during the week. This can be useful to businesses that need ads running to generate leads and sales during specific days and times during the week.

For example, this may be useful to restaurants who are closed on Mondays and don't want people to see an ad and find out they can't get your special free dessert that night. It's also useful for companies running call centers that only have representatives scheduled from 7 A.M. to 7 P.M. on weekdays. They don't want to generate leads after 7 P.M. each day, so they can set them to run only Monday through Friday during call hours.

## HOW THE FACEBOOK AD AUCTION WORKS

Facebook has three goals:

1. Maintaining a wonderful user experience
2. Maximizing ad revenue
3. Maximizing value for its advertisers

On some campaign types you can choose how Facebook will "bid" your ads in the auction.

Many people do not understand the process for how your ads actually get shown.

I (Bob) was fortunate to spend an hour with the head Facebook engineer a while back, and I actually learned way too much about how this works. I will no doubt never need to use all the information I learned. He was more than happy to go deep into the technical wizardry that makes up the process for showing our ads!

As you can imagine, there are hundreds of thousands of advertisers desiring to show their ads to Facebook users. *The ad platform is NOT equitable.* Everyone has an equal opportunity to set up their campaigns, define the parameters of who to show the ads to, and create ads that will get users to respond. However, it's not a given your ad will be shown as often as you like or for the price you want to pay.

Because there is limited ad space, Facebook has a system to decide which ads from which advertisers get shown to each user in their feed. This is called the auction. Billions of auctions are happening every single day on the Facebook Ad platform as advertisers compete to show their ads to their targeted audience.

When competing to show your ad to a given user, Facebook considers your bid and budget, your ad's quality, and your ad's expected performance to determine if you win that auction and get to show your ad. These three elements feed into a formula they call Total Value.

The ad that gets shown will be awarded to the Advertiser that achieves the highest Total Value in a single auction.

In summary, there are three ways you can "win" in the Facebook Ad Auction:

1. Have a higher CTR (clickthrough rate) on your ad than Facebook expects

2. Have a higher engagement on your ad than Facebook expects

3. Have a higher bid

The most effective way to be more profitable with Facebook Advertising is obviously not spending more money. You win when you have campaigns that produce higher response on a budget that is lower than your competition. As you work your way through this book, have the confidence that everything we're teaching you is about how to get High CTR and High Engagement on a limited budget. We're coaching you to win the game!

## CHOOSING THE RIGHT BUDGET AMOUNT

Many advertisers wonder how much budget they should allocate to a campaign and whether to choose Daily or Lifetime. There is no right or simple answer to this. Once you understand how the auction works, you will realize that the higher your budget, the more times you will win the auction and show your ads to your target audience because you are generating higher Total Value.

Money buys time in advertising. The more money you are willing to spend each day on your Facebook Ads, the less amount of time it will take for you to know how effective your ads are.

If you can only afford to spend $5 per day for 30 days, it's going to take a long time to get any good data about your ads. But if you can spend $25 per day for 30 days, you will not only get more data more quickly, you'll get more traffic and more chances to sell.

If you only have $150 to spend, we recommend you spend that in a week versus a month so you can receive more data quickly.

We also recommend that you spend a smaller amount of money on a campaign at first if you are trying a new ad or a new audience. Then, make it your goal to increase your budget to more aggressive levels once you get comfortable with the early results.

We have a bonus training on Scaling Facebook Campaigns on the Resources page available at www.PerryMarshall.com/fbtools. In that training you'll learn a good benchmark for increasing your budget is to never exceed a 20-percent increase and to avoid making changes while a campaign is in Learning Mode. This really only applies once your campaign exceeds $100 per day. Up and until that point, it's OK to go higher than 20 percent.

Learning Mode is the time frame that Facebook uses to test out your ad in the auction and figure out its true Total Value. This can take as little as 24 hours and as much as 72 hours.

We suggest that you refrain from making any changes to campaigns, ad sets, or ads until a campaign is out of Learning Mode.

A campaign that emerges from Learning Mode enters an Optimized Phase. Facebook will show the status as Active. This means your campaign has generated enough consistent results and Facebook is satisfied with your budget, bid, targeting, and results to fully deploy it in the Auction.

## CAMPAIGN BIDDING STRATEGIES

In regard to your Campaign Bidding Strategy, you will want to select the option that most aligns with your financial constraints. With each option, there is a benefit as well as a trade-off.

- If you want to get the most results and volume, use the Lowest Cost method. The trade-off is you will lose the ability to control costs.
- If you want to control the maximum amount you will pay for an action (like a purchase or a lead or a visit), use Cost Cap. The trade-off is that you will sacrifice some volume.
- If you want to average out your cost-per-action over time, use Target Cost. Again, with this strategy you will lose some volume and lower cost results.
- If you want to control your costs at the Bid level, use Bid Cap. You will lose control of cost-per-action, but still control overall cost and possibly get more volume than Cost Cap and Target Cost. See the illustration in Figure 8–2.

Cost Cap, Target Cost, and Bid Cap are advanced strategies. We would encourage you to use the Lowest Cost method for most campaigns until you really start to understand your *cost-per-action* that you are tracking and what you are willing to tolerate to actually make the numbers work.

**FIGURE 8–2.** Bid Cap versus Cost Cap versus Target Cost

For a detailed explanation and more help about the latest bid strategies, you can find the latest Facebook documentation linked in the Resources area at www. PerryMarshall.com/fbtools.

# Chapter 9

# Dialing in Your Targeted Audience Using Ad Sets

It's a little embarrassing to share this, but I (Bob) didn't learn to swim until I was eight years old. I was deathly afraid of the water. My mom doesn't swim; neither do two of my uncles. My grandmother would only shower rather than bathe for fear of drowning. Can you understand why I wasn't jumping off the deep end when four people I trusted wouldn't go into water above their waist?

Some people learned to swim the pioneer way—they got tossed in the deep end and literally sank or swam.

Fortunately, my swim lessons at the YMCA were a tad more humane. We learned first how to tolerate getting our faces under water and holding our breath. Then we learned how to kick using a paddleboard. It wasn't until the third or fourth week we started to learn how to put all those moves together to stay afloat and move on top of the water.

Acquiring new customers is the hardest thing to do in all of marketing. Everyone wants new customers now, but that's like diving into the deep end. Instead of throwing you in and trying to find and convert "cold" traffic, let's use a paddleboard and move through the Facebook waters with "warm" traffic.

Rather than try to do the most difficult thing on a new media, you're going to learn how to have the best chance of success on your very first campaign. You're going to start by advertising to people who already know, like, and trust you.

In this chapter, you're going to get your Ad Sets created. You'll start by targeting traffic that already knows something about you. You will do a deep dive into all the ways you can target customers and prospect via the Ad Set.

## NEVER START ADVERTISING TO COLD (UNAWARE) TRAFFIC

The starting point for your first campaign should be traffic that has some kind of previous relationship with you. You don't want to jump in the deep end first because the most difficult and expensive advertising you will attempt do on Facebook will be to try and convert people who have never heard of you. This is why advertisers use the term *cold traffic*. This is the opposite of *hot leads,* which you've more likely heard before.

You're not starting with cold traffic or hot leads, however. You will target *warm traffic*. These are people that are somewhat familiar with you (Solution or Your Solution Aware).

Start targeting traffic in this order. It's sorted from easiest to convert down to the most difficult.

Work your way down the list and start at the point when you can say "Yes" to one of the audiences listed below.

### If You Have a Customer List

If your business collects emails or phone numbers of your customers, you're going to want to upload that list to create a Custom Audience. (Refer back to Chapter 5 to refresh your memory on Custom Audiences and how to create them.)

Once you have your list uploaded, you'll need an offer. You probably can't use your main offer since many of the people on your list will have already purchased it. Some ideas you could use are a flash sale or holiday sale. If you don't want to discount, you can create a unique bundle or product that is desirable to your existing customers.

The reason you'll advertise to your current customers first is because, of all the people in the world, they're most likely to buy from you again. You can use this revenue to fund your ads while you're learning Facebook Ads.

### If You Have a Prospect List

If you don't have a list of paying customers, but you have a list of phone numbers or emails for prospects, this is your next best option. They already know of you, but they haven't purchased yet.

Upload your prospect list to create a Custom Audience.

Once you have your list uploaded, you'll need an offer. Your main offer should work for this list since they haven't purchased from you before. One of your lower-priced offers would make sense too because the lower dollar amount is usually easier to sell.

### If You Have Traffic Going to Your Site from Another Source or Inside a Mobile App

If you don't have a list of customers or prospects but you get a decent amount of organic traffic or traffic from other paid sources, you can advertise directly to those visitors.

After the pixel is in place, you'll create a Custom Audience based on website visitors. They know a bit about you since they were on your site, but you have no idea how much they like or trust you yet.

We always recommend that you segment your Website Visitor Audiences based on their last visit to your site. Someone who visited yesterday is more attentive to you than someone who visited 30 days ago (or even 90 or 180 days ago). (See Chapters 5 and 21 through 23 about segmenting based on time.)

### If You Don't Have Any Traffic or Lists

If you have a website with little to no traffic and no lists of prospects or customers, you're going to have to start with cold traffic from scratch and use Facebook Ads to create your traffic and prospect lists.

*This is the most difficult way to start.*

Instead of creating a Custom Audience of people who have some connection to your business, you're going to tell Facebook as much as you can about your ideal customer and let Facebook start showing ads to them.

You'll do this by running a Traffic Campaign. (Refer back to Chapter 7 about the nuts and bolts of a Traffic Campaign.) You can only target people based on their demographics, interests, and behaviors. Your offer should try to generate leads or attempt to sell a low-priced product in the $7 to $49 range. Once you get this campaign running, then you can retarget the website traffic, leads, and buyers in one of the Campaigns we described above.

## HOW AD SETS FIT INTO YOUR FACEBOOK AD CAMPAIGN

Ad Sets are one level below Campaigns (Campaigns have Ad Sets, and Ad Sets have ads) and are where you will deploy your audiences along with other useful filters.

Ad Sets are how you direct Facebook to serve ads to your targeted audience. To say it another way, Ad Sets are where you define exactly WHO sees your ad.

For some larger Ad Accounts, it's not uncommon to have hundreds, sometimes thousands, of Ad Sets per Campaign. If you're new to running Facebook Ads, that may seem like an awful lot of Ad Sets. Once you understand all the flexibility and variables available to you at the Ad Set level, you'll understand why that is!

This is one advantage of Campaign Budget Optimization: You can have a single Campaign with a budgeted ad spend and then let Facebook allocate your ad budget to the Ad Sets you build.

For a majority of new advertisers, you will start out with just a single Ad Set under your Campaign.

## DIALING IN YOUR FACEBOOK AD SET

There are several important parameters you will define inside your Ad Set. You will decide where your ad is placed, when the ad will be seen, who will see your ad, and how your ad will be optimized for exposure and cost.

These are areas where an advertiser can gain an advantage over the competition. There is significant leverage for the advertiser that can choose the most strategic placements and targeted audience.

First make sure you set the Facebook/Instagram Business Page or App you are promoting. Every ad must be aligned with a Page or App. You will see all the Pages and Apps you have access to on the lists. Choose the proper one, especially if you are managing several Pages!

If you will be testing various aspects of your creative, be sure to toggle the Dynamic Creative switch to On so that you can do that within your Facebook Ad (the third level of a Facebook Campaign). You'll learn about Testing in Chapter 28.

## SETTING YOUR AD SCHEDULE AND AD SPEND LIMITS

For campaigns with a Lifetime Budget, you must choose when the Ad Set will start and end. It defaults to starting with the current time and date and ending in a month. You can change either of the dates. The ads won't truly start running the moment you hit Publish because they have to be approved by Facebook's editorial team. Leaving the current time is recommended to get your ads running as soon as possible.

*Important Note:* For Lifetime Campaigns with a beginning and end date, it's not recommended that you change the end date without modifying the budget. This will throw off the Optimizer. If you shorten the duration of a Lifetime Budget Campaign, you should go back to the Campaign and lower your budget.

To do this, take the current total budget and divide by the current number of days. Use that number as the amount of spend per day. Then multiply it by however many days you're adding or removing to see how much to add or remove to the new budget.

You can also set spending limits per ad group inside the Budget & Schedule section of the Ad Set. Because your total budget amount is set at the Campaign level and distributed among its Ad Sets, this gives you finer control of your spending. You can set a minimum and maximum spend per Ad Set. It may not reach either the minimum or maximum if you don't have enough traffic.

With CBO (Campaign Budget Optimization), Facebook automatically "load balances" all the Ad Sets inside a Campaign. It will direct the most impressions to the Ad Sets performing best based on the Campaign Objective.

For example, if you are optimizing for visitors to your website and are running a Traffic Campaign, then if you have three Ad Sets inside your campaign and Ad Set number two is producing the lowest cost per visitor to your website, then the Facebook Optimizer will start to give that Ad Set more and more impressions and reduce those to the other two within your specified budget.

This is OK in most circumstances, but if you need or desire a more equitable share of impressions to all your Ad Sets, then you must set Ad Set spending limits as seen in Figure 9-1. If you are not using CBO, then simply set your desired budget for each Ad Set within your campaign.

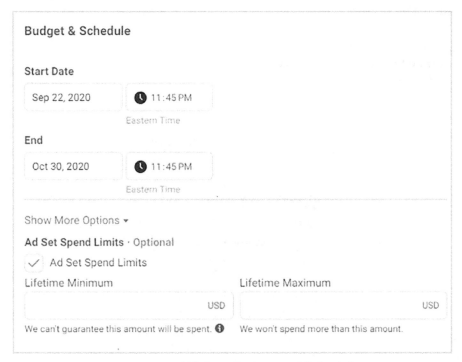

**FIGURE 9-1.** Lifetime Budget and Schedule

## CHOOSING YOUR TARGET AUDIENCE

Once you've chosen your Budget & Schedule, the next step in your Ad Set is to choose your Audience and Targeting options to determine who sees your ads. Chapter 5 covered how to create Custom Audiences.

Click in the Custom Audiences Box to bring up a list of all of your Audiences and choose one.

You don't have to use Custom Audiences, of course, but as you learned, Custom Audiences are extremely powerful ways to target people to see your ads.

You can choose to include any of the Custom Audiences you have created, including Lookalikes. You can also exclude audiences as well.

Here's an example from a client. Seniors in Service wanted to recruit volunteers aged 55 or older who lived in Pasco County, but instead of just targeting everyone in that county, they started with a 1 percent Lookalike Audience created by modeling their volunteer database. Furthermore, they did not want to spend money recruiting volunteers already in their database, so they used the Exclude parameter to exclude their volunteer Custom Audience (the same one they modeled to create the Lookalike Audience). See how this looks in Figure 9–2.

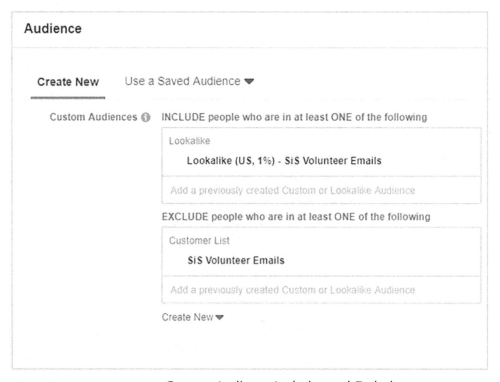

**FIGURE 9–2.** Custom Audience Includes and Excludes

## Narrow by Location

When you are narrowing down a Targeted Audience, you can further narrow by choosing the location of the people you want to reach.

You can choose countries, regions or states, designated market areas, cities, ZIP or postal codes, or even rings around an address or pinned location. You also have the choice to target:

- Everyone in the location
- Just people that live in the location
- People recently in the location
- People traveling to the location (from more than 125 miles away)

When adding a location, you can use the browse button, but that will only allow you to use areas as small as a country. When you type in a location, you can quickly find what you are looking for.

Note that when you select an area to pin on the map, you can narrow your selection down from a 50-mile radius to a 1-mile radius.

This can be very effective at pinpoint targeting a small area around a local business, for example.

You can also select more than one location. For example, you can choose:

- United States and Canada
- Chicago, New York, and Los Angeles
- Multiple ZIP codes
- Multiple pinpoint areas

You can also exclude areas. For instance, if you do business in the continental United States, you can choose United States and exclude Alaska and Hawaii.

This gives you tremendous flexibility and control over who sees your ads based on where they are located.

Figure 9–3 on page 96 shows an example of micro-targeting a one-mile radius. This can be very effective at targeting people in a building such as a convention center where you are hosting a trade show, or possibly expanding it to several miles if you are targeting students and faculty on a college campus.

## Narrow Your Audience By Age/Gender/Language

Once you select a location, you can select the age of the person in yearly increments from 13 to 65, then 65+.

It's a good practice to narrow your age range to at least exclude minors if your product isn't for them and also to dial in your age range if you know your typical customer age range.

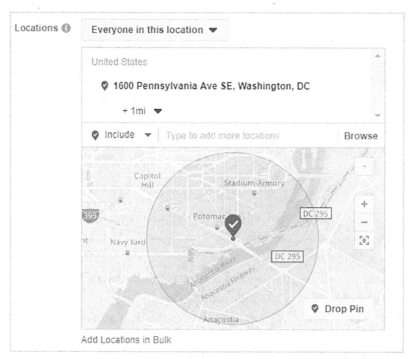

**FIGURE 9-3.** Audience Location Targeting

You also have the option of narrowing down your ad by gender. In many cases, you will leave this set to both. However, for men's and women's products and services it makes sense to exclude one or the other. Note this is unnecessary when targeting a Lookalike Audience because if your model Audience has a gender bias, so will your Lookalike Audience.

Then, in the rare case you want to target people who use a language that isn't common to your location choice, you can specify it here. Normally the language field is left blank.

You don't need to choose English if you're in the USA or another primarily English-speaking locale. Specifically, if you wanted to reach Spanish-speaking people in the USA or French-speaking Canadians, you would choose that language here and then obviously produce your creative in that language.

Let's continue with the Seniors in Service example. As you recall, they only wanted to reach people in a single county who were aged 55 and older. See how this looks in Figure 9-4 on page 97.

## USING DETAILED TARGETING TO BUILD AN AUDIENCE

Detailed Targeting uses demographics, interests, and behaviors that Facebook knows about its users. Facebook has history on the posts you like, share, and comment on and

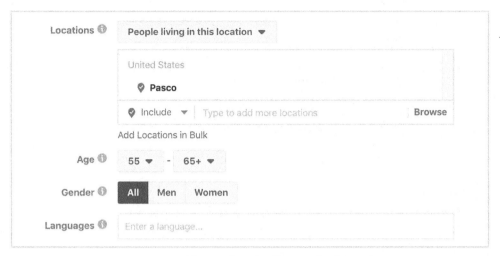

**FIGURE 9–4.** Narrowing Audiences by Location

the Pages you engage with. Your profile contains your age, gender, and relationship status. Your mobile phone's location services let Facebook know where you are and where you are traveling to and from.

Remember, if you are prospecting, you should try to use a Lookalike Audience first. Facebook's AI is better at matching people than the Detailed Targeting in almost all cases.

We're not covering all the different options available to you for Detailed Targeting. Not only are there too many to discuss, they are constantly changing. Something that may be available to you today might be removed next month.

Here are the macro-categories in Detailed Targeting:

- *Demographics*. Includes: Education, Financial, Life Events, Parents, Relationship, and Work
- *Interest*. Includes macro categories like: Business and Industry, Entertainment, Family and Relationships, Fitness and Wellness, Food and Drink, Hobbies and Activities, Shopping and Fashion, Sports and Outdoors, and Technology
- *Behaviors*. Has to do with actions people take on Facebook like using Facebook Payments, clicking on a Shop Now button in an ad, expressing interest in a Facebook event, or being rabid soccer fans based on their post interactions. Behaviors also include non-Facebook activity like recent travelers, having an upcoming anniversary, or people who commute each day.

Here's how Detailed Targeting works: As you add targets to your list, your Audience grows. In terms of Boolean logic, every target you add, there is an "or" placed after it.

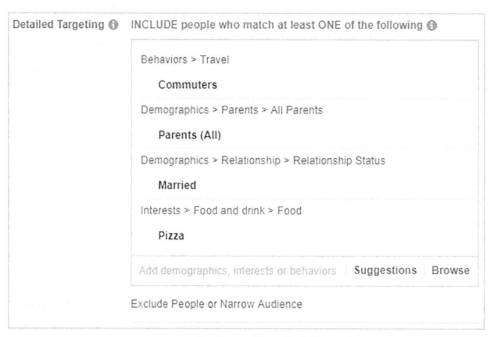

**FIGURE 9–5.** Audience Detailed Targeting

So, if you look at Figure 9-5 you might misinterpret the criteria. A pizza place wanted to target married parents who are commuters and love pizza. This is not the way to build the target. What is actually happening here is that they are targeting anyone who is married, anyone who is a parent, anyone who is a commuter, and anyone who likes pizza.

This is obviously a HUGE Audience and includes more people the pizza place DOESN'T want than actually want.

A better strategy is to use the Narrow Audience option below the targeting box to force the Audience to include a specific target group. In Boolean logic this is adding an "and" versus an "or". In Figure 9-6 on page 99, this is how the pizza place should have built their targeting.

By using the Narrow By/Must Match features, you can match a very specific person. It's still not as powerful as a Lookalike Audience in most cases, but it can help get you started when you don't have the ability to create a Lookalike or when you're doing Audience Layering that you'll learn about in this chapter.

## TARGETING FACEBOOK CONNECTIONS

Facebook Connections allow you to reach people who like your Page or friends of people that like your Page, people who have used your app or their friends, and people who have responded to one of your events.

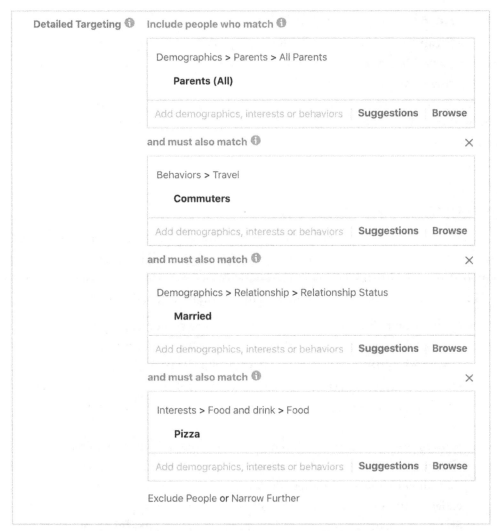

**FIGURE 9–6.** Audience Narrowing Detailed Targeting

This is only really useful in two ways. First, you can prospect to friends of your existing connections. They'll be shown your ad and the top of it will say "Friend's Name likes Your Page Name" for additional social proof. Second, there's a strategy for getting your Business Page Likes count to over 100 (you'll learn this in Chapter 23). Do not use this feature for anything more than this.

## SAVING AUDIENCES FROM THE AD SET INTERFACE

If you will end up using an Audience more than once, it's smart to build it once and then save it for future use. All you need to do is simply click the Save This Audience button at the bottom of the Audience.

## "WHERE ARE MY ADS SEEN?"

Facebook can place your ad in millions of places, including multiple places within Facebook and Instagram (which they own) as well as website and mobile apps owned by third parties unaffiliated with Facebook.

Automatic Placements is the default, and we're warning you to NOT accept this default when you start out. Not only do different Placements have very different users, it also involves having to develop unique creative for ads that run on all these Placements. You'll dive into Placements in Chapter 11.

## EXCLUSIONS AND BLOCK LISTS

Exclusions prevent your ad from being shown along with specific types of content or on specific websites. This only applies to ads on the following Placements: Audience Network, Instant Articles, and In-Stream Videos.

Filters allow you to choose between Limited, Standard, and Full inventory.

- *Limited* won't show your ads with content that shows tragedy or conflict (death, war), all debated social issues (abortion), objectionable activity (drug use), sexual or suggestive (nudity), strong language (none at all), explicit content (violence to wounds), adult apps (alcohol delivery or buy/sell apps like Offerup), streaming (anything live), dating, news, gaming, weather, travel, food and drink apps. It's very strict.

- *Standard* loosens up the requirements and is the default. It won't show your ads with tragedy, social issues with direct attacks or strong language, drugs, nudity (but allows suggestive or revealing content), multiple uses of strong language, violence, and major wounds. It filters alcohol delivery apps, and games that focus on war, drug, or alcohol usage. It's much less strict, but still keeps your ads away from most "objectionable" content.

- *Full* inventory is *almost* all of the content. Your ads still won't show where there are direct attacks on protected characteristics (race or religion), sale or use of any drugs (legal or not), nudity, and excessively violent content.

Block lists prevent your ads from appearing in specific places. You can choose to block apps, Audience Network sites, Instant Article publishers, or video publishers for your in-stream video ads. You can find the list of publishers in your Assets Library, then Brand Safety, then Block Lists. Then you can choose the ones you want to block proactively. Also, under Brand Safety is a report that shows where your ads have appeared so you can use that to block sites reactively once your ad has shown up.

Once you enable a block list, Facebook will also block all of the very low-volume publishers by default. It will also block the preinstalled apps (that are not in the app store, but already come with a smartphone) as soon as you add a block list.

## OPTIMIZATION AND DELIVERY

The last dial to lock in is Optimization and Delivery. Note that your choice in variables will change based on the Campaign Optimization method you choose. We're going to cover all the ways you can optimize delivery and performance of your Ad Sets in the very next chapter.

Chapter 10

# Optimizing Your Ad Sets within Your Targeted Audience

F acebook makes it very easy to get a campaign running quickly. By giving you default settings and automatic functions, they satisfy your desire to launch quickly. Do this at your risk (or peril).

You haven't completed your Ad Set setup at this point. In the previous chapter, you learned the basic settings and spent a great deal of time on targeting your audience. You cannot move on to creating your ad yet until you fully understand Placements and Optimizing for a result.

In this chapter we're going to show what's behind each setting and by the end you will know what settings you can leave on and which ones you don't want to turn on until you've gotten much more experience and test data.

## OPTIMIZATION AND DELIVERY BASICS

We find this setting to be amongst the most confusing parts of a Facebook campaign. You learned about Campaign Objectives in Chapter 7, so hopefully it's pretty clear by now that you should choose an objective to match the goal of your campaign.

However, inside an Ad Set, you can choose different events you want to optimize for.

### Optimization for Ad Delivery

What you select here will affect who sees your ads. For example, you could be setting up a Traffic Campaign but optimize it for Daily Unique Reach, Impressions, Link Clicks, or the default setting: Landing Page Views.

The best explanation we can give is that while you set a goal at the Campaign level, the actual dial that truly optimizes your ads happens here. What you are telling Facebook is to get you as many/much of the selected method result as efficiently as possible.

Quite often, the default choice made for you is the right choice, but as you gain experience you may discover that by trying out different settings, you may improve your results and gain a competitive edge over your competition in the Ad Auction.

### Cost Control

You should only set a cost control if you have a specific cost requirement such as a maximum cost per conversion or average cost per conversion you want to get.

Cost controls are optional, and this is not something you will find you need to manage. You should allow the Facebook Optimizer to take your budget and get the most results at the best price. When you add cost controls, you're limiting Facebook's ability to achieve your goal. For example, you may want to limit Facebook to getting you leads that cost $5.00 or less. That may not be realistic when in fact the average cost per lead in your market is $10 per lead.

We've seen many advertisers try to use this control and end up with campaigns that get no impressions.

Again, the default options for Optimization and Delivery are often fine for the beginner. Facebook will balance efficient spending of your budget to achieve your campaign objective.

## EVERY CAMPAIGN TYPE HAS DIFFERENT OPTIMIZATION SETTINGS

You will learn all the settings for each campaign type and the implications of these settings.

In several cases we share our best practices based on our experiences.

### Optimization for a Brand Awareness Campaign

No options are available for a Brand Awareness Campaign. The default is set to Ad Recall Lift.

## Optimization for a Reach Campaign

As shown in Figure 10–1, with a Reach Campaign, you can choose to optimize for:

- Reach—which is as many people as possible.
- Impressions—which will show your ads as many times as possible to people more than once.

You can also limit how often people see your ads by using a Frequency Cap. The more urgently you want people to see your ad, the higher the frequency cap you will choose.

For example, if you have an audience of people who visited your website within the last day, you might want to set it to show your ad three times every day. For people who visited your site more than two weeks ago, you might only want to show an ad one time every two days.

## Optimization for a Traffic Campaign

With a Traffic Campaign, you can optimize the campaign for four different types of Traffic:

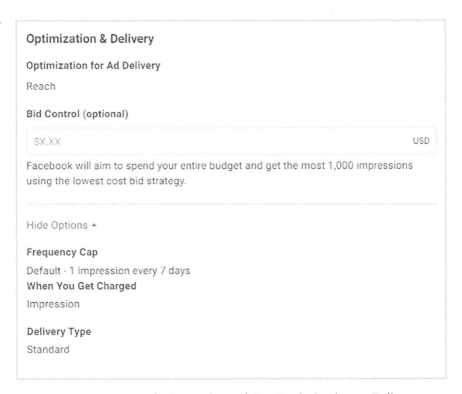

**FIGURE 10–1.** Reach Campaign Ad Set Optimization & Delivery

- Landing Page Views
- Link Clicks
- Daily Unique Reach
- Impressions

Landing Page Views only applies when you're driving people to your website. It will optimize the Audience and show to people most likely to click on your ad and load your website based on their history using Facebook.

Link Clicks will optimize your Audience for people likely to click on the ad. They might go to your landing page, app, or messenger, or they might click to your Page or to see comments. Many advertisers make this mistake. If you want to optimize for people to visit your website, optimize for Landing Page views rather than Link Clicks. Make sure you also include on Landing Page views when you run your reports as shown in Figure 10-2.

Daily Unique Reach will show your ads to as many people as possible, but only be shown once a day to each person. Similar to a Reach Campaign, you might use this when everyone in the Audience is equal in importance, but you still want Facebook to give you traffic. You will only use this type of method when you have Custom Audiences such as customers or prospects and you want as many of them to see the ads as possible.

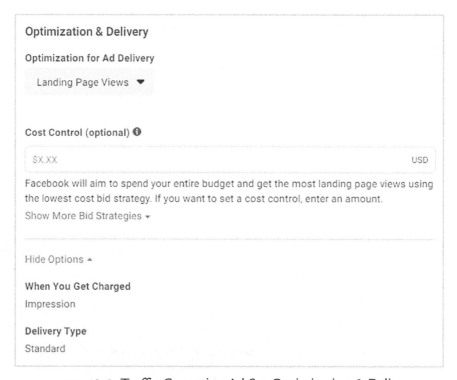

**FIGURE 10-2.** Traffic Campaign Ad Set Optimization & Delivery

Impressions will show your ads as many times as possible and people will see them more than once a day. It's best not to choose this method for a Traffic Campaign because it's given us inconsistent results and higher costs in our experience.

### Optimization for an App Installs Campaign

With an App Installs Campaign, you can optimize the campaign for:

- App Events
- App Installs
- Link Clicks

There are three types of App Events:

1. *Automatically Logged Events.* The Facebook SDK automatically logs app installs, app sessions, and in-app purchases.
2. *Standard Events.* Popular events that Facebook has created for you.
3. *Custom Events.* Events you create that are specific to your app.

You can see these events in Figure 10–3.

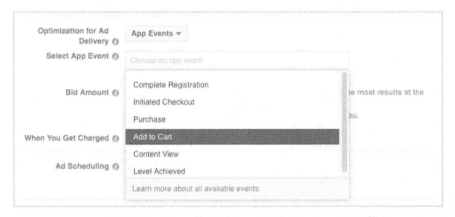

**FIGURE 10–3.** App Installs Ad Set Optimization & Delivery

Before you can publish the Ad Set, you must also choose the app you are promoting (which you already registered with Facebook) and the store/platform you will be sending your visitors to (iTunes or Google Play). This is located right beneath Ad Set Name as shown in Figure 10–4 on page 108.

Next, in the Placements area, you can specify devices.

For Android devices, you can specify all types of Tablets and Smartphones or list individual models. You can also restrict the OS Versions of the devices your ads

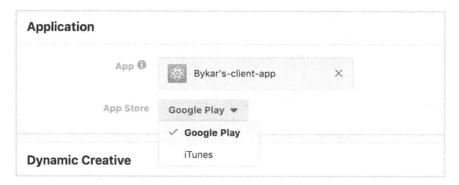

**FIGURE 10–4.** App Installs App and Store Selection

will display on in case your app is only compatible with certain versions as seen in Figure 10–5.

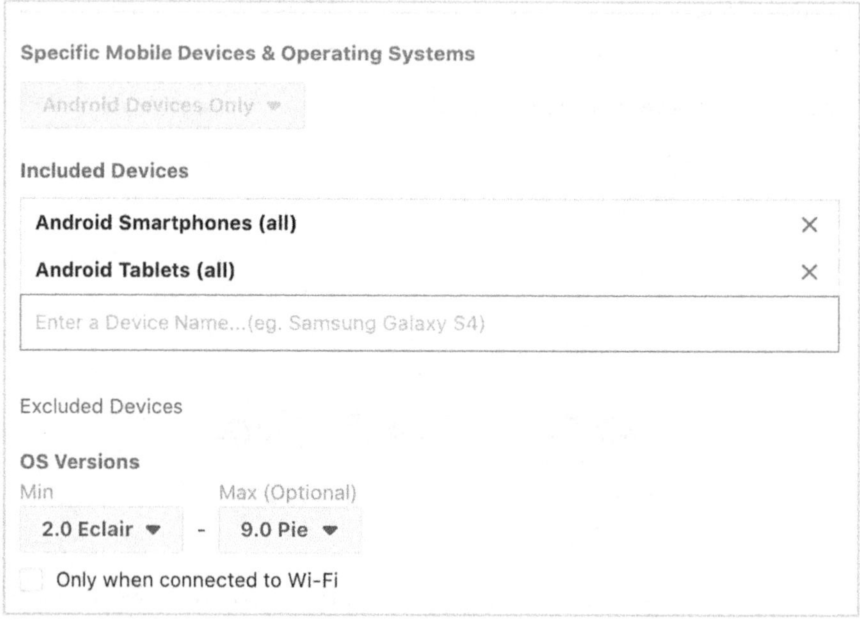

**FIGURE 10–5.** App Installs Android Device Selection

For Apple devices, you can specify all types of iPads, iPhones, iPods, or list out individual models. You can also restrict the OS Versions of the devices your ads will display on in case your app is only compatible with certain versions as shown in Figure 10–6 on page 109.

Optimization for an App Install Campaign defaults to Link Clicks. You should change it to App Installs. You can then scroll down and set your conversion window for

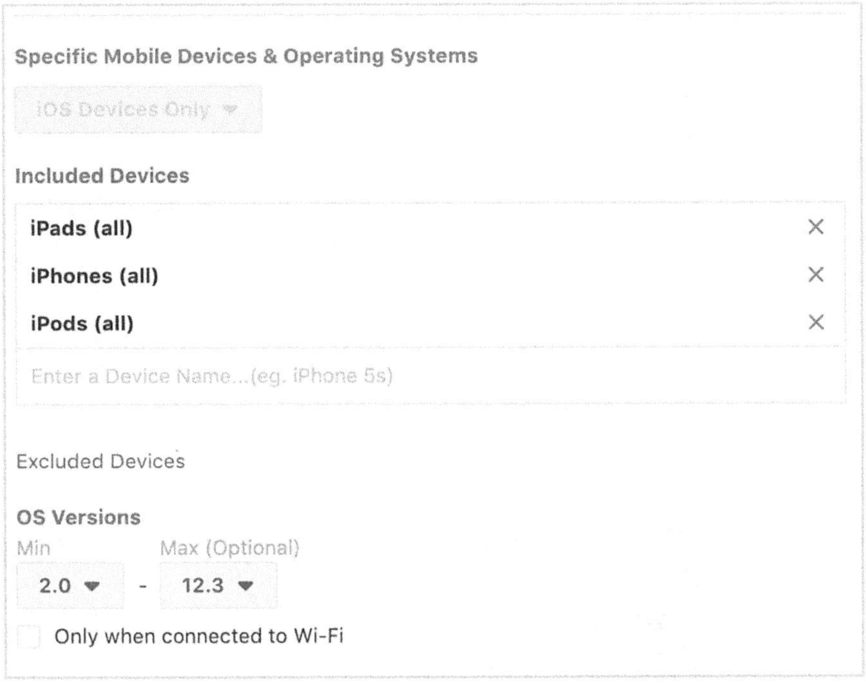

**Specific Mobile Devices & Operating Systems**

iOS Devices Only ▼

**Included Devices**

| | |
|---|---|
| **iPads (all)** | ✕ |
| **iPhones (all)** | ✕ |
| **iPods (all)** | ✕ |

Enter a Device Name...(eg. iPhone 5s)

**Excluded Devices**

**OS Versions**

Min      Max (Optional)

2.0 ▼  -  12.3 ▼

☐ Only when connected to Wi-Fi

**FIGURE 10–6.** App Installs Apple iOS Device Selection

optimization. For installs, the conversion window is only one day as shown in Figure 10–7 on page 110. For all other events, you might want to change it to a seven-day window if you have a free trial.

You can also add an optional cost controls to limit your spend. It can be a Bid Cap, where it simply won't bid more than the amount you specify in each auction and your average will be lower than the cap. Rather than limit the bid, you can have a Cost Cap, which will put a maximum average bid for each app install result. It can be a Target Cost to keep your cost-per-app-install within 10 percent of your limit.

Before you can create an ad for an app install, you'll have to register your app in the App Dashboard on the Facebook Developers' site. Although it's not required, you should also integrate the Facebook SDK into your app so you can track events like installs or purchases and optimize your ads for those.

## Optimization for a Video Views Campaign

With a Video Views Campaign, you can optimize the campaign for:

- *ThruPlay*. Helps you get the most completed video plays if the video is 15 seconds or less. For longer videos, this will optimize for people most likely to watch your video at least 15 seconds.

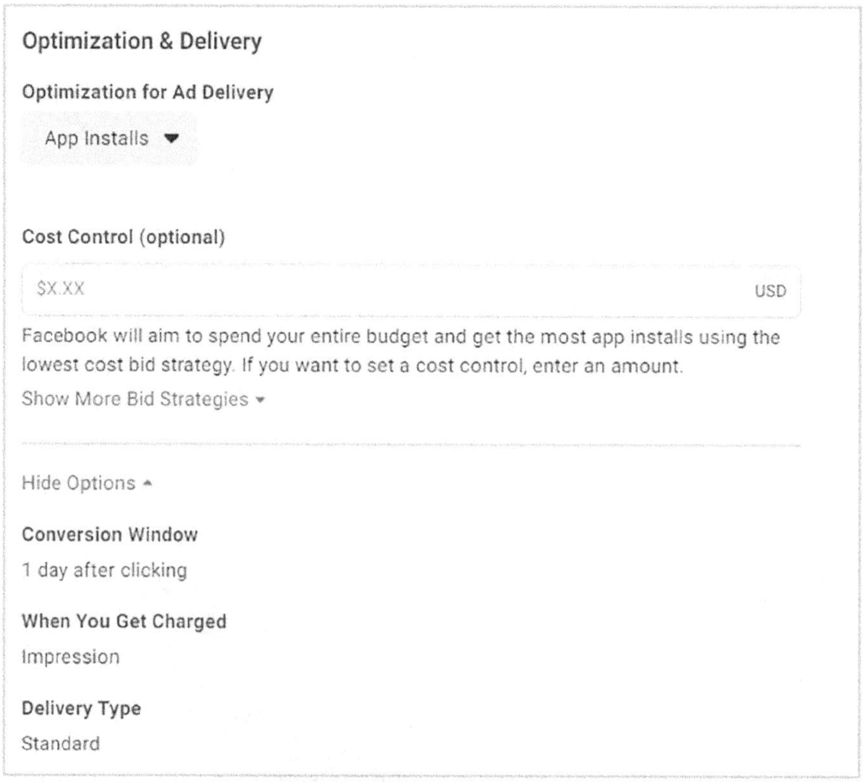

**FIGURE 10–7.** App Installs Optimization

- *Two-Second Continuous Video Views.* Helps you get the most video views of two seconds or more. Facebook says that two-second continuous video views will have at least 50 percent of the video pixels on screen at the least.

We recommend you choose ThruPlay as your method, and in terms of paying for Impressions or ThruPlay, choose Impression as you can see in Figure 10–8 on page 111.

When most people see this option for the first time, they will select to only pay when their video is played because that is the objective. In our testing, it doesn't change the price much to leave it on paying by impression. The advantage of paying by impression is the Optimizer will advertise to a larger Audience because it doesn't have to only show the ad to people most likely to view it. The wider the Audience that the Optimizer has to choose from, the more likely it is to get you better people.

### Optimization for a Lead Generation Campaign

When you choose the Lead Generation object, there aren't any optimization choices to make as you can see in Figure 10–9 on page 111. Facebook will show your ads to people it thinks will become leads.

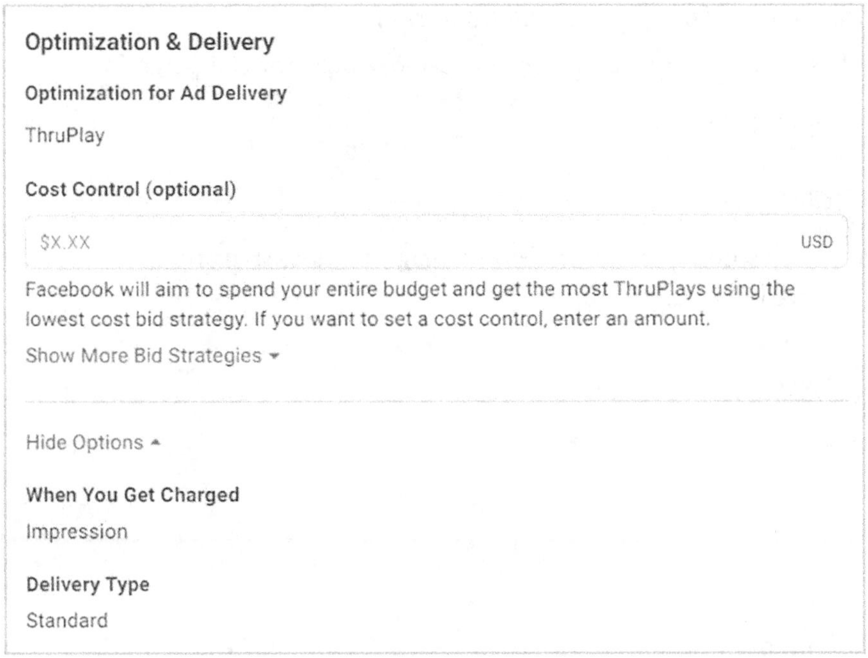

**Optimization & Delivery**

**Optimization for Ad Delivery**

ThruPlay

**Cost Control (optional)**

$X.XX                                                                USD

Facebook will aim to spend your entire budget and get the most ThruPlays using the lowest cost bid strategy. If you want to set a cost control, enter an amount.

Show More Bid Strategies ▾

Hide Options ▲

**When You Get Charged**

Impression

**Delivery Type**

Standard

**FIGURE 10–8.** Video View Campaign Ad Set Optimization & Delivery

**Optimization & Delivery**

**Optimization for Ad Delivery**

Leads

**Cost Control (optional)**

$X.XX                                                                USD

Facebook will aim to spend your entire budget and get the most leads using the lowest cost bid strategy. If you want to set a cost control, enter an amount.

Show More Bid Strategies ▾

Hide Options ▲

**When You Get Charged**

Impression

**Delivery Type**

Standard

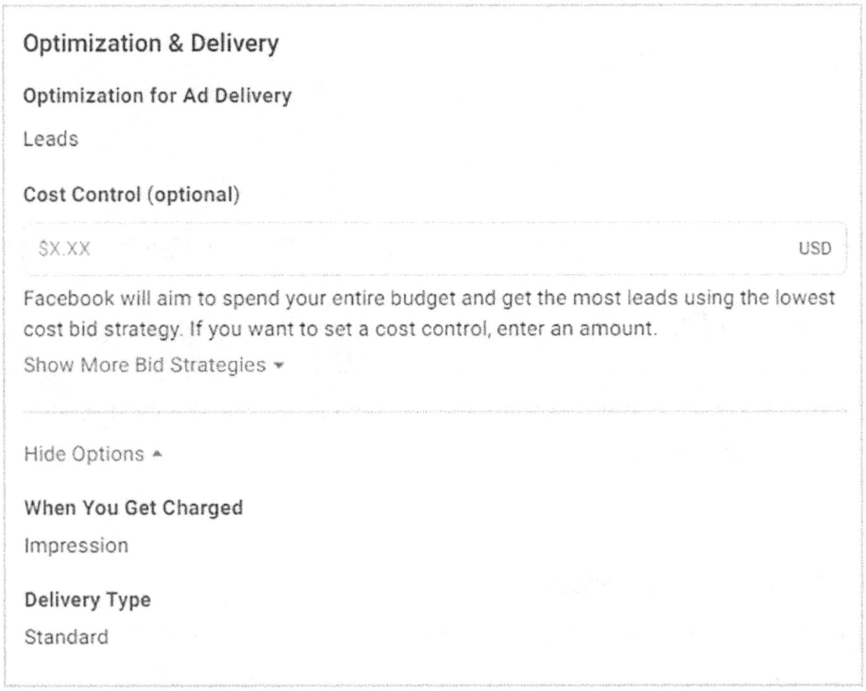

**FIGURE 10–9.** Lead Generation Campaign Ad Set Optimization & Delivery

### Optimization for a Post Engagement Campaign

With a Post Engagement Campaign, you can optimize the campaign for:

- Post Engagements
- Impressions
- Daily Unique Reach

We recommend optimizing for Post Engagements when using this type of Campaign as you can see in Figure 10-10.

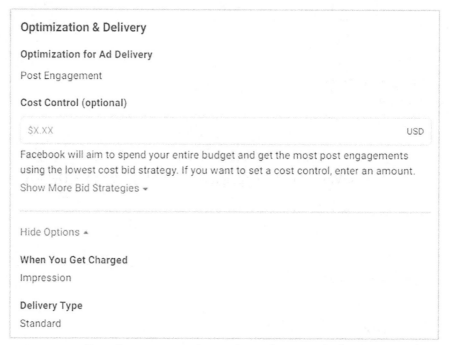

**FIGURE 10-10.** Post Engagement Campaign Ad Set Optimization & Delivery

### Optimization for a Page Likes Campaign

With a Page Likes Campaign, Facebook automatically optimizes for Impressions, and if your Bidding Strategy is anything other than Lowest Cost (at the Campaign level) then you can specify your average or maximum bid per Like as you can see in Figure 10-11 on page 113.

### Optimization for an Event Response Campaign

With an Event Response campaign, you can optimize the campaign for:

- Event Responses

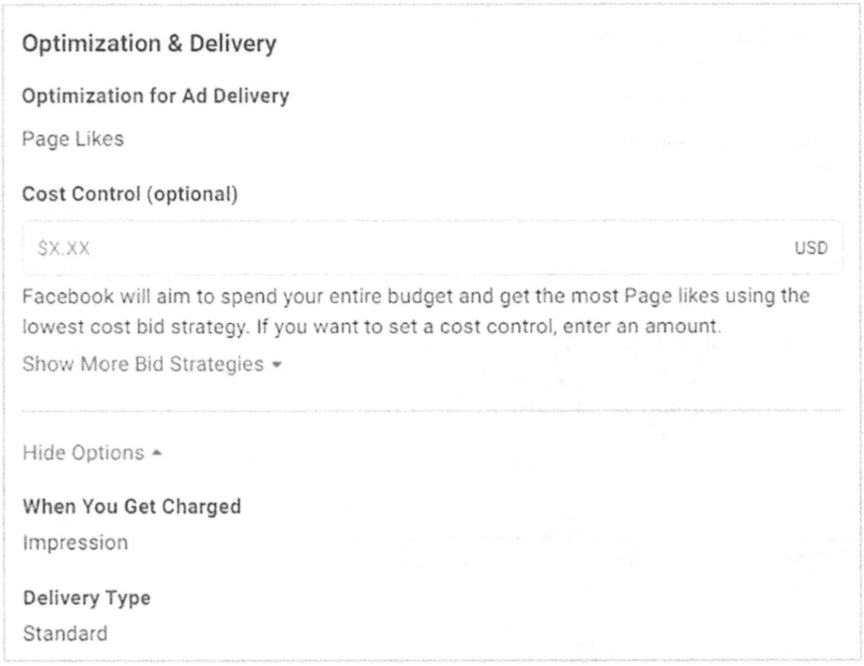

Optimization & Delivery

Optimization for Ad Delivery

Page Likes

Cost Control (optional)

$X.XX                                                                    USD

Facebook will aim to spend your entire budget and get the most Page likes using the lowest cost bid strategy. If you want to set a cost control, enter an amount.

Show More Bid Strategies ▾

Hide Options ▴

When You Get Charged

Impression

Delivery Type

Standard

**FIGURE 10–11.** Page Likes Campaign Ad Set Optimization & Delivery

- Impressions
- Post Engagement

We recommend optimizing for Event Responses when using this type of Campaign as shown in Figure 10–12 on page 114.

### Optimization for a Message Campaign

With a Message Campaign, you can optimize for conversations and leads.

Both would be valid depending on what type of action you really want. You can see the settings in Figure 10–13 on page 114.

### Optimization for a Conversion Campaign

With a Conversion Campaign, you can optimize for:

- Conversions
- Replies
- Link Clicks
- Impressions
- Daily Unique Reach

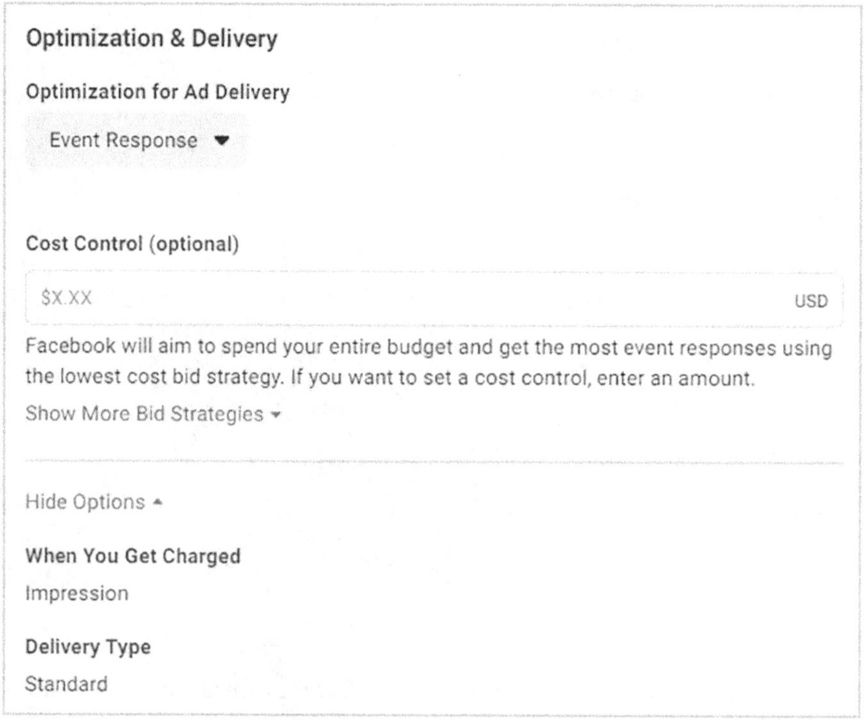

**FIGURE 10–12.** Event Responses Campaign Ad Set Optimization & Delivery

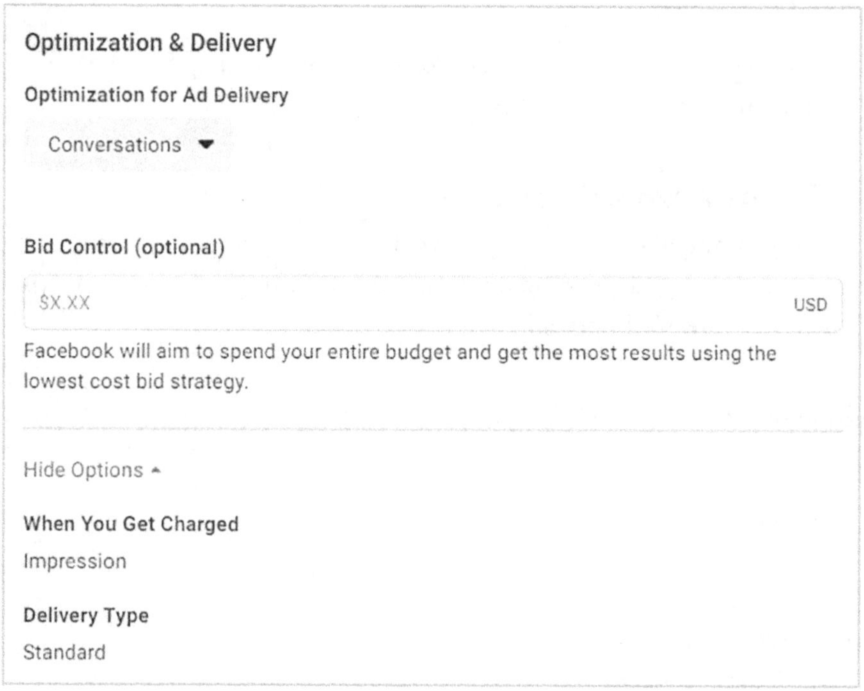

**FIGURE 10–13.** Message Campaign Ad Set Optimization & Delivery

Before we talk about what to select here, you will note that in a Conversion Campaign at the Ad Set level is where you choose the Conversion Event that was briefly touched on in Chapter 3. This selection is back at the top of the Ad Set parameters just under the name.

You can choose any one of the standard events that Facebook recognizes, or you may choose any one of the Custom Conversions that you defined as shown in Figure 10–14.

Remember to choose an event that gets at least 50 actions in a seven-day period. Otherwise, the Optimizer will have trouble calibrating and finding people that will fulfill this event.

Also note that even though there are options for Messenger and WhatsApp, the events only come from your website or app. You can't optimize for events inside Messenger or WhatsApp. These two options still use events on your website or app to optimize for, but instead of sending people to your website, app store, or into your app, their ads drive people into Messenger or WhatsApp.

You can choose any events with a green icon. A red icon indicates that event has not yet been detected by Facebook and there is likely an issue with your pixel that needs to be fixed first.

Conversion Campaigns allow you not only to choose the event to optimize for, but also how long it takes for the event to occur after viewing or seeing your ad. This is called the Conversion Window. It defaults to the longest time of seven days

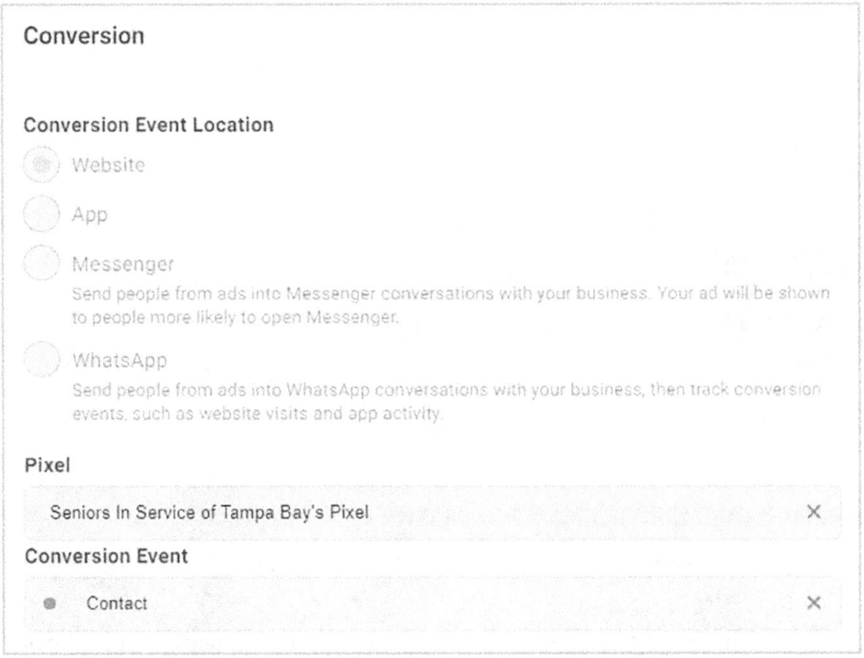

**FIGURE 10–14.** Conversion Campaign Conversion Event Setup

after clicking on your ad or one day after simply viewing it to count the event for the Optimizer.

Events will still happen outside this window and can be tracked. This setting is just what to optimize for. If your event is simple like a Lead, app install, or Page View, you should change the setting to a one-day click. If your event is longer, like an ecommerce purchase, you should leave it at the seven-day click or one-day view as shown in Figure 10–15. This would give you people most likely to buy within seven days of clicking your ad. Again, this is only for the Optimizer and not the overall event tracking.

You can use a Conversion Campaign for both cold (Lookalike) and warm (Retargeting) Audiences. You can use events both at the top of the funnel (like a Page View) and at the bottom of the funnel (like a Purchase). Since the Optimizer does a better job with more events, create your first Conversion Campaigns near the top of the funnel with events like View Content of key pages, then create Add To Cart or Lead event Ad Sets. Then, finally create Purchase Event Ad Sets. Even though purchases are the most valuable, they have the least number of events to give the Optimizer enough data to work efficiently.

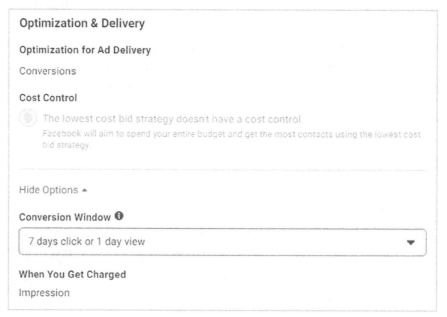

**FIGURE 10–15.** Conversion Campaign Ad Set Optimization & Delivery

### Optimization for a Catalog Sales Campaign

There are unique parameters and variables that become available to you when you choose Catalog Sales.

You should have first created a Product Catalog feed inside of Facebook. As this is an advanced procedure that changes often, we're referring you to the very detailed documentation provided by Facebook which you can find on our Resource page at www.PerryMarshall.com/fbtools.

First choose a product set. The default is All Products. To create a new product set, click the PLUS button as you can see in Figure 10-16.

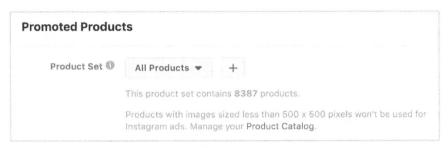

**FIGURE 10–16.** Catalog Sales Product Set Selection

Next, you will notice how different the Audience section looks. You can choose to retarget people who interacted with your catalog or target new prospects. This is a powerful way to retarget non-buyers who visit your ecommerce store.

In the example in Figure 10-16, notice this product set has 8,387 products. By having the catalog registered with Facebook and the pixel installed in the shopping cart, we can retarget people that visited any one of the 8,387 product pages and didn't purchase, added a product to the cart and didn't start checkout, or started checkout but did not complete it.

In the ads section, you can define a template that will dynamically insert the product image, title, description, price, etc. from the catalog and it will customize an ad for the Facebook user for their feed.

This is an extremely powerful technology for ecommerce owners that should be used from day one.

Note, if you are trying to reach a new Audience with a dynamic Catalog Ad, you would define your Targeted Audience just like you always do as you can see in Figure 10-17 on page 118. Figure 10-18 on page 118 shows the events you can use to create your Retargeting audience.

Finally, once you get to the Optimization and Delivery method, you can choose from:

- Link Clicks
- Conversion Events
- Impressions

Although Facebook recommends Link Clicks, we only recommend you optimize for this if you have a low-traffic ecommerce site as you can see in Figure 10-19 on page 119.

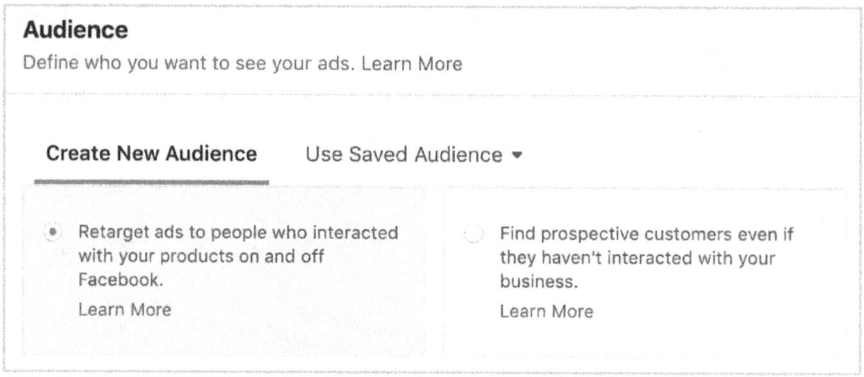

**Audience**

Define who you want to see your ads. Learn More

**Create New Audience**   Use Saved Audience ▾

○ Retarget ads to people who interacted with your products on and off Facebook.

Learn More

○ Find prospective customers even if they haven't interacted with your business.

Learn More

**FIGURE 10–17.** Catalog Sales Audience Creation

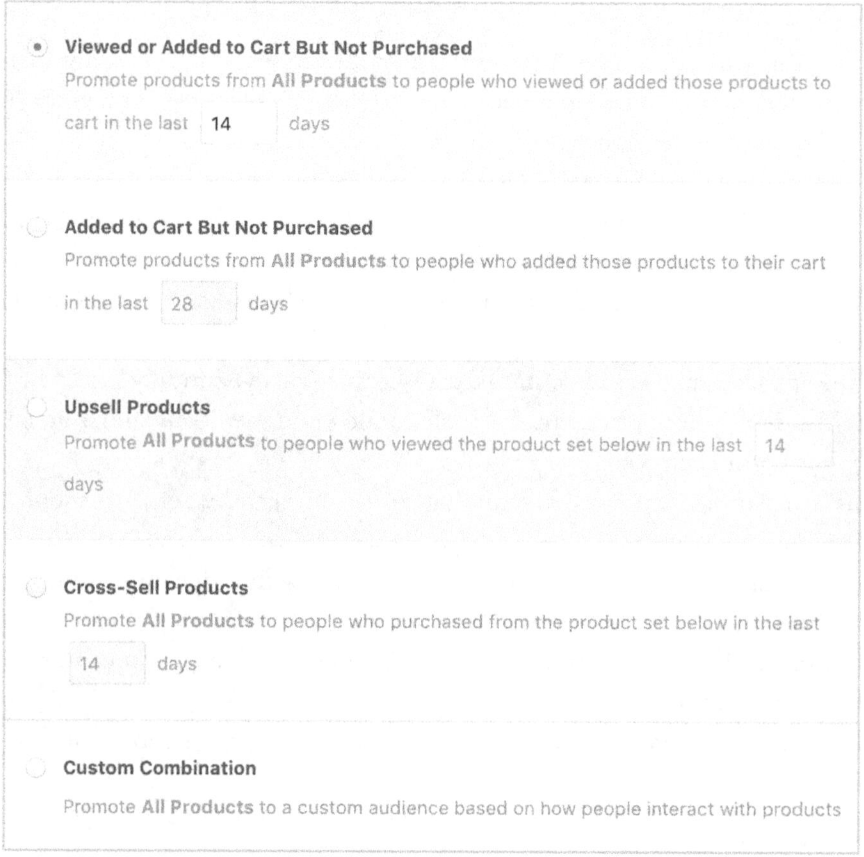

● **Viewed or Added to Cart But Not Purchased**

Promote products from **All Products** to people who viewed or added those products to cart in the last ⬚ 14 ⬚ days

○ **Added to Cart But Not Purchased**

Promote products from **All Products** to people who added those products to their cart in the last ⬚ 28 ⬚ days

○ **Upsell Products**

Promote **All Products** to people who viewed the product set below in the last ⬚ 14 ⬚ days

○ **Cross-Sell Products**

Promote **All Products** to people who purchased from the product set below in the last ⬚ 14 ⬚ days

○ **Custom Combination**

Promote **All Products** to a custom audience based on how people interact with products

**FIGURE 10–18.** Catalog Sales Audience Retargeting Options

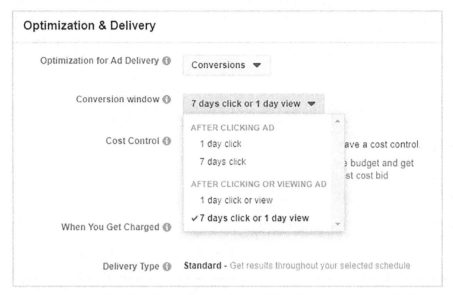

**FIGURE 10-19.** Catalog Sales Campaign Ad Set Optimization & Delivery

You should choose Conversions if your store has a decent amount of traffic (5,000 visitors or more per day).

The reason you should choose Conversion Events versus Impressions like in other Objectives is that you want the Facebook Optimizer to focus its efforts on finding the most likely users to convert at the deepest parts of the funnel here. However, you may choose Impressions if you don't feel that you are getting enough actions to allow the Optimizer to get statistical significance.

# Chapter 11

# Location, Location, Location: Facebook Placements

A dvertisers traditionally have made choices about where to run their ads: TV, newspaper, billboard, or magazines. For TV, they choose the channel and time they want their ads to run. For newspapers, they choose the section and sometimes the weekend or weekday edition for prime placement. For billboards, they choose a physical location (highway, city, etc.). With magazines, they choose which publication and what month.

It's no different with Facebook. Not only do we get to choose WHO sees our ads, we also get to choose WHERE they will see them.

Facebook has many places they can serve your Ads which they call Placements, which are platforms and devices where your ads will show. Your ads can appear in different places on Facebook, Instagram, Facebook's Audience Network (apps and websites), Messenger, Stories, and more.

Each placement has different format (orientation and length) requirements. There are currently seven different categories of placements grouped by format requirements. More importantly, because each placement interrupts the user in a different way, the ad has to grab their attention and enrich their experience in a slightly different way.

Just like a "one size fits all" hat mostly fits most people, but not very well, it's the same for using the same ad in all of the different possible placements—it will work, just not as well as it could if they were slightly optimized for each placement. Not every placement is the same. In this chapter, you'll learn how to select the right Placements for your advertising goals.

## AUTOMATIC PLACEMENTS

The default Facebook chooses for you is Automatic Placements. Automatic actually means all placements. Never use Automatic Placements until you have absolutely exhausted all the traffic from the placements we prioritize here. There are several low-quality locations that will give you cheap clicks but will never convert into sales. We recommend that you ALWAYS edit and choose your placements as you can see in Figure 11–1.

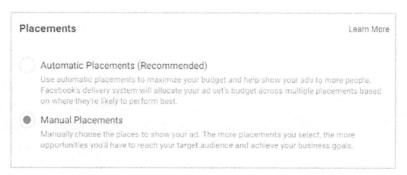

**FIGURE 11–1.** Automatic vs. Manual Placements

The two main placements you'll use are the Facebook News Feed and the Instagram Feed. All the options will be covered, but you should focus your effort on the two feed items because they have the best performance overall.

## DEVICES

In addition to where you want your ads to show (the placement), you can also choose the devices you want to show your ads inside the Ad Set. Your available choices are:

1. All Mobile Devices
2. Android Devices Only
3. iOS Devices Only
4. Feature Phones Only (used primarily outside the U.S.)

The best reason for limiting to mobile only or a specific platform (iOS or Android) is if you have an app and it only works on one of the platforms.

Remember that about 93 percent of Facebook content is viewed on mobile phones these days, so that is your primary focus.

## PLACEMENTS

We recommend that all advertisers manually select the Placements they will run on. As mentioned in Chapter 9, we see such a varied rate of response on each placement. Ads that run in the News Feed are going to perform much differently than the ads you run on Audience Network.

To effectively target, you will want to customize the creative for each Placement. The Facebook Stories format is vastly different from the News Feed, and that's very different than the Instagram Feed.

You'll discover in Chapter 12 that Facebook is starting to make things easier for you by giving you tools inside of Ad Manager to customize your creative by Placement. This may be too much to ask of a new advertiser. It also is too much work for an experienced advertiser to set up a new campaign. There is absolutely no reason to spend hours customizing creative for every Placement on a new campaign. You should test on one Placement, measure the response, and when you're satisfied with the results, then "scale" the campaign by expanding to other Placements. Let's walk through some placements.

*Note:* There is a bonus chapter on our Resource page at www.PerryMarshall.com/fbtools entitled, "Strategically Scaling Your Facebook Campaigns" with basic and advanced ways to scale your Facebook ad campaigns.

### Facebook News Feed Placements

These ads appear along with posts from friends and pages. Your ad will intermix with the normal News Feed scroll. One of the best formats we've found for these are vertical (9:16) videos. The vertical videos help you take up more screen space as people scroll by. The time limit on your videos is an incredible four hours.

### Instagram Feed Placements

These ads appear along with posts from friends. Your ad will interrupt the normal feed scroll. The best format for these are square (1:1) videos. The time limit on your videos is two minutes.

### Facebook Marketplace Placements

Marketplace Ads are not the normal listings for items for sale by individuals. They are ads for anything that appear within the listings. These ads appear on the Marketplace desktop home page or when someone browses Marketplace in the Facebook app. They have the word "Sponsored" at the top and a video will certainly stand out from the rest of the still pictures of items for sale as you can see in Figure 11–2. The best format for these are also vertical (9:16) videos. That makes your video from the News Feed usually good enough for the Marketplace. Ads in Marketplace will also show in News Feed. It's not currently possible for an ad to show only in Marketplace.

**FIGURE 11–2.** Marketplace Placement Ad

### Facebook Video Feeds Placement

Your ads appear in the Suggested Videos while someone is watching another video and they appear in the Facebook Watch feed with the list of other videos in the feed. The best format for these are vertical (9:16) videos as you can see in Figure 11–3 on page 125. They can be up to four hours in length.

*Note*: These are not the same ads that interrupt other videos. These show up in the list of videos to be watched.

**FIGURE 11–3.** Facebook Video Feeds Placement Ad

### Facebook Right Column Placement

This was the original ad placement for Facebook. It's quickly dying. The right column placement is an image-only placement that appears on the right-hand side of the News Feed on desktop browsers only. You can use a .jpg or .png file, and a landscape (16:9) orientation is best. The resolution should be at least 2,292 x 1,200px. Because most people use their phones, this image-only placement doesn't get many impressions. It's only available for Traffic, Conversion, and Catalog Sales campaigns.

### Messenger Inbox Placement

Messenger Inbox ads appear between conversations. They are a condensed ad, and when someone clicks it, they are shown the full ad within Messenger. Both are static images.

The best format is a square (1:1) image as you can see in Figures 11–4 and expanded in Figure 11–5.

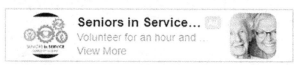

**FIGURE 11–4.** Inbox Placement Condensed Message List Ad

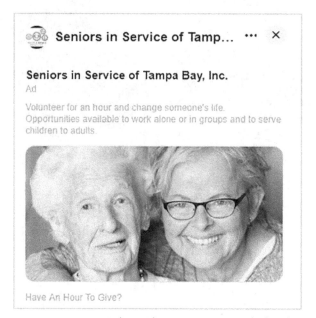

**FIGURE 11–5.** Inbox Placement Expanded Ad

### Stories Placements

Stories are full-screen experiences that show photos and videos that disappear after 24 hours. They're very similar to Snapchat. Photos show for six seconds and videos for up to 15 seconds before disappearing. If someone interacts with your video, it can be up to two minutes long.

Your video should be vertical (9:16) so it can fill the screen like the Story content natively does. You can't choose any of the three Stories placements on their own. They have to be chosen with other Stories or the Feeds placements.

When designing your creative for the ad, keep any text and logos out of the top and bottom 15 percent (250 pixels or so) as you can see in Figure 11–6 on page 127. They might get covered by the profile icon or call-to-action button. It's very important to be sure to preview your ad for these placements.

**FIGURE 11–6.** Facebook and Instagram Stories Placement

Because it uses the same vertical video format as the Facebook News Feed, any videos less than two minutes long can be shared across the placements.

## Messenger Stories

Messenger Stories and Facebook Stories are cross posted to each other. However, Messenger Story ads only show up when someone looks at their stories from inside the Messenger app. The story ad appears between organic stories from friends. These ads basically extend the reach of Facebook Stories and Instagram Stories Ads. You can see one in Figure 11–7 on page 128.

**FIGURE 11-7.** Messenger Stories Placement Ad

### Facebook Search Placements

When people use the general Search function and Marketplace search, your ads will appear mixed in with the results.

As of this writing, this is a fairly new placement. So, as of right now, we do not know how effective this placement is for advertisers.

### Messenger Sponsored Messages

Sponsored Messages are ads inside the Messenger inbox to re-engage people who already have an existing conversation with you. The Sponsored Messages placement runs by itself and will turn off all the other placements. You can only use an image. Videos aren't supported yet. The best image size to use is 1200 x 628 pixels to fill the width of the Messenger screen as you can see in Figure 11–8. Once it's opened, you can see an example in Figure 11–9.

Our guest author Larry Kim has an extensive tutorial on how to code and place these ads. You can find his contribution in Chapter 19.

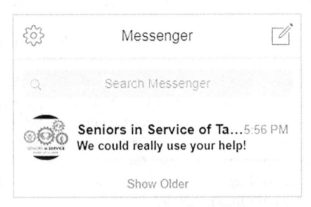

**FIGURE 11–8.** Messenger Sponsored Messages Placement Inbox Ad

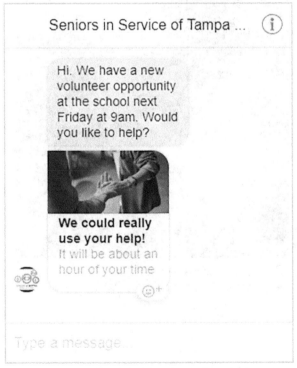

**FIGURE 11–9.** Messenger Sponsored Messages Placement Opened Message Ad

### Facebook Instant Articles

Instant Articles are fast, interactive versions of an article inside the Facebook mobile app that also appear on a publisher's website. They are hosted on the same infrastructure as Facebook, so they load up to ten times faster than standard web pages. Because they're in the app and much faster to load, Facebook says 20 percent more articles are read than offsite links and people are 70 percent less likely to abandon the article.

You can tell when a link goes to an Instant Article by the lightning bolt icon under the main image.

The Instant Articles are in line with the article and take up the full width of the screen. You should format your video to be portrait (9:16), although Facebook is currently cropping them to 1:1 if you have a link to your website or 4:5 if you don't have a link in the ad as shown in Figure 11–10. While you can send someone to your website, this placement makes sense to use an Instant Experience. Since the user is already inside an Instant Article, they will see the speed and look and feel the benefits of loading in Instant Experience from the Instant Article.

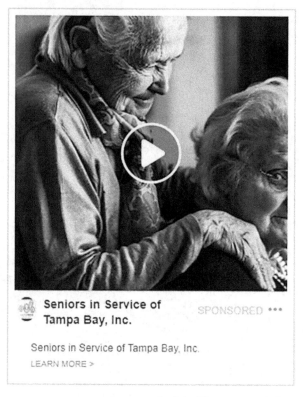

**FIGURE 11–10.** Instant Article Placement Ad

## Audience Network

The Audience Network is where you can run ads off Facebook and Instagram. It includes ads on websites and inside mobile apps. This allows you to run ads created in Facebook Ads Manager with all the same Targeting Audiences and reach people when they're not using Facebook and Instagram. This placement is still growing, but over a billion people a month already see an Audience Network ad each month. And Audience Network ads are running in a third of the top 500 Android apps.

When someone clicks on an Audience Network ad, three things can happen.

1. A link in a new browser window
2. Ask to install an app
3. Launch an existing app

Audience Network native ads allow the designer of a website or app to explicitly set the look and feel of the ad to look like the content of the site or app. Facebook will take your creative and format it to match the site. They are called *native* because they look just like the rest of the content with the exception of the word "Sponsored" in them.

Audience Network banner ads are images and have three sizes:

1. Standard Banner 320x50 pixels—Best for phones
2. Larger Banner 320x90 pixels—Best for tablets or XL phones
3. Medium Rectangle 320x250 pixels—Best for scrollable feeds

You can upload a single image, then use Facebook's tools to crop the image for each size when you create your ad.

Audience Network Interstitial ads take up the full screen. They can be a video or an image. Because they take up the full screen, they should a vertical format (9:16). The videos can be up to two minutes long.

### Audience Network Rewarded Video Ads

Audience Network Rewarded video ads are full-screen ads that users opt-in to view inside an app. In exchange for watching your ad, they get something of value inside the app like virtual currency or exclusive content. The video is 3 to 60 seconds and is not skippable. It has a call -to-action button at the end. Because most games are played in landscape mode, make the video landscape (16:9). If your Audience mostly uses apps in portrait mode, then make the video in portrait mode (9:16).

## In-Stream Video Placements

In-Stream Video Placements interrupt a person watching a video in the middle of the video (like a TV commercial). They're available both on and off Facebook. Since most videos people watch are widescreen (16:9), you should also use the widescreen (16:9) format. The video is required to have sound. The ads show up only on videos longer than three minutes and won't show up until at least one minute into the video.

### Facebook In-Stream Video Placements

Facebook In-Stream Video Placements are 5- to 15-second videos that interrupt someone viewing a video on Facebook in the middle of the video.

### Audience Network In-Stream Video Placements

Audience Network In-Stream Video Placements are five-second to two-minute videos that interrupt someone viewing a video off Facebook in the middle of another video or game.

That's all of the placements as of mid-2020. Facebook's biggest changes relate to adding placements. Be sure to check out the Resources page at www.PerryMarshall.com/fbtools for an up-to-date list of placements.

# Chapter 12

# Leveraging Creative in Your Ads to Maximize Response

A single, well-created ad could change the course of your business forever. There are numerous ones we could look at, but one that we love to share is Dollar Shave Club. This is a company that has embraced creativity and built a large subscription company and a brand around a $5 razor. Look at one of their ads in Figure 12–1 on page 134.

At any given time, they are running hundreds (yes, hundreds!) of ads.

They have such a good handle on balancing humor with a need in the marketplace. They not only have a great offer ("Try a Razor for $5") but they also match their offer to segments of the marketplace using creative that appeals to their chosen target audiences.

A new advertiser, or one with a creative block, could do wonders by spending an hour studying this company's work. (We show you exactly how to do this in Chapter 13.)

When it comes to ads and creative, it's more art than science. With Campaigns, Audiences, and Placement, it's more science than art.

Facebook Ads people are most familiar with are mixed in with posts you see from friends and family. These posts called News Feed Ads were a brilliant innovation by Facebook because they match the format of the existing content from friends. Once they launched these type of ads, Facebook's advertising growth skyrocketed.

**FIGURE 12–1.** Dollar Shave Club Creative Built an Empire

Today, new ad formats and places for them to show are continually being added.

In this chapter, you're going to start with learning the scientific part of ads such as the format of your ad and how ads work. Once you have that knowledge, then you'll learn skills for developing the artistic and creative part of ads—the part people see and respond to.

## THE ELEMENTS OF AN AD

All ads have common elements. Every ad on Facebook will be identified with a Facebook Page (or Instagram Profile). Most ads will have a headline, a visual element like a video or still image, and a call to action. An example of a mobile News Feed Ad is shown in Figure 12–2 on page 135. This is the most common ad you'll learn how to create.

This News Feed Ad is designed to be viewed on a mobile phone. In any ad, the imagery or first second of the video catches the user's attention. The headline is in bold at the bottom.

**FIGURE 12–2.** Sample News Feed Ad

The call-to-action button (Learn More) is also at the bottom.

We learned in school that people read left to right, then top to bottom. However, this isn't the case with a Facebook Ad or post. Most people scan the image area first and if it's interesting, they look at what Page posted the ad. Next, they move down to the headline, then back up to the primary text above the visual area, and finally back down to the call-to-action button.

If you've studied ads in other media, you've been told the headline is the most important part of the ad. On Facebook, the visual is the most important part. It's what attracts attention and stops the user from scrolling by.

A very important rule to be aware of is the visual area can't contain too much text, whether it's a still image or a video thumbnail. Facebook states that it has to be less than

20 percent text. If you violate this rule, an automated bot is easily able to process your image in real time and generates a warning.

This warning lets you know that Facebook will severely cut back on the number of impressions your ad will get if your text saturation is over 20 percent in the visual area. Facebook used to disapprove your ad 100 percent of the time when this happened, but now they usually allow it to run with "the brakes on."

It's best to create an image that fits within the guidelines. However, you have the ability to submit your ad for a manual review and possibly get it overruled and run your ad if you think they are incorrectly penalizing you.

Again, this applies to both images and the thumbnail image of your video. Note that once a video starts, it can have as much text in it as you want! This is another reason to use video versus images if you need to use a lot of text in the visual area of your ad.

Also note that if you're creating a Carousel Ad with multiple images, all of the images have to comply with the 20-percent-or-less text rule.

Your headline should be short. Usually four to six words works best. It will be bold type and its job is to sum up your ad. Try not to repeat what you put in the body text in the headline.

The call-to-action button typically leads to an external landing page or some action within Facebook like Messenger, an Instant Experience, or a Lead Form. This same call to action will appear at the conclusion of your video.

The text on a call-to-action button lets users know what to expect. Match your button to the action you need the user to take.

## CHOICES OF VISUAL MEDIA

Single ads give you the choice of still images or videos, while Carousel Ads give you the choice of both still images and videos. Remember, Facebook considers themselves a video company. They make it very easy to upload a video by accepting 25+ file formats. Video tools are built into Ad Manager, making it easy for novices to do video editing.

In our testing at Feedstories, we've seen video consistently outperform still images a majority of the time. And as you learned in the previous chapter about Audiences, video allows you to build a "Video Viewers" Audience that allows you to advertise to people who simply watched your video without clicking on anything.

With all that being said, you should focus on video for the visual aspect of your ads. Even if you have absolutely no experience with video, Facebook makes it easy to create an eye-catching video. If you can get good with video, you can easily also test still images.

Facebook allows you to use many different sizes of video within your ad. We have a list of recommended sizes to use the most screen real estate to attract attention in the Resources at www.PerryMarshall.com/fbtools.

The number-one job of your video is to catch users' eyes and stop them from scrolling past the rest of your ad. In order to do this, you have to be interesting enough to catch someone's attention. Facebook likes to call this "Thumb-Stopping Content."

I (Bob) first heard this when I was at Facebook headquarters in 2016. The presenters used this term multiple times during various presentations. It refers to the way that people use Facebook on a mobile phone. They scroll with their thumbs, and your job as an advertiser is to stop their thumb with your creative imagery so that they pay attention to your content. This is why it's critical to have an image or video that catches their eye.

If you think of what people expect when they're scrolling through their feeds, they look for happy pictures of friends and family. For this reason, visuals of happy people often work well.

However, just a video of happy people isn't enough. Happy strangers aren't usually compelling enough to stop someone from scrolling. You have to add something unusual to catch their attention. It shouldn't look and feel like a vanilla, boring stock image. We've all seen too many of these and keep scrolling.

Here are some examples:

The ad in Figure 12–3 is a video thumbnail image for one of our clients who is in the sporting goods space. They sell physical education equipment to schools and park districts. This thumbnail works because it's visually different. PE teachers might even recognize this because they might have either used these in the past or heard about them.

**FIGURE 12–3.** Unusual Image

This thumbnail in Figure 12–4 is from a video clip of our Rosetta Stone Seminar. Interest is drawn to this image due to the gestures and the words on the display.

**FIGURE 12–4.** Gestures and Words Make for Interesting Images

Figure 12–5 shows a thumbnail from a video showing our client on a roofing job. It's clearly not stock and the blurred background and gesture of the subject draws the user's eyes.

**FIGURE 12–5.** Not Stock Photography and Blurry Background

Figure 12–6 on page 139 is a snapshot of an entire ad. This is an unusual way of presenting a product (a tank top). The company's slogan on the back is visible, plus you're seeing the back of the model, which is unusual. The image is vertical, so it takes up space in the News Feed. We also used emojis in the ad text to give the ad even more sizzle.

**FIGURE 12–6.** Unusual Presentation of a Product

Chapters 13 through 17 dive into creative and how critical it is to your overall success.

## AD FORMATS

In addition to choosing whether you use video or a still image, you also choose an Ad Format as you can see in Figure 12–7 on page 140. Your choices are:

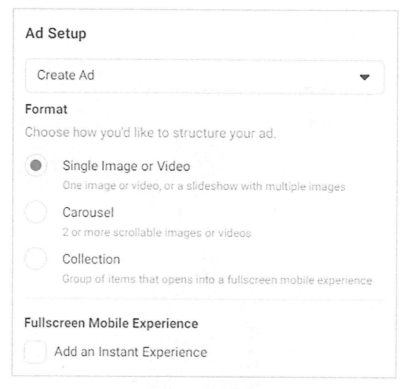

**FIGURE 12–7.** Ad Formats

- Single image or video (which includes a video slideshow of multiple still images).
- A Carousel of two or more horizontally scrollable images or videos.
- Collection format that opens a group of items into a full-screen experience.

When creating your first ad, it's fine to start with the single-image format. The Carousel format is also a nice option for featuring several images if you want to tell a deeper story or feature a couple of your most compelling products. The good thing about Carousel format is that Facebook has an option to order the images if you don't know which one people will find most compelling. You can also turn this feature off if you need the order of the images to stay fixed to tell a story.

If you want to get started with collections, Facebook has four templates. There's an Instant Storefront template that allows you to display a catalog in a grid with one main product at the top. You can create a Lookbook when you want people to see your products in action or to imitate a print catalog. You can use a Customer Acquisition template when you want to drive people to a landing page and have multiple images or videos that show off your single offer. And finally, there is the Instant Storytelling template to show people a series of visuals that will help tell the story of your product or business.

## YOUR PRIMARY TEXT

With your focus on mobile News Feed Ads, you have three lines of text to work with before you get a "... See More" link to expand the text. There are three major ways these are used. The first is just a sentence or two, the second uses a bulleted list, and the third way is as an intro to a long copy story as you can see in Figure 12–8.

**FIGURE 12–8.** Three Uses of Primary Text

Notice in our example how the bullets are replaced by emojis. Related emojis usually work better than the simple black bullets or no bullet points at all.

## CALL-TO-ACTION BUTTONS

Facebook allows you to have about 20 different predefined call-to-action buttons depending on your situation. It will even let you have no button at all with a little more space for your URL and headline. Having no button will be confusing for the user because it makes the ad look like a regular post and doesn't let people know they can click on the ad. We recommend choosing a button that makes sense for what you want the visitor to do next.

Some common ones are Learn More, which leads to another source like a landing page where they see a continuation of the content from the ad. A Buy Now usually leads to a sales page. A Download leads to some type of downloadable asset like software, PDF, or an app. Never try to trick your readers with the button text. Make it as clear as possible with what you expect them to do and you will get higher conversions.

## NEWS FEED VIDEO TECHNICAL REQUIREMENTS

Facebook wants you to upload the highest resolution source video available without any black bars on the top or bottom. Almost all file types are supported, so upload any video files you have without worrying about file types at first. Your video can be between one second and four hours long. That's quite a range! We recommend your first videos be between 15 and 60 seconds. Facebook will take almost any aspect ratio (width to height). For mobile, a 9:16 or 4:5 ratio (full portrait/vertical format) works very well. It allows you to take up as much space as possible on the screen when users are scrolling by. Otherwise, a standard 16:9 landscape format always works well.

## VIDEO THUMBNAILS

Thumbnail images are still shots that are taken from a video. They are used as the preview before the video starts playing. These have to follow the same rules as images and not have more than 20 percent text. Facebook automatically creates them for you, but you can select your own thumbnail if you want too. Facebook will automatically test different thumbnails if you let them to try to find the one that leads to the most video views. In most cases it's best to let them do that.

## CAPTIONING YOUR VIDEOS

Facebook says a staggering 85 percent of videos are played without any sound. That makes it important to turn on captioning (also known as subtitles) for your videos so people can read the dialog without having to turn on their sound. Captions are a great benefit to you as they allow you to tell more of your message. Studies have shown people are more engaged with videos with captions versus without. Facebook believes captions are so important, they make it easy to add captioning for free. You'll learn how to do that in Chapter 15.

## USING MULTIPLE ADS PER AD SET

Even experienced advertisers cannot predict what creative will resonate best with their audience. We cannot tell you how many times we've fallen in love with a particular video or image and it completely falls flat when we launch it. That's why it's critical that you always test multiple creatives to see what resonates the best with your audience.

Remember that audiences and targeting are defined in the Ad Set level so it's very easy to test multiple ads at once against the same audience. The best practice is to create two to six ads per Ad Set. *Note*: This is different from split testing, which will be covered in Chapter 28.

Facebook will begin distributing impressions of each of the ads under your Ad Set when you publish it. Ads will enter what Facebook calls the *Learning Phase*. As users respond and engage with the ad, eventually Facebook will begin to give more and more impression share to one, possibly two ads that will eventually get all the traffic for that Ad Set. Facebook is handling the heavy lifting for determining which of your ads are the best at generating responses for the best cost.

This simple testing method is the best for testing imagery. While you can run ads with different imagery and text and headlines, it's better to test one parameter. However, the imagery is the most important element in generating response. You will see the most variability in response with different images. So, test imagery first. Once you have a winning image or two, then try changing up the text area. Finally, try different headlines and calls to action.

## SPECIFIC AD CONFIGURATION BY PLACEMENT

As discussed in Chapter 11, you can allow Facebook by default to show your ads on all placements. While this is easy, it's important to understand what happens to your creative. Remember, an Instagram Story Ad looks different from a Facebook Desktop News Feed Ad. If we use a video in landscape format (16 by 9), it will look stunning on Desktop, but it will be cropped and resized to be unusable as a Story Ad on Instagram. You may be surprised what it looks like (hint: not always what you would want).

There are two big problems with a one-size-fits-all approach to your ad. The first is that important parts of your ad may get cut off or distorted when it's fit to all of the possible placements. The second is that there is a major difference in the people viewing the ads.

Someone scrolling through their News Feed wants to be engaged and entertained or informed with no particular interest. If that same person is scrolling through the Marketplace, they're interested in buying or selling stuff. Then when they are watching a video, they're *already* entertained when your in-stream video shows up. That's why a creative that works in one placement doesn't always work in another one. That's also why the News Feed gives the best results. People actively want to be interrupted with good content.

Facebook is constantly innovating in terms of new placements, but also default sizes of creative on these placements. Because this changes so frequently, we keep an updated matrix of ad specs (size, duration, etc.) at www.PerryMarshall.com/fbtools.

## INSTANT EXPERIENCES: HYPER-FAST LOAD WHEN THE CUSTOMER CLICKS

As the name implies, Instant Experiences load instantly within the Facebook App when your ad is clicked on. You can think of them as a mini landing page within Facebook instead of your website. Since it's on Facebook, it's mobile-optimized and full-screen. People can watch multiple videos and photos, swipe through carousels, even tile and pan an image all within the ad.

Facebook's Collection Ads always lead to an Instant Experience. You can optionally add an Instant Experience to a Carousel Ad or even a Single Image or Video Ad. There are four templates ready for you to customize, or you can design your own. The existing templates are for:

1. Customer Acquisition
2. Storytelling
3. Selling Products (without a catalog)
4. Augmented Reality Experience

If any of those will work for your goals, it's quite easy to customize the template and get going. You'll need plenty of images and videos. If you have an existing landing page, many times you can take the assets from that page and turn them into an Instant Experience with very little work.

If you're more advanced, you can start with a blank Instant Experience and design your own. The building blocks are shown in Figure 12–9.

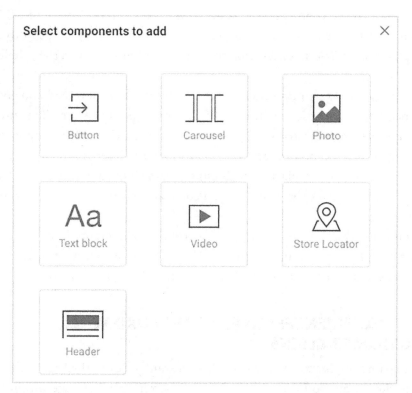

**FIGURE 12–9.** Instant Experience Building Blocks

The Header allows you to upload a logo at 882 x 66 pixels or just title the experience with text. A Video should have captions and be under two minutes. A Photo should have a width of 1080 pixels and can link optionally to a website, app store, or another Instant Experience.

The Text Block will hold as much text as you need to tell your story or describe a picture, video, or product. A Carousel is just like a Carousel Ad format. It holds from two to ten images, and any or all of them can link to a website, app store, or another Instant Experience.

A Button will take someone to a website, app store, or another Instant Experience. You can use chain Instant Experiences together to create a multipage landing experience all without leaving Facebook and loading instantly.

The Product Set links to your catalog and allows you to show info of up to 50 products once you map the fields from your catalog to the set. Finally, the Store Locator will direct people to the location of your store(s) based on their current location. This does work even if you only have one location.

# Chapter 13

# Sources of Creative Inspiration for Facebook Ads

It's time for a study break!

The last few chapters have been roll-up-your-sleeves, hard-core execution. Now we're going to have some fun, expand your horizons, and make you some money . . . all at the same time.

There is nothing worse than staring at a blank Facebook Page when you're trying to come up with an ad. In this chapter, you'll get several great resources of creative inspiration for your Facebook Ads. These resources will not only give you an idea of what's possible, but also insight as to what is working for other advertisers.

## HOW IMPORTANT IS CREATIVE TO ADVERTISING SUCCESS?

One of the most impactful meetings of my (Bob's) career occurred at Facebook Headquarters in Austin, Texas, in the fall of 2016.

I was surrounded by around 100 advertisers and agencies that all had the distinction of managing over a million dollars in ad spend over the past year.

For three days, we networked with each other and heard presentations from the VPs and head engineers of every major Facebook unit such as the Facebook News Feed, Instagram, and Ad Platform.

Pertinent to the topic at hand—Facebook Ads—is the fact that the head engineer of the Facebook Ad Platform told us, and I paraphrase,

*There are three things that determine the effectiveness of your ads—bidding, audience, and creative. Don't try and be cute. We've automated and engineered two of these three. Our algorithm can do a better job of bidding than you can manually. Our Lookalike Audience technology will do a better job than you finding targeted customers. However, the only thing we cannot automate and therefore should be 80 percent of your effort is creative.* Your creative is the most important part *of determining whether your ad is successful or not.*

That sentence changed the trajectory of my career. It's the 80/20 of Facebook Advertising. Working on improving your creative should be 80 percent of your focus like it is mine. The other 20 percent involves strategy and structure, which is covered extensively in this book.

Creative is where you, the small-time advertiser, can compete and defeat bigger advertisers by having more effective creative that connects with your Target Audience.

## ADS FROM COMPETITORS AND SIMILAR BUSINESSES

Due to the privacy scandals and alleged tampering by Putin during the 2016 U.S. elections, Facebook introduced a new concept called Page Transparency that allows any user to see what ads are running for any Facebook Page. It also shows the history of ads for Pages that have run ads about social issues, elections, or politics. This includes how much was spent. An example is shown in Figure 13–1 on page 149. As of the end of July 2020, notice how much each candidate had spent on ads in total, and over a seven-day period!

You can do this same kind of research on competitors or anyone that might be running ads on Facebook. To start looking for inspiration, visit a Facebook Page of a competitor or similar business from your desktop browser (not your mobile device). Scroll down the right column until you find the Page Transparency section as shown in Figure 13–2 on page 149. From there, click See More.

At the bottom of the summary there is an Ads From This Page section. If the Page is currently running any ads, you will see a link that says Go to Ad Library as shown in Figure 13–3 on page 149. Click that link.

Once you are there, you can see all of the active ads that Page is running. If there are any videos, carousels, or collections, you can interact with them. You can see how long they've been running as well as where they link to. Once you click on See Ad Details, you can bookmark the Facebook Page to end up with a collection of ads you'd like to use for inspiration as you can see in Figure 13–4 on page 150.

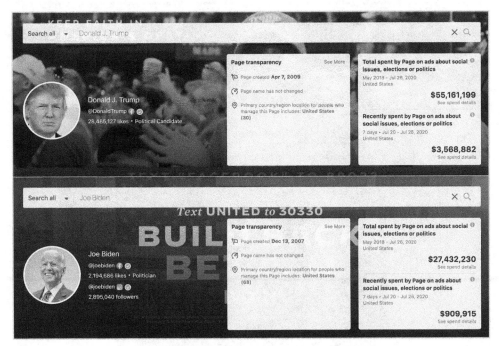

**FIGURE 13–1.** Page Transparency Data

**FIGURE 13–2.** Page Transparency

**FIGURE 13–3.** Go To Ad Library

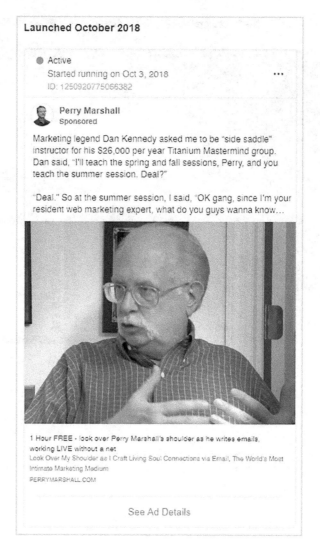

**FIGURE 13–4.** Ad Sample

After collecting ads you like, it should be much easier than staring at a blank page. You can access the library directly if you like at https://www.facebook.com/ads/library/.

## FACEBOOK BUSINESS SUCCESS STORIES

Facebook curates great case studies at https://www.facebook.com/business/success. They're sorted by business size, campaign objective, industry, product, and region. You can search for keywords or just browse. Each case study contains a story about the brand itself, the results of a campaign, a detailed explanation of what they did, and a list of the products they used.

## FACEBOOK CREATIVE HUB

You can create mock-ups in the Facebook Creative Hub outside of a campaign. That allows you to use them in multiple places and preview the ad in all 27+ placements in real time. You can access the Creative Hub directly at https://www.facebook.com/business/inspiration/creative-hub or by choosing Creative Hub under the Plan heading in the top navigation of Business Manager.

## FACEBOOK ADS INSPIRATION

You can see some of the coolest ads that are selected by Facebook's Creative Shop at https://www.facebook.com/business/inspiration. It will let you see some amazing ads from big brands. You can sort by ad type or placement.

# Chapter 14

# Creating Your First Facebook News Feed Ad

If you have not placed a Facebook Ad yet, the time has come. You are ready! It's time to swim. We're taking away your paddleboard and waiting for you to kick off the wall and take your first lap in the Facebook pool!

The good news is you can create your first ad in less than five minutes, and people anywhere in the world can be responding to it within minutes after Facebook approves it.

In this chapter you will set up a Campaign, Ad Set, and Ad for the Facebook News Feed. It may be helpful for you to have Ad Manager open and work alongside us as we show you step by step how to do this.

If you've run a Facebook Campaign before, this might be review. It may be best for you to skim this chapter and see if there's anything you can glean that perhaps you might have been missing.

Let's get started!

## BASIC CAMPAIGN SETUP

Let's go step by step in creating your first News Feed ad. We did not repeat all the details of these steps for creating campaigns, so if you get stuck on something, you might need to refer back to Chapters 7 through 12.

1. Create a new Campaign. Set your Objective and Budget.
2. Create a new Ad Set.
3. Choose your Audience.
4. Remove all of the placements except the Facebook News Feed and Instagram Feed.

Now, open up your ad and start by naming it. The name should be related to either the creative or to what you're promoting. Examples of ads named based on creative might be:

1. Testimonial—Joe
2. Testimonial—Megan
3. Testimonial—Becky
4. Video—Fast
5. Video—Cheap
6. Video—Easy
7. Thumbnail—Black and White
8. Thumbnail—Bright Red
9. Thumbnail—Looking Back

Again, it really helps with tracking and reporting if your Ad Name makes sense when glanced at in a reporting view. The Ad Name is at the top of the Ad Setup.

Next up is the Identity box. This allows you to choose which Page is promoting the ad. Most people only have one Page and it defaults to be your only Page. It also shows your Instagram account.

Moving down the list of options, the next choice is Create Ad. In the Format section, make sure Single Image or Video is selected.

Under the Media section, click the button that says Create Video (not slideshow). A wizard will pop up in the new window.

## CREATING A VIDEO FROM A STILL IMAGE

Choose the Vertical Templates. Then pick a template you like. In this example, you'll choose the Spotlight an Image template (shown in Figure 14–1 on page 155) since you'll only need one image. The template will automatically generate a vertical video for Facebook and a square video for Instagram. Click Customize once you've chosen the template.

Now you'll see the three scenes that make up the video as you can see in Figure 14–2 on page 155. The first one is a still image that takes up the entire ad, the second one is

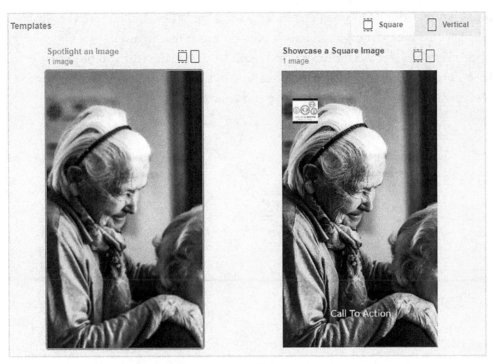

**FIGURE 14–1.** Spotlight an Image

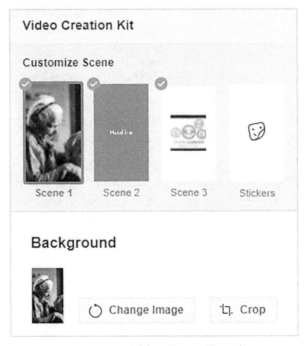

**FIGURE 14–2.** Video Scene Creation

some text, and the third one defaults to your logo. When you choose the first image, make sure it's eye catching and doesn't contain much text (if any).

Scene two is text as you can see in Figure 14-3. Usually this will be a benefit to the viewer. It could be a discount, sale, or calling out a problem you solve or solution you have. Here you can change the font size and color and the background colors.

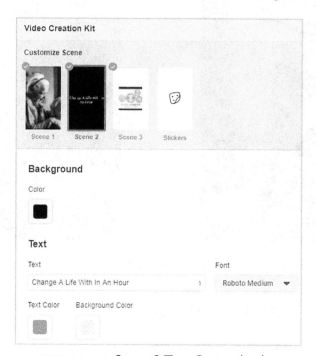

**FIGURE 14–3.** Scene 2 Text Customization

The final scene is for another image and a background color. This is a good place for your logo. You can push the Play Button to watch a preview of the movie you've created. As you can see, the motion is much more eye-catching than the same still image. The video allows you to have a longer message with more text. It's overall more engaging. Click Use Video and the video will be created and added to your ad.

It will take a few seconds for the video to be created. As soon as it's available, click the Edit Video button as shown in Figure 14-4 on page 157.

The button brings up a menu that will let you set the thumbnail image and create the captions as seen in Figure 14-5 on page 157. Click on Thumbnail and look at what Facebook automatically created. It is usually fine. Since this is simply a slideshow with no dialog, the captions will be empty and there's no need to create them.

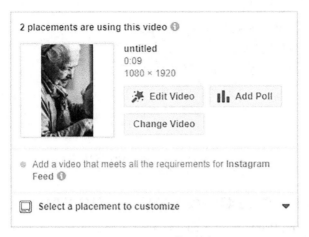

**FIGURE 14-4.** Edit Video

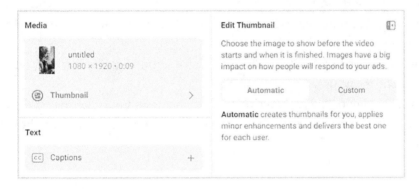

**FIGURE 14-5.** Thumbnail and Captions

## Captions

Captions consistently increase engagement with your videos. You can either have Facebook generate these automatically and edit them yourself, generate them automatically and have Facebook edit them for you, or upload a specially formatted SRT file with the captions inside it as you can see in Figure 14–6 on page 158.

We recommend generating them automatically and editing them yourself for the first few short videos you have. If you use a professional video company, they may have the ability to send you the SRT files. Use those if they provide them. If you use Facebook to review them, it will take extra time before your video can run.

**FIGURE 14–6.** Caption Setup

## ADDING YOUR AD TEXT, HEADLINE, AND CALL TO ACTION

Next, you'll create the Primary Text for your ad. In advertising circles this is also known as your *ad copy*.

It's easier for beginners to create a bulleted list than try to fit a story. Find three benefits of what you're offering and use them. Remember, it adds a See More after three lines. You may see the Add Another Option box link. Ignore that for your first ad. We like to use initial capitals for each letter. You don't have to, but we think it helps the text stand out more.

Now, you'll need a Headline. This should be about four to six words and be your biggest benefit to the user.

These placements have a Description field. It shows up sometimes when Facebook chooses to show it and uses it near your website name. You can see these fields in Figure 14–7.

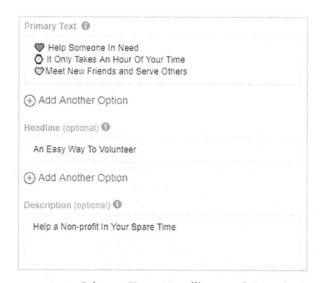

**FIGURE 14–7.** Primary Text, Headline, and Description

Next, fill in your website URL. This is where people will go when they click on your ad. Copy and paste it from your website so you don't accidentally have a typo and send people to a broken link. Right underneath it is an optional Display Link. This is just a shorter version of your URL if you don't like how it's automatically displayed.

Choose your Call to Action button text. Remember to choose one that matches what will actually happen on your landing page. You can see these in Figure 14-8.

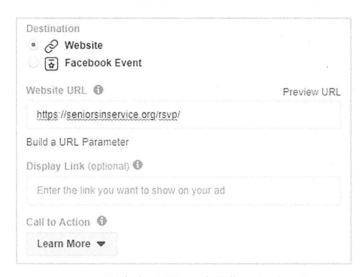

**FIGURE 14-8.** Website URL and Call to Action Button

In order to get reporting on how well your ad works, you'll need the Facebook Tracking Pixel to connect your website to your ads. Make sure your Facebook Pixel is toggled on and selected in the Tracking Box as shown in Figure 14-9.

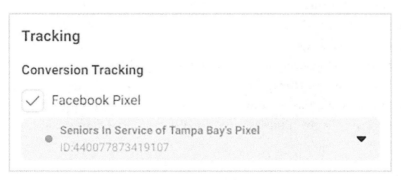

**FIGURE 14-9.** Tracking Pixel

Finally, you'll want to preview it on both the Facebook and Instagram placements to make sure it was cropped to fit their sizes correctly. Below the video is a drop-down menu that says Select a Placement to customize. Choose both the Facebook News Feeds and the Instagram Feed.

Once you look at the previews, it's finally time to run the ad! Click the green Publish button and your ad will start running as soon as it's reviewed.

## QUICK SHORTCUT FOR CREATING YOUR FIRST AD USING AN EXISTING POST

If you already have a popular post that you'd like to use as your first ad, follow the steps above. Instead of clicking Single Image or Video, click Use Existing Post. Once you get there, click the Select Post button as shown in Figure 14–10.

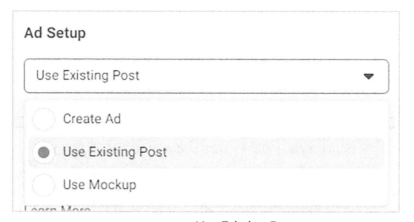

**FIGURE 14–10.** Use Existing Post

Once you click that, you'll get a list of possible posts as shown in Figure 14–11 on page 161. Choose the one you want to turn into an ad and click Continue.

Once you have your post selected, the final step is to go through and manually crop the visual area for each placement. It only takes a few minutes and you're guaranteed to crop it correctly vs. Facebook's auto-cropping algorithm. Figure 14–12 on page 161 shows what happens sometimes when Facebook auto-crops a video.

Finish the same steps as you did with the new video by choosing the correct Tracking Pixel. Then hit the big green Publish button and you've got your second ad running!

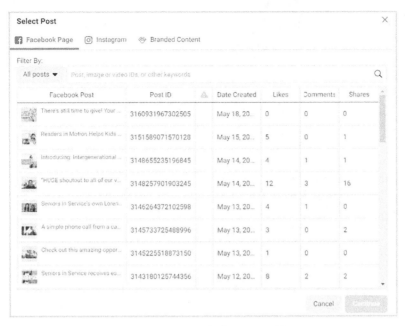

**FIGURE 14–11.** Existing Post List

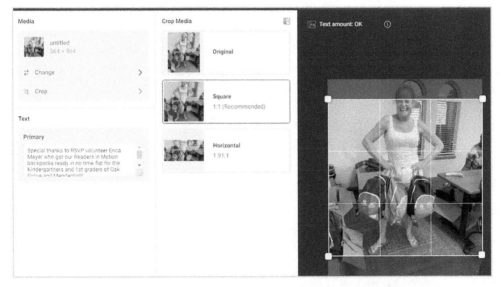

**FIGURE 14–12.** Bad Auto Cropping (Head Cut Off)

# Chapter 15

# The Strongest Persuader of All: Facebook Video

## Guest Author Brandon Boyd

It's no secret that there is no greater media for influencing an audience than video. We are experiencing the greatest shift in history in how video is consumed as people now carry their televisions and movie theaters with them in their pockets and can stream video from virtually anywhere.

Traditional video advertising (television) relies on having a reasonably captive audience and follows a formulaic approach, whether it's a 30-second commercial spot or a full-blown infomercial. Smartphones, of course, have changed all that. The question has become how to use video on a platform where people not only have extremely short attention spans, but have little patience for anything that does not immediately engage them.

The good news is that you as a Facebook Advertiser have access to audiences while users are interacting on social platforms. You can place video content right in the middle of their experience.

In this chapter, you will learn how to use video to grab attention in a crowded marketplace. You'll also learn a valuable tool for creating compelling video content that engages your audience. Lastly, you'll learn how to integrate your video into Facebook Ads.

## INTERRUPTION VS. DIRECT OFFER

The core philosophy behind any advertising has to do with putting an offer in front of people who are experiencing a problem that a given product or service can solve. Effective social media advertising begins first with the understanding that, in general, no one goes on any social media platform primarily looking to solve a problem. The type of social advertising that works is not necessarily a direct approach but rather interruption and takes the form of entertainment or education.

Your objective as a social media advertiser is to invoke and leverage curiosity first, then sales second, with your content. You're not necessarily going to take a direct approach in most cases but rather soft sell in terms of creating a story around what you are offering. You're first going to get their attention, then warm them up with additional interesting and relevant content. Finally, after you've earned their attention and made an impression, you will have earned the right to make a sale.

The good news is there's a methodology you can use that will ensure your ads and content are designed for gaining the maximum attention on social media platforms.

## THE THREE Cs OF CREATING THUMB-STOPPING CONTENT

A shift occurred for us over three years ago when my business partner (and this book's author) Bob Regnerus had a meeting with Facebook at their headquarters in Texas. About 80 percent of what they talked about was Video Ads. Bob told me that the VP in charge of the News Feed stood up and proudly proclaimed, *"We're essentially a video company now."*

Facebook coined the term "thumb-stopping content" because of how people consume information on their smartphones (scrolling with their thumbs until they find something interesting).

Your job is to construct your video ads in a way that garners the attention your product or service deserves. In order to do that, you've got to make sure that your content includes the following three factors: contrast, curiosity, and comedy.

### Contrast: Standing Out in a Crowded Space

The definition of contrast is the state of being strikingly different from something else in juxtaposition or close association. In advertising terms this can include:

- Your ad vs. your competition's ad
- Static images/text vs. video—i.e., movement
- The common perception of an industry and its opposite
- The style of your ad vs. a normal ad

When you're thinking about your ad campaign and beginning to develop creative for it, ask yourself how you can position your product or service in a way that is starkly in contrast to the general market perception of it. Does what you are marketing generally have a serious perception? Think about how you can use humor or levity to create contrast and differentiate yourself. Are there common elephant in the room, issues around the product or service's industry that other competitors are afraid to talk about? You can be the one who openly addresses them by creating content around them.

## Curiosity: Invoking a Sense of Wonder and Interest

Curiosity is a strong desire to know or learn something and usually begins with getting someone's attention by offering them a strange or unusual piece of content. Some ways that people leverage curiosity in advertising can include:

- The "Birthday Card Effect"—anticipation of what's next
- Interesting or unconventional style—filming on a smartphone vs. high-end video production
- A compelling offer that may border on seeming too good to be true
- A report, book, or video that offers uncommon or hidden knowledge

Curiosity taps into our primal desire to learn more and to know what we don't know. This is why in traditional direct marketing the idea of secrets are so powerful for getting people engaged. Free reports and white papers have been leveraged by countless businesses because they draw on the never-ending desire of people to educate themselves. People are always looking for a slight edge, for making and saving money, for creating an advantage for themselves in some way. Address these inherent desires in your content.

## Comedy: Entertainment as a Way to Earn People's Attention

Entertainment is a pillar of any effective social media ad campaign, and at the core of entertainment is humor. The huge benefit of creating entertaining video content for Facebook is that people share it. For example, people might share:

- Parody: deliberate exaggeration for comic effect
- Superbowl ads: people watch the commercials, not the game

People are going on social media for amusement provided by their social connections, not to look at ads. They are likely looking to escape some form of boredom in the moment. Your video ads, if they're going to work in any capacity, have to qualify to earn their attention by having some element that relieves that boredom, and usually this takes the form of humor. The great news is if your ad provides amusement it will get shared. No other advertising platform exists where people will freely promote your ad if it has entertainment value.

## THE CONTENT CREATION MATRIX: THE SIMPLE GUIDE TO CREATING COMPELLING VIDEO CONTENT

The diagram in Figure 15–1 is the guide we use at our studio to make sure the video content we produce contains all the elements for creating effective engagement.

Your goal as a video content creator is to touch on as many segments as possible within the circle. Specifically, some segments on each side of the circle are covering what

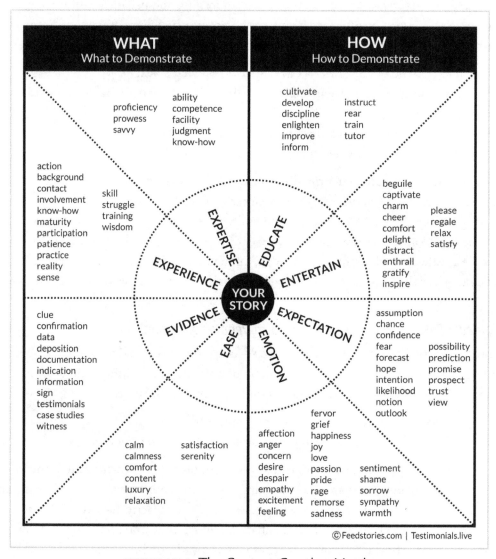

**FIGURE 15–1.** The Content Creation Matrix

and how to demonstrate your product or service offering. The more segments covered, the more effective your videos will be. The goal is not necessarily to attempt to hit all of these segments at one time in one video, but rather divide and deploy them over time to match how people buy over a sales cycle.

### What to Demonstrate

In your videos, you are looking to show the viewer what it is like to experience your product or service firsthand. You do that by demonstrating the following:

- *Expertise.* Share your knowledge and experience.
- *Experience.* Demonstrate what your business does to transform people's lives.
- *Evidence.* Prove your products and services solve problems by featuring testimonials and case studies.
- *Ease.* Show your customers how simple, easy, and fun your product is to use.

### How to Demonstrate

How you present your product or service is critical to your success and encompasses the three Cs discussed earlier. The below elements bring your business to life when infused into what you are demonstrating:

- *Educate.* A good video will teach a person something they didn't know before.
- *Entertain.* Some of the most memorable videos combine selling with entertainment.
- *Expectation.* Set up a future event and build anticipation. Our guest author Jeff Walker dives into this in Chapter 24.
- *Emotion.* Create impactful videos that use emotion to connect with your customers.

You'll notice in Figure 15–1 we've included words underneath each element that act as a thesaurus to give you additional words to help you define each element. Hopefully it helps you create the right types of videos for the objective you have in mind. Having the right video at the right time for a prospect is what will help you achieve success in using video in your Facebook Ads.

## WHY USE VIDEO?

Yes, you should absolutely use video in Facebook Ads. Facebook prefers video, as stated by Facebook and thousands of dollars of tests. Here's why:

- Video increases engagement.

- Video produces better cost-per-action.
- Video connects with people better and tells a better story.
- Video is best for mobile. Multiple sources report 80 percent of social media is accessed via mobile devices.
- Videos get shared by Facebook users.

In our testing at Feedstories, we've seen video consistently outperform still images a majority of the time.

Remember, the number-one job of your video is to catch users' eyes and stop them from scrolling past the rest of your ad. In order to do this, you have to be interesting enough to catch someone's attention. Remember, Facebook calls this Thumb-Stopping Content.

You've learned a lot about copywriting in this book, but understand that video is copywriting, too. Copywriting isn't just written words; it's also spoken words. Video gives you the added bonus of imagery, gestures, body language, and facial expressions to convey even more emotion to supercharge your copy!

## FACEBOOK IS MAKING VIDEO EASY

There are a number of ways Facebook has made video easy for non-video advertisers. We showed you some things already in Chapter 14, but we'll highlight that and more here for your convenience.

The slideshow, for one, is a way to create motion from still images. Slideshows don't always outperform still images, but it's something you should test because it's simple to do.

Catering your video for different Placements is another way to gain an edge. Instagram feed videos should be formatted differently from Facebook mobile News Feed videos and differently from Facebook Stories videos.

If you are using Auto Placement or just using two Placements, you can customize the way each video is formatted by selecting it from the drop down box as you can see in Figure 15–2 on page 169.

You can also do a lot of editing and enhancements to your video now by clicking Edit Video. You can see some of them in Figure 15–3 on page 169.

Use Trim if you want to shorten a long video and test a shorter version without needing an editor or software.

Use Cropping to trim your video to different sizes. We find that 4:5 works well for Facebook Mobile and Facebook/Instagram Stories Placements. 1:1 works best on Instagram Feed.

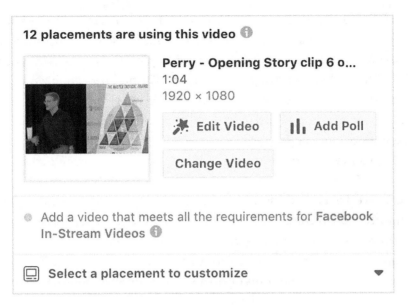

**FIGURE 15-2.** Customize Video by Placement

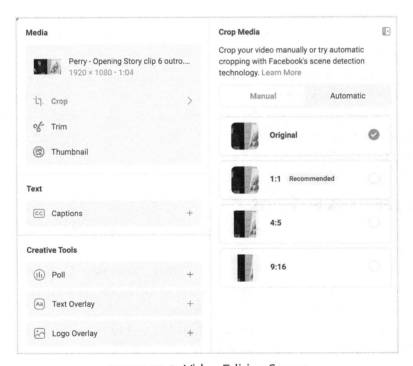

**FIGURE 15-3.** Video Editing Screen

Be careful cropping a video that's 16:9 to 4:5. It doesn't always convert well because the main subject often gets cut off on either side. This is also why we caution you in your use of Automatic Cropping, which can sometimes produce strange cropping where the main areas of focus (like your subject) are cut off. The best bet is to have a video editor/company produce these sizes natively from your original video files.

We used to painstakingly select a thumb-stopping thumbnail image for our videos, but we do not anymore and just let Facebook automatically choose a thumbnail for us. However, you can choose a thumbnail from your video or upload one using the interface.

The Creative Tools: Text Overlays and Logo Overlays are ways to enhance a video without the need for an editor or software. The Text Overlay is a particularly interesting option when you want to emphasize things within your video.

Polls are an interesting way to create engagement and interaction with users. It's a very simple way to ask a question or do a simple survey without needing a service or software.

### Captions

The most important function here is Captions, and we recommend using Captions whenever possible. Facebook says that 85 percent of its users watch videos with sound off. Imagine going through all the work of producing a video and then only 15 percent of the people listen to the audio portion!

We recommend that you always place captions on videos. Use Facebook's Tools to auto-generate the captions and then be sure to review and edit every screen to be sure the text makes sense. Hint: If you don't like doing captions, use a service like Rev.com or similar service that can produce SRT files (".srt" is a caption file type that video software can display over your video).

## VIDEO LENGTHS FOR ADS

Many people ask us how long their videos should be. We'd be wrong to give you a single number because it depends.

A general rule of thumb is to use the Customer Awareness Timeline. The further they are to the left, the less they know you. We have found success with 30- to 60-second videos as a way to introduce someone to a business.

As a prospect moves right on the Customer Awareness Timeline, your videos can be a little longer or, in some cases, even really short! The people that are most aware of you will tolerate longer videos, sometimes lasting three to five minutes or even an hour. Recently we ran a 75-minute video as an ad that detailed how to get prepared for an

SBA Loan during the 2020 Covid-19 crisis. Since it was such a complex and hot topic, it worked well.

We also like to use short, 7- to 15-second videos in the middle of the funnel when we want to push someone to a FAQ, article, landing page, or promotion. Think of these videos as "pattern interrupts" to get someone to turn their attention to you for a moment.

A general rule is that if someone is a stranger, keep it succinct. If someone is a growing or existing friend—(client, prospect, member) give them the depth they want. Try to always be efficient with your words but give them enough depth to really know what's inside your heart and mind.

## VIDEO STYLES

There are several questions to consider when it comes to deciding what style your video should be:

- Should you hire a professional to get a polished look, or should you shoot it on a DSLR or even a smartphone to give it an organic look?
- Should you use animation? Should you do face-to-camera or interview style?
- Should you use a green screen, solid background, or natural background?
- Should you shoot in a studio, your office, or outside?

All these are great questions, and the right answer is—YOU SHOULD!

Your video style will be determined, among other things, by:

- Your audience
- Your product
- Your personal taste
- Your budget
- Your expertise
- Your schedule
- Your objective
- Your offer

The very best answer we can give as experts in this field is to first find the path of least resistance to getting your first videos done. A completed video that is running in your Ad Account is far superior to an idea that exists in your head. So, get something done quickly that fits your budget.

You can always find your style by finding videos that you like and then creating a video in that style for your company.

Once you get experience, you can expand your horizons and venture into new types of video and also consider hiring a professional agency like Feedstories.

There is a bonus chapter included with the Resources on www.PerryMarshall.com/ fbtools called "10 Practical Ways Businesses Are Sharing Their Stories Using Video." This is a visual chapter showing you examples of using video in practical ways to generate more sales on and off Facebook.

Brandon Boyd has been involved in creative design and direct marketing for over 20 years. Leveraging creative design skill to drive marketing campaigns and branding efforts, his influence has been felt in several different industries including retail space leasing and management, transportation, health insurance, higher education, medical associations, and publishing.

Brandon continues to provide creative direction, copywriting, and marketing strategy as the cofounder of Feedstories, a Video Sales and Marketing Agency that turns stories into sales. Learn more at Feedstories.com.

# Chapter 16

# Creating Killer Ad Creatives That Reflect Your Hook

## Guest Author Molly Pittman

Creativity isn't something you can teach step by step. However, by walking through how we do this at Digital Marketer and sharing a lot of examples, good and bad, you can learn the thought process and get helpful tips to use while you are developing your own creatives.

The creative, other than targeting, is probably one of the most overlooked aspects of the campaign. People outsource a lot of their images or videos, which is fine. Companies like Design Pickle do a good job, and you can get unlimited designs from them. Tools like that can be a little expensive, but it's nice if you don't have a designer on your team. That being said, probably the best thing that ever happened to our ads was hiring a designer that just creates our ads. Even if you're managing multiple brands, having one person that you can communicate with who understands how advertising works is super important. Keep in mind that you can't rely on the designer, whether it's an outsource or someone on your team, to come up with good ads. That may sound counterintuitive, but it's true. Designers are not marketers; instead, they like to create pretty pictures. However, that doesn't always mean that the pretty picture is going to be a high-converting ad creative. The designer is there to produce the image or the video, but they need a lot of instruction. This isn't because they're bad at designing, they just don't understand marketing. Realizing your role in this whole system is very important. A lot of thought goes into the creatives that we produce at Digital Marketer and our different sister properties.

A great book I read about this process that I highly recommend is called *Big Magic: Creative Magic Beyond Fear* by Elizabeth Gilbert (Riverhead Books, 2015). It taught me a lot about how to think about being creative, because whether you know it or not, you actually are creative. You just need to understand how creativity comes to you. It has helped me understand how our designer thinks, how I should be thinking, and how ideas come to play.

In this chapter, you'll continue to study creative and how to leverage imagery and copywriting to produce responsive ads.

## SIX CREATIVE MUST-HAVES

An important thing to remember is that the creative doesn't necessarily need to be all about the offer. Make sure that your creative reflects the marketing message or *hook,* the message you're using to sell or to get someone to take action on, that's in your copy. A lot of people mess up on this aspect of the creative by setting up an ad campaign and telling their designer that they need an image of the product or something that just looks good. While using an image of the product may work in some cases, that's not always what's needed for a high-converting campaign. You want to start getting into the mindset that the image and video creatives are just the visual elements that should be supporting the rest of your campaign as a whole.

There is a lot of thought that goes into this process, and there are six important things to think about whenever you are working on your creatives. All of them don't have to exist in every creative, but number one definitely does.

### 1. Your Creative Should Be Reflective of Your Hook

Your hook is not your offer. Whatever you are trying to get your customer to do, whether it is download a lead magnet or buy a product, is the offer. The hook is the way you sell and market your offer. One offer could have ten hooks if you're testing ten different marketing messages to get someone to take action. Your creative should always convey the marketing message or the hook.

If your image isn't doing that, you're just using your image to catch eyeballs. Using a puppy or a pretty woman might get a bunch of clicks, but they will likely be from people who do not care about what's on the other side. Five to seven years ago, that might have worked because it was the Wild West of the internet, but now it is not. Do not use an image simply to try to draw attention or clicks. It is just not going to work because the ad scent will be terrible once they get to your landing page or wherever you're sending traffic.

## 2. Tell a Story

In your ad, try to tell a story about how your offer can change or affect their life. Carousel ads are a great way to tell a story using your creatives.

## 3. Display the Product

If you are selling physical products or something you can literally demonstrate, it is acceptable to show the product. Those are the easiest images to create because, for example, if you sell makeup brushes, you can demonstrate what your makeup brush does. This won't work for all business types; however, if you can show your product and it's further down the funnel, a simple demonstration or image of the product can work.

## 4. Stand Out in the News Feed

Although you don't want to use creatives that stand out for the sole purpose of standing out, there are some ways to stand out in the News Feed. Our designer uses contrasting colors, so whenever she's creating an ad she makes sure that whatever colors she uses contrast with one another because that catches people's attention. Little video ads or gifs can also be used to catch people's attention because they move. If you convey the marketing message while making it a little bit flashy, but still on brand for whatever company you're running ads for, that's great. If you're running an image in the News Feed, and it doesn't stand out, you're probably going to have trouble because it's going to blend in with everything else.

## 5. Be on Brand

A lot of big companies are talking about this now, but what does that really mean? We have a really simple style guide at Digital Marketer with the fonts and different colors we use. We don't always stay on our brand colors and images, but when you're working with a client or for your company, make sure that you know what being on brand means. The more campaigns that you run, the more people are going to start recognizing your brand, so if you can, make sure your images have something that really stands out and it's something that's across all of the images. You'll notice that we use a flat cartoon style at Digital Marketer. The ads and colors may be a little bit different, but when you see the ad, you know "that's Digital Marketer." I have brand recognition there. Make sure you establish that because if you start running completely different ads across different campaigns that look different, that's not good for brand lift. People aren't going to recognize your brand and, as much as that's sort of a vanity metric, it is important.

### 6. Play Off Emotions Already Associated with an Image

This is something we've really found to work over the past year, and it's done by figuring out what associations people already have in common that we can play off. What icons or images do people already have a relationship with?

For example, in Figure 16–1, we ran an ad with an iPhone battery that was low. If you have an iPhone, which most people do, you have an emotion associated to that battery being low. You know that you need to plug it in. If you can use these different icons or images that we're all familiar with and use every day, it's really helpful because people already have an emotion associated with that. For example, if you want to portray scarcity, find something that has already done that in our culture like a low iPhone battery or a low bank account. You have found something that already creates scarcity in people's lives and are using that to convey your own hook.

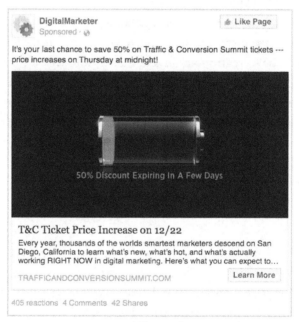

**FIGURE 16–1.** iPhone Battery Ad

## WHAT NOT TO DO

We have a room in Slack where we're putting ads that we do and do not like every day to educate our designers. The two ads shown in Figures 16–2 on page 177 and 16–3 on page 178 are examples where the creative failed.

**FIGURE 16–2.** Cat Hook for MLM: Fail

Figure 16–2 with the cat is pretty obvious. A lot of people will set up a great campaign, but then get lazy on the creative and just pull a stock image. This is the biggest part of your ad and definitely not where you want to be getting lazy.

The reason why this one failed is because the cat has nothing to do with their hook or offer. What they are going for is playing off of something warm and cuddly that people love, but that cat has nothing to do with network marketing even if it's sitting in front of the keyboard. This mistake is costly and will end up being terrible for your brand because you will get a lot of unqualified clicks.

## GRADES AND REPORT CARDS

In Figure 16–3 on page 178, we had a lead magnet for social media managers you can use to audit social media profiles. There were a lot of different hooks and avatars at play with this one because the social media manager could use it, the supervisor of the social media manager could audit the social media manager, or an agency could use it. The offer was a lead magnet for a social media audit, but one hook we came up with was "get a grade." Everyone has an association with grades in some form from school. This is a good example of a hook because we didn't literally say, "this is a social media audit; go do it." Instead, we said, "This is a social media audit that you can use to grade your accounts, your social media manager, or clients before they hire you for an agency." To convey our hook in the creative, we simply created

**FIGURE 16–3.** Get a Grade

an image that shows a report card. Instead of showing the lead magnet, it just says social media and an F.

Whenever we create these hooks, we pull the biggest keywords. In this example, it's "grade." Then, we think about what people associate with grades—report cards. We'll then type "grade" or "report card" into Google or Dreamstime and see what images are coming up first. Google works great for this because the images coming up first are the ones that people have clicked on the most in regard to that keyword. Since Google has so much data, you can see the images that already have association with your keyword. Instead of making assumptions, let Google tell you what people are clicking on in relation to that word.

When we Googled "grade" and "report card," we got the idea for the grade F. It's a simple image that absolutely portrays the marketing message of a grade. It's not just a bland image showing a mockup of the lead magnet; instead, we took it a step further by pulling a key word out of the hook and made sure the image reflected that. We have tested this image with an A as well, but F works the best because people have a more emotional association with the F grade.

This image can be used multiple ways across all of our different avatars as well. If you want to flip this and run to bosses of social media managers instead, your first line of copy can change to, "How does your social media manager score?" The same image can be used no matter who you're targeting, and it still portrays the hook of getting a grade.

Figure 16–4 was a "create a report" hook. We took the audit and positioned it as a report that you can actually give to someone else. We used the same concept but changed it slightly to portray someone actually handing over a report. This seems very simple, but remember that someone scrolling through is going to look at your image for only two to three seconds. Your goal is to make this simple and make sure it really portrays what you're trying to say. The copy is, "yYou should receive a weekly report from your social media manager to ensure their strategy is not only working but actually improving over time. Send this ten-minute audit to your social media manager today and ask them to report back weekly." The image conveys that simply by showing a social media manager handing over the report.

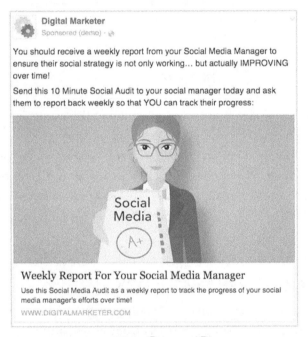

**FIGURE 16–4.** Create a Report

We were able to come up with multiple hooks for the same offer. This one was a little bit more fun. The hook in Figure 16–5 on page 180 is about grading your competition. The copy says, "Take the audit and go and grade your competition's social media profiles to see how you stack up against them." We pulled the keyword of "stack" or "stack up," and the image that came to mind from that was stacks of pancakes. This all sounds really silly, but this is exactly how we come up with our images. For our creative, we had

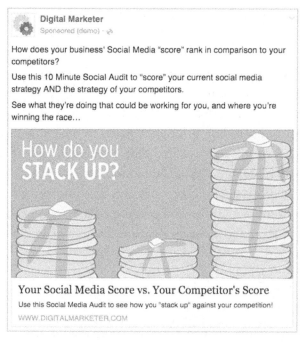

**FIGURE 16–5.** Stack Up

stacks of pancakes, and this one converted really well because it's visually appealing. People understand when they read it, and it's kind of funny.

Finally, in Figure 16-6 on page 181, the hook was knowing your goals. This was targeted for a corporate audience, asking, "Is your social media strategy actually in line with the goals you set for your business?" The image we used with "Are you hitting your social goals and showing progress week to week?" really conveyed the marketing message.

## ANALYZING CREATIVES THAT WORK

Here are examples from other companies I really love. All of these portray the marketing message so well. Figure 16-7 on page 181 is from Hired, and they're saying, "If you're counting down the hours until you get to leave the office, it might be time for a change." The hook in this ad is to get more out of your work/life balance. How they decided to portray the marketing message was to put work on one side of a gauge and life on the other. It's so simple, yet effective, which is why I love it. One way to enhance this creative even more is to make it a GIF where the gauge is actually moving because it would really catch someone's attention. However, this still works because instead of just putting a stock photo of people in an office counting down the hours until they leave, they took it a step further.

**FIGURE 16–6.** Knowing Your Goals

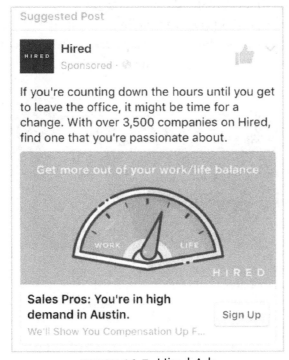

**FIGURE 16–7.** Hired Ads

The ad example in Figure 16–8 also does a great job on that same thing. Their hook is, "Don't bottle up your emotions." The keyword they pulled from that hook was bottle, and they have portrayed the bottles as sad to fit their marketing message. You can see that these companies are using very similar strategies.

**FIGURE 16–8.** Bottle Emotion

This is also true with Figure 16–9. The hook is "Not all wounds are visible." A common image that's associated with wounds is bandages. This is really simple, and it's also on a background that really stands out.

Figure 16–10 on page 183 is an example from a wine delivery company. I love this image because it shows the product and it's a pattern interrupt because of the way they have the wine arranged in a pattern that makes you stop and wonder what it is. Your

**FIGURE 16–9.** Bandages

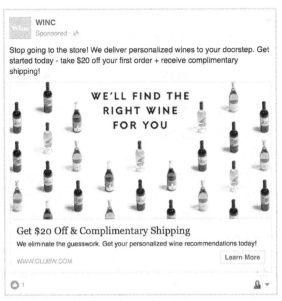

**FIGURE 16–10.** Wine Delivery

brain is just curious. A way they could have taken this a step further is showing someone actually delivering the wine, but I love the pattern interrupt aspect of that image.

Figure 16–11 is an example from us at Digital Marketer, and this shows how literal we get while creating our images. The copy is "YOU can create a blog content plan in 60

**FIGURE 16–11.** 60-Second Blog

seconds or less by filling in these five simple blanks." We were targeting bloggers. We took it a step further and thought about what platform most bloggers use—WordPress. We decided to make the image look like WordPress because it's something they're familiar with. We then added in the clock because it speaks to the 60 seconds. This is one of our highest converting ads of all time, and it's really simple. It took our designer about 20 minutes to make, but it was effective because we were playing off of psychology by using something that these people already knew because they're probably in WordPress every day. By recreating it we can easily catch their attention.

The example in Figure 16–12 is great. The copy reads, "We can't build Rome in a day, but in less than 24 hours, we can find someone to build it for you." In this example, they took the word build and ran with it. They have little ninjas coming down and building the app. It's a very simple idea that's very literal to the hook.

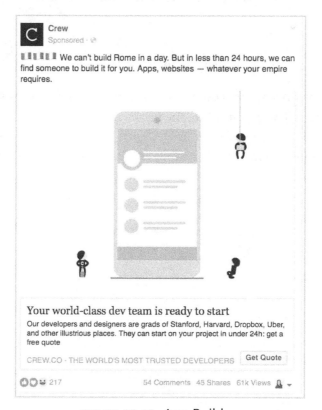

**FIGURE 16–12.** App Builder

Figure 16–13 on page 185 is one that I think is awesome. This example circles back to the stacking keyword with "How does your metabolism stack up." In this case, it's showing progression with different colors. The image really stands out against the background and is great.

**FIGURE 16–13.** Metabolism

In Figure 16–14, you can see we were really being literal with the "rock star" keyword by having a band playing. There are also marketing icons up in the music notes to really speak to the marketing message and our target audience.

**FIGURE 16–14.** Rock Star

Figure 16-15 is an example from SamCart. They are saying, "Are you trying to sell your stuff online, but overwhelmed by the idea of setting up a sales funnel?" In this example, they're playing off the fact that this market is overwhelmed by sales funnels. The image portrays what we're told it's like vs. what it's really like. This is imagery that people know because they may have seen it used in different markets, but they're applying it to funnels. Brian, the founder of SamCart, has told us that this ad has done really well. This ad also has great shareability because their target audience can relate to it.

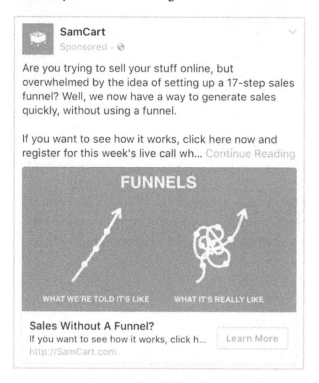

**FIGURE 16–15.** SamCart

While the ad copy in Figure 16–16 on page 187 could be better, the image fits their hook perfectly. This is a financial app, and this sort of graph is familiar in culture. They're playing off what most people do when it comes to their finances. The first of the month you stick to your budget, in the middle of the month you're terrible, and then at the end you try to get back on budget. They chose a very literal way to depict their marketing message.

The Wag example in Figure 16–17 on page 187 is very simple, but I love it. This is a Retargeting ad after I visited their site. Here is an example of where you should use dogs in your creative because this company is a dog walking app. There's nothing wrong with using dogs if it actually relates to what you're doing. For this ad, they decided to use an

**FIGURE 16–16.** Financial App

**FIGURE 16–17.** Wag

image of dogs, but they still incorporated the offer of 50 percent off your first walk in the image as well. It's very simple but portrays the marketing message.

Figure 16–18 on page 188 is a video from our sister company over at Survival Life. There's rain coming down and the lighter is still going, because the hook is that the

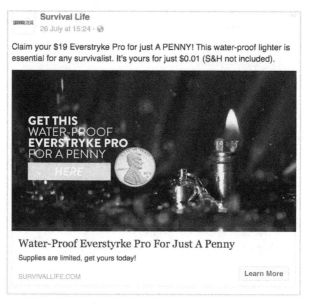

**FIGURE 16–18.** Survival Life

lighter is waterproof. This is so simple because they're just displaying what the lighter does. They've added the penny because you can get the lighter for a penny, and then, there's just a call to action. This ad has done really well for them.

Hired (as seen in Figure 16–19) has some great examples of ads that are reflective of the hook in a simple way. Each of these portray the marketing hook in a literal way that's very simple yet extremely effective.

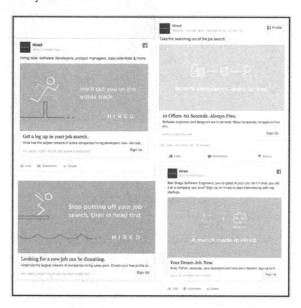

**FIGURE 16–19.** Hired

**FIGURE 16–20.** Library

Figure 16-20 is a great example of being really literal. This was a Facebook Ad template library, so we made the image look like a library. It's very simple and literal, but it works very well.

Figure 16-21 is for an offer called a Customer Avatar Worksheet. One of the hooks we came up with was, "Can you guess where your customers are hiding?" so we pulled

**FIGURE 16–21.** Guess Who

out the word "guess." Something a lot of people associate with that word is the game Guess Who. Our designer didn't pull an image of the game directly from Dreamstime, but she simply mocked it up with different customers.

Another example for this offer is Figure 16–22, which is an image playing off of the image from the television show *Brady Bunch*, and it fits right into the hook. The colors are great, and people become curious wondering, "Who are these people?"

**FIGURE 16–22.** Brady Bunch

Figure 16–23 on page 191 is a great example of how to display a physical product without being boring. Instead of just showing the makeup brush, it has pink blush coming off it, which makes it really eye-catching. This is a market that requires really good design, and they are drawn to good-looking, high-quality images. This ad absolutely speaks to that audience.

The Jimmy Buffet ad (Figure 16–24 on page 191) is another great example of successfully showing the product. This ad is being run to his fans. It's simple with the item they're getting and the sizes on the bottom. The engagement on this ad was insane because many of his fans had to stop on it.

Something to keep in mind, which this ad is a good example of, is when you're using people in your imagery, make sure they are looking at you or at your CTA. In this ad, Jimmy is directly looking at you, so when you are scrolling through the News Feed, his eyes catch your attention when they're looking right at you. Whenever you are using people in your ads make sure they're either looking at you, the CTA, or whatever you want people to actually click on. If they're looking in a different direction, you're going to look at what they're looking at, so you just want to make sure they're looking at whatever you want the customer to look at.

**FIGURE 16–23.** Makeup Brush

**FIGURE 16–24.** Jimmy Buffet

## WORKING WITH A DESIGNER

Giving our designer projects takes a lot of work from me, but it's worth it. You can't just tell the designer that you need ads for your product; there should be a system in place for this. What I start with is Google. In this example I was Googling things like "social media for your brand," and I found an image that I thought was really cool. I take screenshots of whatever I like inside of Google and then I put them in a document like Figure 16-25. I do my own drawings of what I'm envisioning because I don't want the designer to knock off the image I found, on top of the fact that I don't always want exactly what they were doing. I'm just taking the concepts from what Google was telling me works and then applying it to our ads. For this ad I thought of something that shows the brand with social media icons coming out of it, because this lead magnet was a ten-minute social media audit. I wanted to take that concept but tweak it to fit our marketing message by putting the ten-minute clock in the middle, because I knew that it worked with the blog plan ad before. I took what works, put that in the middle, and then had her add the icons around.

The process we use to come up with our concepts is the Ad Grid. With this process, I figure out the different avatars and hooks and then, using Google and my own creativity, I think about each of the hooks and how they can speak to different people. I spend a lot of time brainstorming what these creatives should be and then write them out.

In hook one, I have all the different images that I want. I usually have about three to five depending on the campaign. Then I always have our designer come up

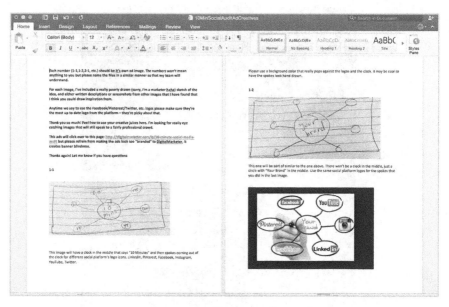

**FIGURE 16–25.** Designer Example

with a wildcard on her own because after she's gone through my suggestions, she knows where things are headed with the concept. The more she does, the better she gets, and some of the ones she comes up with now beat mine. This takes a lot of time because I'm doing research for every single hook and coming up with three to five ideas of creatives that could portray that message. While you may not need more than one or two ideas in your business, it's important to always be taking whatever you're trying to sell, coming up with the hooks, and then using this process through Google or Dreamstime to figure out what images really portray what you're trying to say.

Once I have completed the document, I send it to our designer, and she follows up with the first draft of the ads. Sometimes, they're not what I was looking for at all, and it's usually because I didn't explain it well. These documents have become really detailed to try to avoid situations like that. I will not only write it out, but I also sit down with her or get on a call to go back through everything and make sure she understands exactly what I'm envisioning for each of these images. If you don't explain your concept well enough, your designer might run with it on their own, which is not usually the best idea. They might be able to create a pretty picture but not necessarily a high-converting ad. Sometimes, we go through three to five revisions, and sometimes, they're perfect right off the bat. We put a lot of time into this process, and it's not something you should just create in Snagit or outsource on Fiverr anymore. I really believe this is a super important step in your campaigns and a big investment that that you should make in your business.

Something that's important to keep in mind is to always test your creatives. Sometimes, the winner is the one I liked the least, but it doesn't matter what I like as long as it portrays that message.

## TELLING A STORY WITH YOUR CREATIVES

A powerful thing to do while creating your ads is to create a story that your viewer can put themselves in. You have to be careful while doing this so you don't make your copy too direct at your audience. Using the word "you" in your ads may have a negative effect because it may scare people into thinking that you are directly calling them out. Figure 16–26 on page 194 is a great example of talking about a person without using the word "you." You can create a fictitious person instead, so in this example, it says, "Jeff wants to grow his business. He downloads the Kabbage App to get a line of credit up to 100 grand." Even though the pictures are kind of like stock photos, this is a great ad because the images tell a story. In this case, you can actually show this app in action. "He applies first thing in the morning right." Even

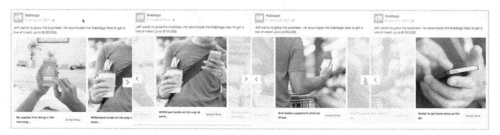

FIGURE 16–26. Kabbage App

though you're talking about "Jeff," the person is thinking about themselves. On the next image, you have Jeff withdrawing funds on his way to work, so it has an image of a guy walking to work. It then finishes with a nice call to action. This is kind of silly, but it's telling a story.

If I were them, I probably would have done a little bit more with the images. I think stock photo images become hidden in the News Feed because most of what your family, friends, and people that you actually care about on Facebook are doing is sharing pictures that look similar. When you use imagery that is a photo, it can get buried in the News Feed because it's blending in with actual photos from your friends and family. I do think they did a great job here telling a story, and carousel ads are an effective way of telling a story in your ads because you can document whatever the before and after is of your product, hook, or service.

We would do something like Figure 16-27 because it's true to our brand. It's the same concept as the Kabbage App, but it fits our cartoon style, and it's a little more marketed. Since we put a little bit more thought into it, it stands out more in the News Feed and catches people's eye. This is for our Digital Marketer HQ products, which is for larger companies who want to train their marketing team. This is also a story-based ad, and each of the images takes them through the multiple steps you need to take. If you are the avatar for this ad, you can see yourself taking each of these steps yourself. I actually got the idea from the Kabbage ad, but I wanted to spice it up a little bit. Adding text onto the actual image for the carousel really helps because it stands out more, so that's what I would do in terms of the carousel ads.

FIGURE 16–27. DM Carousel

## AD CREATIVE CHECKLIST

Our designer created a checklist for Facebook Ads that walks through the thought process behind each creative.

### 1. Create a Powerful Message and Conceptualize Images

This is the step where you take the hook, do your research, and make sure the image portrays that hook. This is where you search Google and your competitors to see what they are doing. You also want to figure out what benefits your offer provides, who you want to target, who your audience is, what the end result is that your customer can receive, and what emotions/feelings you want to convey.

We have a perfect example of playing off of people's emotions in Figures 16–28 below and 16–29 on page 196.

The first ad was run to people who visited our website for our Traffic and Conversion Summit event but didn't buy tickets. As we were getting close to increasing the price of tickets, I started running this ad that reads, "We're excited you visited the site, we're sad you didn't purchase, but there's still time. Batteries don't last forever, and neither will our 50 percent off deal." Silly, but it works. At this point in the campaign, the battery is green, so they know that it's going away soon but there's not a lot of scarcity yet.

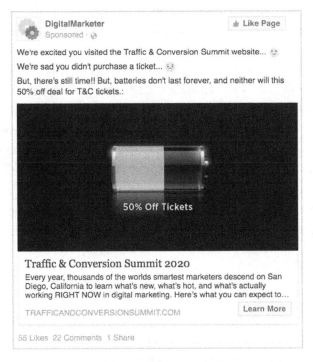

**FIGURE 16–28.** Battery Ad 1

**FIGURE 16–29.** Battery Ad 2

A week before the price actually increased, the same people started seeing the second version of this ad where we had the battery about to die because it was getting really close to the end of our sale. We needed something that portrayed the marketing message of scarcity, and this worked really well because it's something people are familiar with.

Figure 16–30 on page 197 is another example of taking something that people can relate to or are familiar with. This was a messenger ad, and what we were trying to convey is that if you click on this ad, you can actually chat with someone. When we thought about how to show that our designer mocked up an image to look like a message, of course you don't want it to look exactly like Facebook, but you see right away that it's some sort of message conversation that's happening. An extra aspect we added to catch people's attention even more is that we made the image move to look like you're having a conversation in real time. When you see the text bubble come up, we all associate that with someone who is talking to us. It's something that everyone's familiar with, and it's a very effective nine-second video ad that portrays the message of "Do you want to have a conversation?"

## 2. Sketch Out Ideas Before Laying Out any Design Elements

This is the step in the process where we use the document with all of my ideas and sketches. At this stage, you don't want to worry about colors or font choices yet. I never really tell our designer what color or font choice to use because that is where she really

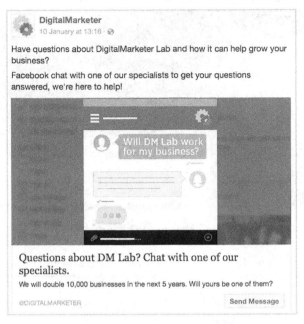

**FIGURE 16–30.** Messenger Ad

is good. My job in the process is to make sure all the elements are in the image that I'm looking for from a marketing perspective.

### 3. Use Complementary or Contrasting Colors

Facebook Ads have to pop, and using only a few complementary color choices will help obtain this goal. You don't have to add ten different colors to your ads, and you don't want to because it can get very busy.

### 4. Choose Your Fonts

It's important to only use one or two different font families for your image. Figure 16–31 on page 198 is an example of why it can be bad to use too many fonts in one image.

In this example, there are so many different fonts that it's hard to read. It's kind of cute and it's definitely on brand for her, but you can't really read it. In this case, it's not because of the black background, it's because of the use of multiple fonts. Using only one to two fonts is really important for readability if you're putting text on your ad.

### 5. Add Text and Call to Action (CTA) to Your Image

Almost all of our images have a text or call to action on them because we've found that that works best. A lot of people actually aren't reading your ad copy; instead, they're

**FIGURE 16–31.** Too Many Fonts

going right to the image. If you can take a few words of your hook that are the most important and put them onto the image it's going to work really well. We either put a little line of copy or a button with a CTA. This will engage those people that prefer to look at images more than read the copy.

### 6. Make Sure Your Image Is Congruent with Your Brand

You really want to make sure you are consistent overall with your designs. When someone clicks on the image and they go over to your landing page, or wherever you're sending traffic, the design elements should be similar. At Digital Marketer, we are able to maintain a certain brand because our ads are similar to the featured images on our blog. Everything is congruent so when someone sees it, they instantly have a connection and know it's Digital Marketer.

## ANALYZING CREATIVES THAT DON'T WORK

Figures 16–32 and 16–33, both on page 199, are examples of something you shouldn't do and how you can fix it. The offer is a social media swipe file, and the hook is that it's a headline swipe file. In the updated version, we played off of newspapers because that's what people commonly associate headlines with. We made the image look like a newspaper, and the headline is "Ultimate Social Media Swipe File." We tested it in multiple colors, but the black and white did the best. It definitely stands out in the News Feed. This was an upgrade from the original because the first one doesn't help convey the hook or have anything to do with the actual offer.

**FIGURE 16–32.** Outdated Ad

**FIGURE 16–33.** Updated Ad

**FIGURE 16–34.** Otter

The ad creative in Figure16–34 failed because it had nothing to do with content marketing or a crash course. Sometimes people will choose something, like the otter in this example, because they think it's cute and that people will click because of that. While the colors are great because they grab your attention, the concept is lacking.

## GETTING INSPIRED

While learning about what works with creatives, you have to realize that this is not a process or a system; it's something you have to continuously study. AdEspresso has a great library of Facebook Ads you can use to study, which is something I do almost every day. I'm constantly in Facebook taking screenshots of ads. Ryan, Britney, and everyone on the team sends me ads. We are always circulating what we think is good and bad, and this takes constant attention and practice to learn what's working.

The creative comes down to being a good marketer. It's pretty simple once you start to get in the right mindset. Just remember to always ask, "How can I convey a marketing message that will get someone to do what I want them to do?"

Molly Pittman is the CEO of *Smart Marketer* and the founder of Train My Traffic Person. She uses her wide range of business communication and deep understanding of the customer journey to create profitable, scalable traffic campaigns. She can be reached at molly@mollypittman.com.

# Chapter 17

# How I Know When My Copy Is Ready—Power Questions

## Guest Author Ryan Deiss

The theme that keeps coming up again and again is the idea of how to keep the focused attention of your prospect. As marketers, so often when we're writing copy and marketing pieces, we just start with the assumption that people are going to see what we're creating and just automatically consume it.

"He's going to read this," or, "Of course they're going to watch this video."

Nothing in life is as important as you think it is while you're thinking about it yourself. As humans, we are taught to believe that what is in front of us, that which is focal, that which is salient, that which is top of mind, is really important.

Even if it isn't.

It is one of the reasons there is so much focus on Retargeting ads in Facebook. When you run Retargeting ads and people keep seeing those same ads over and over and over again—even if the ad is only being shown to them and a small group of people—they are thinking, "Wow, this brand is a really big deal. It's really important."

How do we do this as marketers? How do we draw focused attention from our prospects?

In this chapter, you'll learn the list of seven questions that I ask myself before I finish any piece of ad copy. The most ideal situation would be to have a good answer to all seven questions, but if at least one or two of them are effectively answered, the end result will be a much more powerful piece of marketing, a much more powerful piece of copy, and a much more powerful ad.

Why? Because it's actually going to get viewed. And that's the biggest thing of all.

How do we make sure that our brand and our message become focal? How is this done so that the brand and message become so obvious they begin to permeate the prospect's mind? In researching this for myself, I created these seven questions that I ask myself before releasing any type of ad copy to ensure that the brand and message have a prospect's focused attention. Here they are:

## 1. NOVEL, UNIQUE, AND DISTINCTIVE

The first focusing question when writing ad copy is, "How do we make our offer appear novel, unique, and distinctive?" This is really, really easy if the offer happens to be novel, unique, distinctive, or brand new—something that the market has never seen before. It's more challenging if it is a commodity or something that has been on the market for a while.

One of the best open rates for an email subject line is something like: "Major announcement." In using a subject line like "Major announcement," people are going to open it even if they don't really care what the announcement is. Cable news has figured this out, "Breaking News . . ." At the bottom or top of the screen are the words "Breaking News."

Everyone wants to know what's new, what's novel, what's unique. Looking at human biology and why humans react this way, it is because "the new" is something that might try to kill us. Humans are taught to pay attention to something new for their own survival. If it's unfamiliar, it's going to capture our gaze. It's going to draw that focused attention. And that's the same type of attention that marketers seek to attract.

If your offer is something new, that's great. But if your offer is not new—if it is something people are used to seeing—here are some questions to ask in order to attract the prospect's focused attention:

1. What's a way to make the offer feel new and noteworthy?
2. What's a way to make the offer new?
3. What's a different angle?
4. Are there any current news stories that can be used to help attract attention to the offer?

## 2. SIMPLE AND EASY

Question number two: how can you make your offer simple and easy to understand?

This is SO important, and it's something easily overlooked. The challenge is that what seems simple to us is not simple to our customers. What seems like such an obvious and compelling idea to us isn't that obvious to them.

The challenge is to make it simple and easy to understand. This is critical because when people grasp something quickly and effortlessly, they not only like it more but they tend to ascribe more validity and worth to it. In other words, when people grasp the idea, when they understand it, they don't just like it, they believe that it's worthier. That's how arrogant human beings are.

It's like this: "Well, if I understand it, then it must be true." And it's the reason why things like rhythm and rhyme can make messages more consumable. Going back to the OJ Simpson trial, "If the glove doesn't fit, you must acquit!" People could get that concept and easily understand it. That's why it was so effective.

Making ideas simple and easy is really hard to do because sometimes it means pulling back on claims in your ad. It means not explaining every little nuance and detail of the product. For some people, this is really, really hard to do, especially if the offer is for your own business. Most potential customers just don't care about the details.

You must be wondering, "How can I make my offer seem simple and easy to understand?" Think back to every major hit song—go back and listen to them. Google the top 100 most popular songs of all time, and then listen to the chorus. They're made up of single-syllable words. As humans, we don't just like things that are simple, we ascribe more worth and validity to them. As a bare minimum, try to be simple when writing ad copy.

## 3. TRIGGERING A DESIRE

In the ad copy, what will trigger a desire for consistency that will drive a sale or action? As you can see, this question is a little bit complicated and requires some explaining. Robert Cialdini talked about this concept in his book, *Pre-Suasion: A Revolutionary Way to Influence and Persuade* (Simon & Schuster, 2016). He illustrated this with an example about a survey company—a company that big brands pay to send people out to the street with clipboards and say, "Hey, would you mind taking a survey?" Most people when approached by these survey people usually say something like, "No, I really don't want to," or "No thanks." Either way, it's a little bit awkward for both the person asking the question and the person saying no.

To overcome this awkwardness, they changed the question to, "Pardon me—do you consider yourself to be a helpful person?" It was a question that when asked, people had a hard time saying no to. When asked, they were likely thinking, "Yes, I am a helpful person."

Once people answered that question, the surveyor could say something like, "Great! If so, I can really use your help. I'm trying to get answers to this survey, and it would really mean a lot to me if you could help out." When the survey company made this change, their survey completion percentage went up 70 percent.

This type of questioning triggers this need for commitment and consistency. "Yes, I'm a helpful person, and because I'm helpful, I'm going to remain consistent to that, and I'm going to help you with your survey." Here's an example from a recent promotion for a workshop that used this same technique. The start of the sales letter read:

"Let me ask you a question. Is your product or service good? Does it work? If you put it in their hands, if you put it in front of the right person, will they get a good response? If you answered yes to that question, then I want to show you how to sell a whole lot more of it."

The triggering of desire for consistency by using the question, "Is your product or service good?" means that everyone who reads this question should be like, "Yeah, it's good." Then the subsequent line in the copy of, "I want to show you how to sell a whole lot more of it" is the push toward driving the sale.

Questions are compelling. Questions in and of themselves will draw some attention. For instance, asking a general question engages the mind. But it doesn't engage heart. And it doesn't engage identity. When asking someone, "Are you brave? Are you helpful? Is what you're doing good?" the person is saying something about themselves. Whatever it is they're saying about themselves, if that informs the next action that you would like for them to take, then all the better.

For some of you, this may seem manipulative. And you're right; it can be taken too far. For instance, the surveyor in the example above walks up to folks and says, "Do you consider yourself to be a helpful person?" For me, I wouldn't want to do that. There are better ways to get the same outcome. That example is an instructive example, but to say to somebody, "Hey, is what you're doing good? Yes or no?" If they're sitting there really questioning themselves and ultimately answer, "I don't know," then they are someone that I won't be able to help.

When you ask someone, "Do you consider yourself to be brave?" and they answer "Yeah, I do," then you can move them toward the desired action like this: "Cool. Then are you brave enough to end one of the biggest schisms that has been in business between sales and marketing?" "Yeah, I think I am." Prior to that, they weren't really considering it as much, but by engaging not just their mind but their heart and their identity, now they want to take action. Now they want to do something to show that they really, really mean it.

## 4. PRE-EXPOSURE

Question four is, "How can marketers pre-expose their audience to a concept linked to the desired emotional stimulus?" When thinking about how to pre-expose the audience to a concept linked to a desired emotional stimulus, the first thing is to uncover the desired emotional stimulus. In other words, how do we want our audience to feel so that they will want to make a purchase? What does their emotional state need to be if they're going to make that final purchase decision?

Figure 17–1 is the concept in a Facebook Ad by Digital Marketer that you read about in the last chapter. The ad was for an early bird sale that was about end. The ad image was of the low battery warning on the iPhone. If you've ever pulled your phone out of your pocket and it's at 10 percent battery life, the image is just a little sliver of red. If you

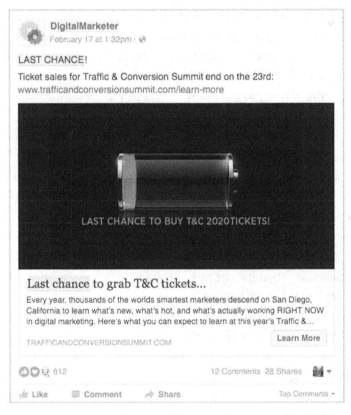

**FIGURE 17–1.** Pre-Expose Your Audience Using Metaphorical Imagery

own an iPhone, you've seen that low battery warning icon, and the emotion that you feel in that is this sense of urgency like, "OMG. I've got to plug it in."

What does your phone running out of juice have to do with the fact that this event is nearly sold out? They have nothing to do with one another. The low battery image exposes people to the idea, to the emotional stimulus, which in this case is nervous energy, urgency, and the need to act now. In using this commonly known image, it exposes the desire to emotional stimulus, which causes the action to take place.

## 5. MENTAL LINKS AND ASSOCIATIONS

The fifth question is along the same lines as question four. With number four, the focus was on how to pre-expose the audience to the desire to emotional stimulus. With number five, the focus is on identifying mental links and associations. In other words, what kind of nostalgia can be tapped into and positively associated to the offer? In question five, it's not just tapping into emotions but into memories. It's a much deeper feeling. If you've ever listened to a song that almost made you cry, it wasn't because of the sadness of the song. It was because the song brought you back to a moment in your life when you were feeling sad. That's what nostalgia is all about.

The reason that happens is because we as human beings create thought through associations. That is how thought occurs. It is by associating one thing with another thing. It's, "I know to fear this because it kind of reminds me of this other thing that hurt me at one point in time, so I'm going to fear it, too." This idea of association is big. How can you associate your product, your service, with a known common experience? That's really what is being asked in question number five. What mental links and associations can be tapped into and positively associated to the offer?

Great ads do this all the time. They tap into the memories and the feelings of an entire group of people and then associate a product to that. That's basically the way that Coke has been selling brown sugar water for decades. They've been associating this product to people's lives, whether it's family or friends or good times. Even if you never had that exact experience, it brings you back. To accomplish associating a product with a memory, it's necessary to know the positive associations the audience has experienced and finding a way to take them back there.

A good way to do this is through metaphors. When creating a metaphor, it is associating one thing to another thing that appears to be irrelevant. One way to do this is through imagery. An image, even if it's just there subtly in the background, can harken back to a memory, to something that happens every day, or to somewhere memorable. By mentally associating a product with this positive experience, either a past experience or desired future experience, this is the idea in question five.

Again, what mental links and associations need to be tapped into and positively associated to the offer? Ones that are just beyond emotion. Emotion is so powerful. In associating the offer to a real lasting memory or to a deep-seated future desire, this is where the power lies. With positive mental associations, whether the person experiences it, whether they know someone who experienced it, or if they could imagine themselves experiencing it, it's those same positive feelings that are transferred to the product and it becomes instantly understood, like what was discussed in question number two. The concept is grasped more easily. And, therefore, it's trusted more rapidly.

## 6. OPEN LOOPS

How can open loops be used to hold attention and leverage through the close? How can the idea of an open loop or a cliffhanger be introduced? Introducing mystery is another way to capture attention. What's a compelling mystery that can be leveraged at the beginning of a message to hold the audience's attention? This is something that has been used extensively on TV. Soap operas are famous for this. Right before the big thing happens, it fades to black to a commercial or that episode ends.

This idea that humans need closure was developed by a psychologist named Bluma Zeigarnik. She actually was eating lunch with a group of other colleagues one day, and they noticed that there was this waiter that had an almost uncanny ability to remember everyone's order. We've all been to restaurants where everybody at the table is throwing different combinations of their order to the waiter, they're not writing anything down, and yet they manage to remember it all. Well, the story goes that they had this waiter, and they were wondering what it was about this person that allowed them to memorize everybody's order. They were going to ask the waiter about it. But what they realized a short time later was that the waiter didn't actually remember their order anymore. Once the waiter delivered their meal, and came back around, they asked him, "Hey, by the way, how did you remember that I wanted this and this and this without writing it down?" The waiter was like, "Honestly, I don't remember even what you ordered."

What Zeigarnik realized is before you have closure, the brain keeps it open. The brain is hyperactive, and it can hold attention on a subject, even a fairly complex one, really well. The waiter was able to keep in his mind this multiple-person, complex order, but the second that the plate hit the table, Boom!, cognitive closure. Job done. Erase. Clear. No more keeping that info in random access memory. Clear it. Let's move on to the next thing.

In leveraging a story in marketing, don't tell the story and then go into the sales or marketing message. Tell the story and then weave in the message. If you close the story too early, the audience is done. Brain off. They're no longer paying attention. Cognitive closure to the story needs to occur at the point of sale or when the sale close happens.

## 7. PORTALS

This is the last and possibly the creepiest technique of all. How do you create a visual or mental portal for the prospect to pass through that will make them more open to new opportunities? This may seem a little bit weird, but the reality is you probably have experienced it yourself. You're sitting on the couch, and you get up because you need to go into another room to get something. You get up, and you walk into the new room, and when you get there you're like, "Why the heck did I come here? What was I looking for? I don't remember."

There is something fascinating in how our brains work when moving from one room to another, passing through a door. It really does change the way that we think. It is an attention reset. This has been proven and studied in dogs. Robert Cialdini, in *Pre-Suasion*, talked about the infamous Pavlov's dog experiment where Pavlov was able to associate a ringing bell to get dogs to salivate. What most people don't realize, however, is that there was another conclusion to this experiment.

Anytime Pavlov would take his dogs into a different room to show another researcher, "Look at this thing that I figured out. I've trained these dogs because I would ring a bell and then feed them meat. Now anytime I just ring a bell, look, they salivate because they've associated bell ringing with meat eating." Pavlov would take the dogs into a new room to show this behavior to one of his colleagues, but the dogs wouldn't salivate at the ringing bell. The ringing bell no longer had the same effect. What Pavlov realized is that when the environment changes, there is a mental reset.

This is very useful to know as marketers who are trying to get people to take action. Salespeople realize this. By getting someone to move from one place to another, they're more likely to make a decision. And this is the notion of portals—this idea of passing from one place to another. You've probably seen this if you've watched a product launch or something like that. You've seen the marketer driving in his car, and there you are in the car, and he's explaining some stuff. You're riding with him. You're passing from one place to another visually. The image of riding in a car while you're talking to your prospects is a type of portal.

The best film and video directors in the world get this. They get the idea of portals. One of the most obvious examples of this came from the movie, *The Wizard of Oz*. When Dorothy is transported from Kansas to Oz in the tornado, her house lands, and she goes to the door. Now you're seeing the world through her eyes, it's worth going back and watching, as the door swings open, and instantly everything changes from black and white to color as she passes from Kansas, the real world, into Oz. That passage through the doorway is a portal.

Portals can also be created with sound, too. Changing the background music just slightly as a transition occurs is one way this happens. For example, in the *Wizard of Oz*, there's no background music as Dorothy is walking through her house, but as soon as she opens the door, music begins. That's a visual-auditory portal.

To help illustrate this further, here's an example you could use for a local plumbing business. The video starts outside of the building. The plumber says, "Hi, I'm Fred, the plumber. We're really excited. We're doing some great stuff, but come inside. I want you to meet some people." Now the camera follows Fred, the plumber, as he opens the door and goes into the store. That's a portal.

We as human beings tend to make decisions after we have moved from one place to another. We are trained to do that.

The ceremony of walking down the aisle when getting married is a portal. The portal is of friends and family. The bride starts at the back of the crowd behind everyone and walks through this narrow portal. When the couple leaves, they exit back through that same portal. The bride and groom arrive separately, but they leave as husband and wife.

All these little subtleties denote that, "Hey, something has changed. What was before is not the same anymore. It's OK to act and to pursue a new path." In not giving a visual or auditory portal the audience is less likely to make a change. Just think about it. A visual portal could be really, really subtle like a background color change. Whether subtle or more obvious, there needs to be some type of mental cue that, "Hey, we're passing into something new together. It's time to make a change."

## THE SEVEN QUESTIONS SUMMARY

1. *How do I make the offer appear novel, unique, and distinctive?* Basically, how do you make the offer appear new? That's the first thing. Remember, the goal is focused attention. It doesn't matter how great the product is. It doesn't matter how compelling the message is. If people don't focus on it, if they don't hear it, if they don't pay attention to it, it's not going to convert them.

2. *How do I make the offer simple and easy to understand?* Humans love simple. We love easy to understand. If we understand it quickly and effortlessly, we like it more, and we ascribe it more validity. How can things like rhythm and rhyme be leveraged? Children learn the alphabet by simple and easy songs. It's a simplifying mechanism, and people like it because of that.

3. *What's an opening question that, when answered, will trigger a desire for consistency and drive a sale or action?* What's an opening question that, when answered, will make

the prospect say, "Yeah, this is who I am, and this is how I'm going to answer." It's questions like, "Do you consider yourself a helpful person? Do you consider yourself to be brave? Is your product or service good?" Good opening questions draw attention, but the questions that when answered drive consistent action and, specifically, action that's consistent with the desired action, those are even better.

4. *How do I pre-expose the audience to a concept linked to a desired emotional stimulus?* In other words, how to pre-expose the audience to make them feel a certain way? How can a link be established to a product or service and then to the desired emotion? This is best illustrated by the ad that had the iPhone battery almost dead to denote that tickets were about to be sold out. The emotional stimulus there was urgency. The battery image denotes urgency even though it's unrelated to the early bird sale. How about the, "Can you tell me how to get to Valentine Street?" example. Remember that example? The mention of Valentine made middle-aged men feel more romantic, which made them willing to throw themselves into harm's way for a woman they did not know.

5. *What mental links and associations can be tapped into and positively associated to the offer?* Question four looked at emotional links. With question five, the focus is mental links. It's all about memory. It's all about identity. Mental associations like the metaphors, memories, common shared experiences, and nostalgia that become associated with a product in a positive way—that's the focus of question number five.

6. *How can open loops be created to hold attention and leverage the close to create that cognitive closure that the customer's brain so desperately desires?* Here it's about things like mystery. It's about a story, but a story where the ending isn't offered until the message about the product or service is complete. To capture and hold attention, that's how to truly leverage a story. Don't just tell a story. Tell a story; talk about the product, close the story, and then the close of the story draws them to the action.

7. *How do I create a visual or mental portal for the prospect to pass through that, when they do, makes them open to new opportunities?* Is it a visual thing, such as walking with the prospect? Are they passing through a door? Is it a change in background, tone, and music? What is the signal that will make people say, "Now it's time to make a change?"

By using these seven questions before you finish writing a piece of copy and before you finish crafting an ad, you're going to have much more powerful messaging. You're going to find hooks that you had previously missed or ignored or not capitalized on. If your product or service is good, then you're going to make a lot more people happy. If you can get one or two of these questions answered, you're going to be doing a heck of a lot better than your competitors.

Ryan Deiss is the founder and CEO of DigitalMarketer.com. Over 36 months Ryan and his team have invested over $15 million on marketing tests, generated tens of millions of unique visitors, sent well over a BILLION emails, and run approximately 3,000 split and multi-variant tests. Learn more at DigitalMarketer.com.

# Chapter 18

# Capturing Leads Using Facebook Lead Ads

O ne of the difficult things with generating leads is that we're often asking the user to leave Facebook and do something else.

Do you think Facebook wants users to leave their platform?

Do you think Facebook users want to leave, either?

The only person who really wants the user to leave is the advertiser!

What if all three parties could have the best of both worlds?

Lead Ads and Messenger Ads solve that problem. These are very special kinds of ads whose sole focus is to collect leads for the advertiser without a lot of friction and without requiring the user to leave the Facebook platform.

In this chapter, you'll be introduced to Lead Ads, and in Chapter 19, our guest author Larry Kim will introduce you to Messenger Ads. By the end of each chapter, you'll have two powerful strategies for generating leads for your business without ever building a website.

## GETTING STARTED WITH LEAD FORM ADS

Facebook's Lead Generation Campaign Objective allows you to add contact forms to your ads.

The contact forms are part of Facebook, so your leads will never have to leave Facebook to give you their contact information. Additionally, the contact form is pre-filled with any info Facebook already knows about a user. For example, if you want to collect a person's name and email address, that information will already pre-fill into the form based on their Facebook information, and the user simply has to click a Next and Submit button.

This is a low-friction way to collect leads. You avoid disrupting your lead's user experience by keeping them on Facebook instead of switching to your website and back again. They never have to check their email or spam folder for a confirmation. It's a simple and elegant way to collect leads, especially on mobile devices.

When you choose the Lead Generation Objective, there aren't any optimization choices to make, as you can see in Figure 18–1. Facebook will show your ads to people it thinks will become leads.

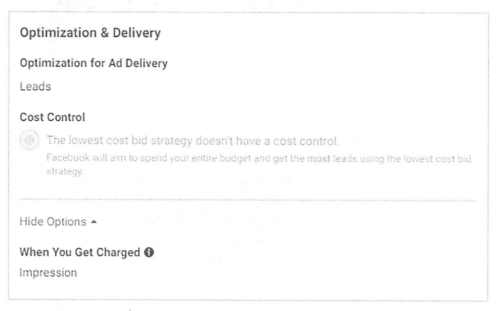

**FIGURE 18–1.** Lead Generation Campaign Ad Set Optimization and Delivery

In order to collect leads, you'll need to have a privacy policy. Even though you'll collect leads directly on Facebook, you'll have to have this privacy policy on your website. If you don't have a privacy policy, you can create one online for free by Googling "privacy policy generator."

You'll also have to create a lead form to collect the leads from your campaign. To do that, go into the setup for your ad inside the Lead Generation Campaign. Scroll down past the ad creative section and find the section that says Instant For. From there, you'll click on Create Lead Form. Choose a New Form and click Next.

## Set Your Lead Form Type

You can choose between a More Volume form type and a Higher Intent form type. Both form types are made up of three screens:

1. Questions
2. Privacy Policy/Review
3. Thank You

The Higher Intent form type adds an additional review section on the Privacy Policy screen and forces the user to slide to submit rather than just tapping Submit before sending you their contact information.

## Create the Lead Form Intro

There's an optional section above the questions at the top of the form that you can use to share the benefits of what the user will receive for filling out the form. Use this area to provide a bulleted list (or paragraph) of benefits the user will get for submitting the Lead Form, as you can see in Figure 18–2.

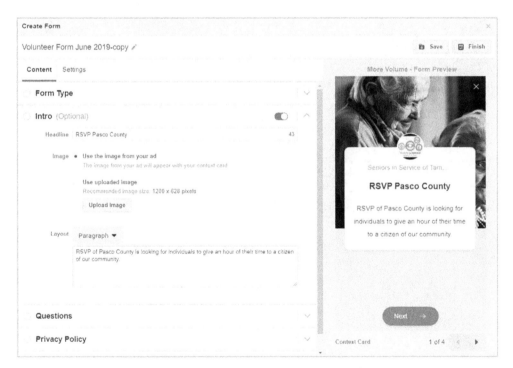

**FIGURE 18–2.** Instant Form Intro Section

You can change the image at the top of the form. You should either use an image from your ad or use your logo if the users are familiar with your business.

### Set Up Lead Form Questions

Both form types default to having email and full name fields that are pre-filled by Facebook. You can add different kinds of questions in a short answer, multiple choice, or even add conditional logic. It's very powerful. Facebook will automatically prefill demographic questions like date of birth, gender, marital status, relationship status, and military status. It can also prefill work information like job title, work phone number, work email, and company name. These are pre-filled with the information the user gave to Facebook, but the user can always change the responses.

If you have multiple locations, it has a store locator built in to show the nearest locations. Finally, you can even use the Lead Form for appointment scheduling to set appointments or schedule a store visit.

Generally speaking, the more fields you have, the less leads you'll generate, but they will be more qualified. You can see the question setup in Figure 18–3.

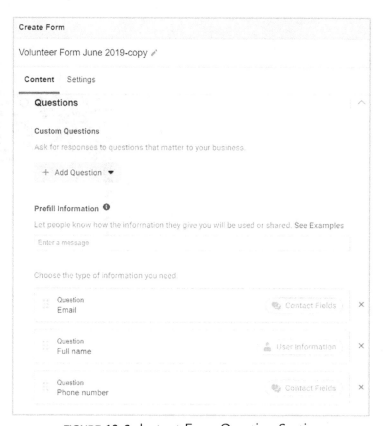

**FIGURE 18–3.** Instant Form Question Section

## Link to Your Privacy Policy

In the next section, you'll need to link to your privacy policy on your website. You can simply put Our Privacy Policy in the Link Text box. If you would like to have even more disclaimer text, you can also add it here. Most businesses don't have to do this, though.

## Review Screen

The Review Screen is only shown for Higher Intent form types. It is one extra step that shows the user what they filled in and allows them to go back and edit. It still links to Facebook's privacy policy (and yours). Both types are shown in Figure 18–4.

## Thank-You Screen

The Thank-You screen is shown last, after the user submits their form. Most users will leave the form and go back to their News Feed. For the people who are left, you can send them to your website, offer a download, or give them a click-to-call phone number for your business, as you can see in the example in Figure 18–5 on page 218.

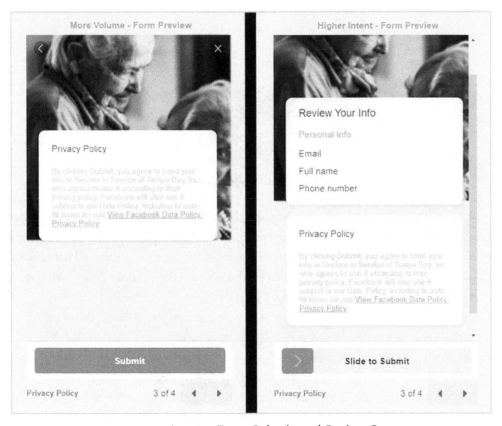

**FIGURE 18–4.** Instant Form Submit and Review Screens

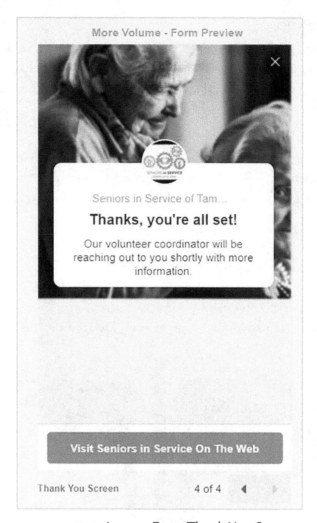

**FIGURE 18–5.** Instant Form Thank-You Screen

Now that you've set up the form, there are a few more settings to change. Go to Settings at the top of the Create Form window. Under Form Configuration, you'll probably want to change the Sharing setting from Restricted to Open. This will allow anyone who wants to fill out the form to be able to. Otherwise, only people who saw the ad can fill it out and it can't be shared by its viewers.

If you use a Customer Relationship Management System (CRM), you might have to match the fields from what Facebook calls them to what your CRM uses. For example, Facebook calls the Phone Number field "phone_number" and your CRM might call it "phone1." This is where you can match them up if you need to.

You can also add tracking parameters to this Lead Form. This allows you to pass additional fields of information to your CRM along with the lead's information, but without having the lead see it. A simple example is that you have multiple Lead Forms for different services and want to know which lead goes to which department. Facebook gives you the ad name and ad ID, but it's much easier to look at a field that says Dave or Sue to know who to give the leads to. Again, these are completely optional. Finally, click the Finish button in the top right corner of the window to save your form.

## RETRIEVING YOUR LEADS

Now you have a Lead Generation Campaign with a Lead Form, but where do the leads go? They're not in Ads Manager. They're stored under your Business Page. Go to the page you created the Lead Form for. Then along the top menu that says Page, Ad Center, Inbox, etc., choose More, then click on Publishing Tools. Once you click that, choose Forms Library in the left-hand menu.

You should see your form listed with a count of the leads that have filled out the form (see Figure 18–6). You can manually download a CSV of the leads right here.

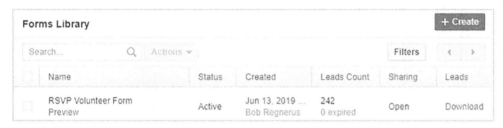

**FIGURE 18–6.** Forms Library

Facebook will only keep your leads for 90 days. If you don't have a CRM to receive them in real time, you have to go to this page and download them as often as you need them.

Because of their speed and simplicity for users, these Lead Forms are quite powerful. You can then nurture the people who filled out the form via email or phone and retarget those who opened or filled out the form. You'll see how to do that in Chapter 20.

# Chapter 19

# Converting Clicks to Facebook Messenger Conversations

## Guest Author Larry Kim

In the previous chapter, you learned about using Lead Form Ads to generate prospects for your business without the need for a website. In this chapter, I'm going to give you an additional way to generate leads without a website by using Facebook Messenger ads.

There are two ad tactics that have resulted in lower cost-per-lead acquisition and higher engagement and conversions for my clients: Facebook Click-to-Messenger ads and Sponsored Messages ads. You'll find both of these ads tucked into the Messages Objective when you're creating a new Facebook Ad in Ads Manager.

Both feature the Facebook Messenger messaging app as the stage for superior ad performance. And these two ads have a few more things in common that make them stand out in the Facebook Ads landscape. They are:

- *Interactive.* Instead of sending the ad audience to a website landing page like traditional Facebook Ads, these ads send people to an interactive conversation in Facebook Messenger.
- *Automated.* The advertiser is able to engage those who click on the ad through a Facebook Messenger chatbot programmed to capture and qualify leads automatically.

■ *Scalable.* When messaging-focused ads are connected to a chat marketing automation platform, businesses are able to achieve a limitless scale of one-to-one conversations.

All these elements come together for unicorn levels of ad performance. Dennis Yu defines "unicorns" as Facebook Page Posts that exponentially outperform other posts when you measure the engagement and reach. Here are the ones we've experienced at MobileMonkey:

■ MobileMonkey reduced cost-per-acquisition 97 percent using the Click-to-Messenger Ad objective.
■ Car Loans Canada increased lead acquisition 75 percent using MobileMonkey and Click-to-Messenger Ads.
■ Blenders Eyewear increased ROAS 7.5 times over using Facebook Sponsored Messages Ads.

You do not need MobileMonkey to use Messenger Ads, but we created it to help advertisers manage this strategy with much more ease.

## WHAT ARE FACEBOOK CLICK-TO-MESSENGER ADS?

Brands use Facebook Click-to-Messenger Ads to acquire top-of-funnel leads at a fraction of the cost of other Facebook Ad types. In fact, MobileMonkey reduced cost-per-lead 97 percent using Click-to-Messenger Ads vs. traffic ads.

Visually, Click-to-Messenger Ads resemble the traditional Facebook Ads you're used to. You have the same options for ad creative (image, video, carousel) and ad placement (Facebook News Feed, Instagram News Feed and Stories, Facebook Marketplace, Audience Network).

However, once a user interacts with the ad, they don't go to a website landing page. Instead, they are whisked over to Messenger, and that's where something special happens.

Facebook Click-to-Messenger Ads feature Instant Lead Capture. Immediately when someone messages your Facebook Messenger chatbot you collect valuable lead information. By default, advertisers instantly receive this info about every new Messenger contact:

■ First and last name
■ Region where they are located
■ Language
■ Gender
■ And, importantly, the ability to follow up with them in Facebook Messenger chat

Advertisers can program a chatbot to have a conversation in Messenger that saves answers to a rich user profile in MobileMonkey's Messenger marketing management

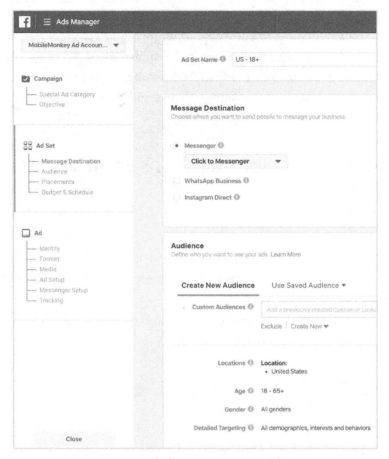

**FIGURE 19–1.** Click-to-Messenger Ad Setup

platform and moves new leads through your sales funnel. See Figure 19–1 for an image showing how to set this up.

## WHEN TO USE FACEBOOK CLICK-TO-MESSENGER ADS

Facebook Messenger chatbots today are being used to do many of the same things users do on a static (read: easy-to-abandon) website landing page. But instead, the chatbot allows for the lead capture or conversion to be done in a personalized, interactive conversation. This includes signing up for a webinar or an event, subscribing to blog or newsletter updates, and of course, capturing lead information and integrating that lead contact info into other business systems like a CRM.

If you're looking for top-of-funnel leads, combine Facebook's interest-based and demographics-based audience targeting with Click-to-Messenger Ads and a MobileMonkey chatbot to capture leads instantly.

If you're looking to convert site visitors to leads you can directly follow up with, use Facebook Custom Audiences to convert your anonymous website traffic into a named lead you can qualify and nurture. You can do the same for your Facebook Page fans, too.

However, you can technically use Click-to-Messenger Ads for any audience, whether cold or remarketing. Just consider your goals and add audience filters to narrow down in accordance with who you're trying to reach.

## CREATING CLICK-TO-MESSENGER ADS IN AD MANAGER

Messenger Ads have the same creative setup as the ads you've created before. They require additional setup to create the automated chatbot part of the conversation.

### Create Your Campaign and Ad Set with the Messages Objective

Following the steps you learned in Chapter 7, select Create a Campaign and choose the Messages Objective.

Create your Ad Set as you learned in Chapters 9 through 11. As in Figure 19–2, your destination will be Click to Messenger.

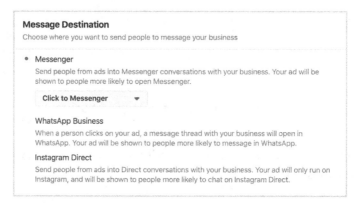

**FIGURE 19–2.** Message Destination within Ad Set

You will also need to change the default optimization method from Conversations to Leads, as shown in Figure 19–3 on page 225.

### Create Your Messenger Ad

Next you'll create your Messenger Ad. Everything about setting up your ad is the same. Follow everything you learned about ads and creative in Chapters 12 through 17. The unique difference with a Messenger Ad is that you will be creating a chatbot to collect information from your leads.

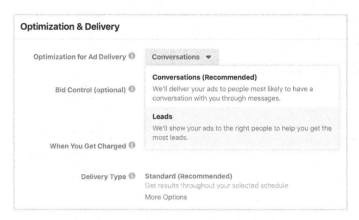

**FIGURE 19–3.** Messenger Optimization

Scroll down to the Messenger Setup section of your ad inside of Ad Manager and choose Generate Leads under the Create New option, as shown in Figure 19-4.

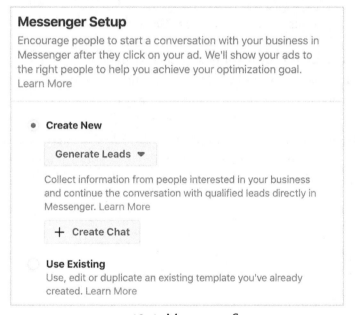

**FIGURE 19–4.** Messenger Setup

## Build a Simple Chatbot

To create your chatbot, click the Create Chat button and a dialog will open, as shown in Figure 19-5 on page 226.

In the intro section, you will first set up the opening message the user will see. It defaults to text only, but you can also add an image or even a video here.

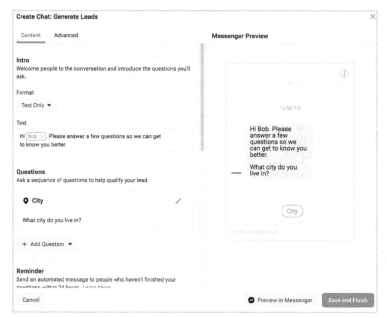

**FIGURE 19–5.** Create Chat: Generate Leads, Page 1

Next you'll add on your questions. Facebook has some preset fields that make it easy to replicate what you would ask for on a landing page form: phone number, email, address (city, state, ZIP, country), job title, company name, and gender.

You also have the ability to add your own custom short-answer questions or options. To add questions to your chatbot, simply click the Add Question button.

As you see in Figure 19-6, you have the ability to customize a Reminder message to the user in the case they fail to complete the entire chat.

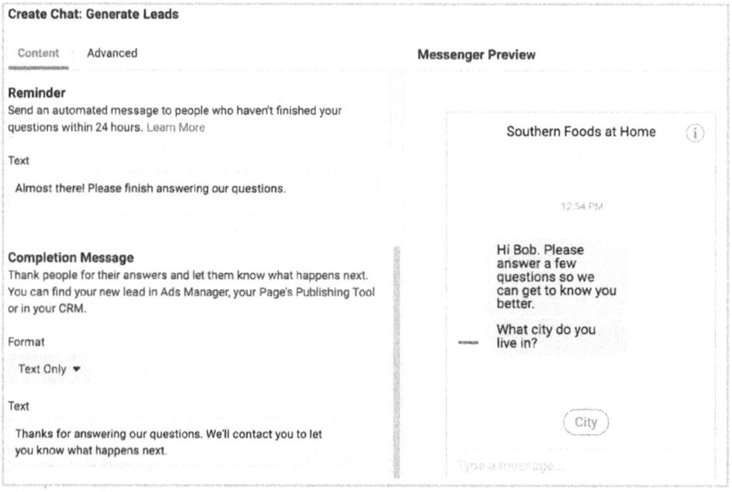

**FIGURE 19–6.** Create Chat: Generate Leads, Page 2

Enter a customized Completion Message next. You can use text only or add an image or video with it.

Scrolling down, this is the place you can connect an app, as shown in Figure 19-7. You will be required to accept Facebook's Lead Ads terms the first time you set up a chatbot. When you've done it successfully, you'll see the message in Figure 19-7.

In order to run these ads, you must have a link to a privacy policy somewhere on the web. Enter that URL in the box provided.

Click on the Advanced tab as shown in Figure 19-8 on page 228.

If you will later be using a form similar to the one you just created, enter a name and click Save Template. Here is where you can customize the Pause Questions if a user decides to pause a conversation with you.

Lastly, if you are connecting your CRM to Facebook (and having Facebook automatically send these leads into your CRM) this is where you can customize the field IDs to match your CRM.

Just like with Lead Ads (as you learned in the previous chapter), you can connect your CRM to automatically export your leads and can choose one of the service providers Facebook connects with or download them manually.

## CREATING CLICK-TO-MESSENGER ADS IN MOBILEMONKEY

As long as your Facebook Ads Manager and MobileMonkey accounts are linked (a process you can complete in Settings > Advertising), getting started with Facebook Click-to-Messenger Ads is straightforward.

There are two ways to create Click-to-Messenger ad campaigns in MobileMonkey.

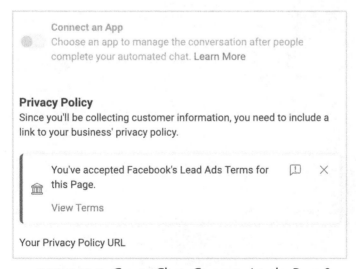

**FIGURE 19-7.** Create Chat: Generate Leads, Page 3

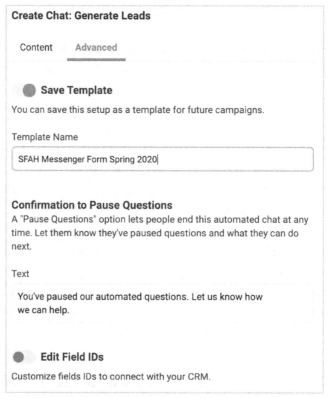

**FIGURE 19–8.** Create Chat: Generate Leads, Advanced

You can either create a new ad from scratch or you can use a clone of your existing ads that MobileMonkey will create for you (See Figure 19-9 below.)

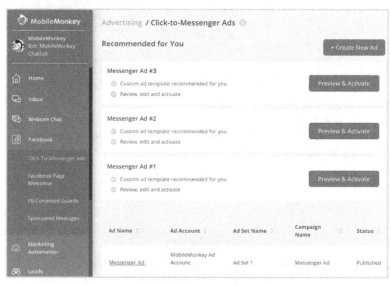

**FIGURE 19–9.** Create a New Ad from Scratch or Clone

When an advertiser clones their existing ad, MobileMonkey transforms it into a Click-to-Messenger Ad. It will have all the same ad creative; you just create the chatbot to respond to the audience.

Here's a step-by-step guide for creating Click-to-Messenger Ads in MobileMonkey.

### Step 1: Create a New Messages Ad Campaign

First, go to MobileMonkey > Facebook > Click-To-Messenger Ads and click Create New Ad.

The ad builder guides you through the steps, starting with giving the ad a name in MobileMonkey. Here you'll connect this ad to the Facebook Ad Account you're running the ad in. See Figure 19–10.

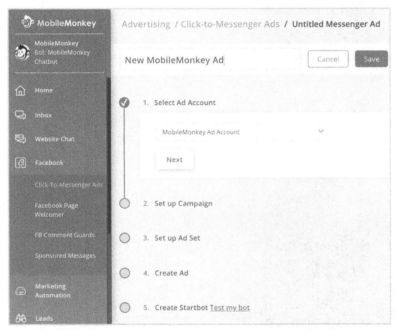

**FIGURE 19–10.** Click-to-Messenger Ads Step 1: Name Ad and Select Ad Account

### Step 2: Set Up the Facebook Campaign

Next we're going to name the campaign for Facebook Ads Manager and set the budget (see Figure 19–11 on page 230). Just as if you were creating the ad in Facebook Ads Manager, you can select a daily or lifetime budget.

### Step 3: Set Up the Ad Set

Usually, when you're setting up a new Facebook Ad campaign, you get to the part where you build your Ad Set (as seen in Figure 19–12 on page 230), which includes setting up your audience targeting.

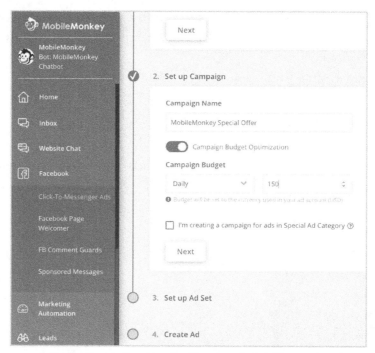

**FIGURE 19–11.** Set Up the Facebook Ad Campaign

**FIGURE 19–12.** Set Up the Ad Set

The MobileMonkey Click-to-Messenger Ad builder will allow you to clone the Ad Set of one of your existing ads to select from a trusted audience targeting setup you've used before.

You'll also name the Ad Set, enter a maximum bid cap if you'd like, and schedule the ad to run continuously or within a given start and end date.

## Step 4: Create the Ad

At this point, it's time to get creative. You get to choose the visual aspects of your ad and how it's displayed for your target audience.

As you can see in Figure 19–13, you can select a format. The standard Facebook Ad formats are Carousel, Single Image, Single Video. Once you choose a format, upload any media elements and craft your text, headline, and description.

In the Call-to-Action dropdown, Send Message is the default option. While that will certainly work, there are others to choose from, like Subscribe or Contact Us.

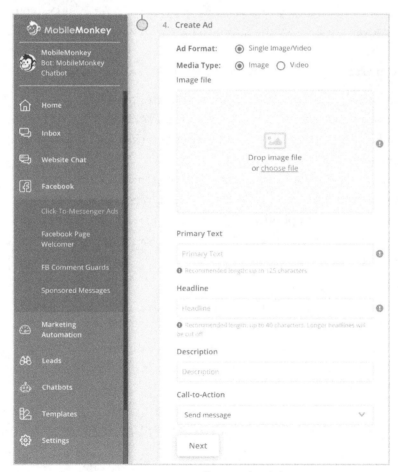

**FIGURE 19–13.** Create the Ad

If you want, you can try a few out. See which one drives the most engagement for your brand and use that approach for a results-driving advantage.

While you could publish now, that isn't a good idea.

If you did, people who clicked would end up in your Facebook Page Inbox. That's not what you want.

You'd have to reply to every message (or have another person do it), and that can be cumbersome. Instead, create a custom chatbot to follow up with folks who message you from the ad.

### Step 5: Build a Facebook Messenger StartBot

By writing a MobileMonkey chatbot conversation, you are automating your Click-to-Messenger Ad experience in a way that causes engagement to skyrocket. Anyone who clicks the ad can discover new information, subscribe, or handle a range of other tasks immediately, all thanks to the handy-dandy bot.

In Step 5 of the MobileMonkey Click-to-Messenger Ad builder, you're going to design the conversation for your chatbot to have with your new contact who clicked on your ad.

Here's an example of what that conversation might look like:

1. Start by asking a simple question and providing a button that the reader can tap to respond without any hassle. As soon as they click that button, they have become a new contact and the advertiser gets their lead info like their name and where they're located.
2. Next, ask for an email address, and save that email address to the user profile.
3. Also ask them how you can help and accept free-form text responses.
4. Finally, ask for their phone number because that's helpful to have when following up with this lead. And thank them and let them know someone will be reaching out soon.

See Figure 19–14 on page 233.

Of course, advertisers can write any conversation flow that makes sense for the purpose of this ad.

After the ad is activated, when a person engages with this Click-to-Messenger Ad, the advertiser gets their lead info. You can connect this lead to your other business systems and send it straight to your sales team as well.

## WHAT ARE FACEBOOK-SPONSORED MESSAGE ADS?

One of the newest ad formats available on Facebook is Sponsored Messages. They are an incredibly effective choice for brands with an existing Facebook Messenger contacts list.

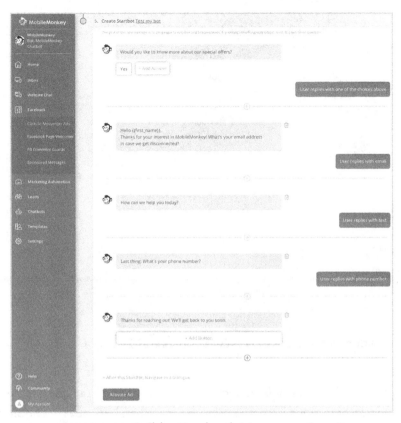

**FIGURE 19–14.** Build a Facebook Messenger StartBot

For example, Blenders Eyewear is an online retailer of sunglasses. They ran Sponsored Message Ads to their existing Facebook Messenger leads and got a 7.5 times higher return on ad spend compared to ads run to other audience segments.

Not only do Sponsored Messages let you engage with users who've shown an interest in your brand, unlike other Facebook Ads, they won't get lost in the noise of a News Feed. Instead, they only appear in Messenger as a message alongside all their organic Facebook Messenger messages. There's no sign that it's an ad until after the user clicks the message, giving the ad a very native feel and increasing the odds the target audience will see it. You can see how to create one in Figure 19–15 on page 234.

## WHEN TO USE FACEBOOK SPONSORED MESSAGES

There is one trick with Sponsored Messages: You can only use them to reach users who've already engaged with you on Messenger. That means this approach won't work in all situations.

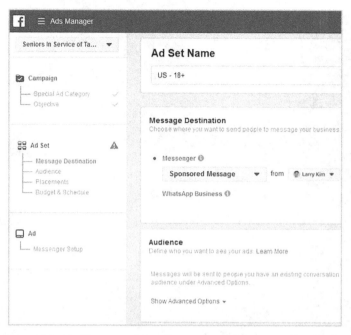

**FIGURE 19–15.** Create a New Sponsored Message Campaign

That's what makes these ads perfect for re-engagement. You can use them to keep users up-to-date about your brand, stay top of mind, and encourage contacts to move forward in your sales funnel.

## CREATING SPONSORED MESSAGES ADS IN MOBILEMONKEY

Now that you know how powerful Facebook Sponsored Messages Ads are, it's time to put them to use. Here's a detailed step-by-step guide.

### Step 1: Create a New Sponsored Message Campaign

Start by opening MobileMonkey (as seen in Figure 19–16 on page 235).

Next, navigate to Facebook and choose Sponsored Messages.

Once you open the Sponsored Message Campaign builder, name your campaign. That way, you can find it again with ease. And select the Ad Account you want to run this ad through (see Figure 19–17 on page 235).

### Step 2: Choose Your Messenger Contacts Custom Audience

After naming your campaign, it's time to define your audience for your Sponsored Message Ad Campaign (as seen in Figure 19–18 on page 235).

FIGURE 19–16. Create a New Sponsored Message Campaign in MobileMonkey

FIGURE 19–17. Select the Ad Account Sponsored Messages

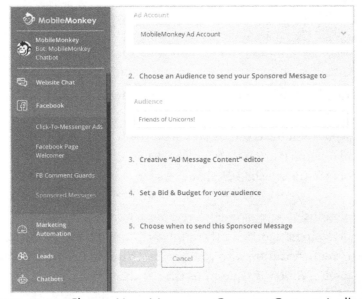

FIGURE 19–18. Choose Your Messenger Contacts Custom Audience

The default setting has it going to all of your contacts. If you want to choose a different custom Messenger contacts audience, now's the time.

### Step 3: Craft Your Sponsored Messages Ad Content

Now that you know which audience you're targeting, it's time to create the actual ad. You'll be adding the message, images, and buttons your contacts are actually going to see. Figure 19–19 shows you what that looks like.

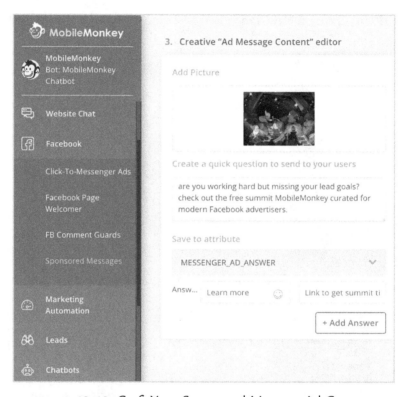

**FIGURE 19–19.** Craft Your Sponsored Message Ad Content

By adding a question instead of a statement, you'll increase engagement. It prompts your users to take action, and that's what you want.

The text portion can only be 125 characters long. That means brevity is your friend, so be concise.

Then, give your users access to quick response buttons.

Create a few options that move them forward through the funnel. For example, if you're driving event registration with your campaign, make one button Learn More and have it link to a set of follow-up questions that let them register.

## Step 4: Set the Facebook Sponsored Messages Ad Campaign Budget

As with all Facebook Ad campaigns, you'll set a budget in this next step (see Figure 19–20).

Start with a conservative budget to serve as a test-run. After you see how it performs, you can tweak your approach to achieve maximum engagement. As a general rule of thumb, Facebook says brands should expect 1,000 impressions for $30.

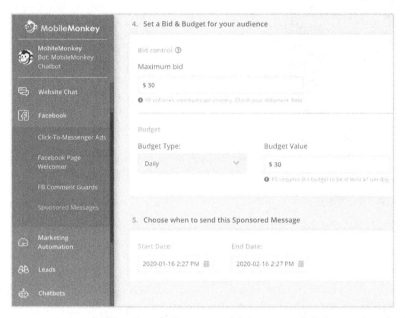

**FIGURE 19–20.** Set the Facebook Sponsored Messages Ad Campaign Budget

Consider the size of your audience and set a budget that makes sense. You can either choose a daily budget or one for the life of the campaign.

## Step 5: Set the Schedule and Publish Your Campaign

Your last step is to define when you want your Facebook Sponsored Messages Campaign to run, as seen in Figure 19–21.

Facebook is the one that chooses which members of your audience will receive your message and when they get it. If you want to tap everyone, then you'll want to set a large window.

Once you have the start and end dates set, all you have to do is click Send.

Your campaign will publish to Facebook Ads, where it will get reviewed. When it's approved, your messages will start to roll out to your targeted Messenger contacts based on your schedule.

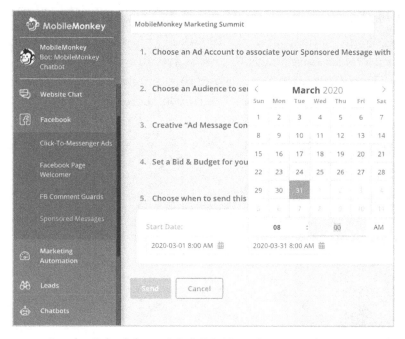

**FIGURE 19–21.** Set the Schedule and Publish Your Sponsored Messages Campaign

Since Click-to-Messenger and Sponsored Message Campaigns have different functions, they both have a place in your brand marketing. Consider which goals are a priority and then choose the approach that works best in that situation.

Don't miss the power of an automated chatbot landing page when you connect your Click-to-Messenger Ad and Sponsored Message Ads to MobileMonkey. MobileMonkey is a power platform that allows you to set up the Facebook Ad as well as the automated chatbot follow-up, saving all your lead info and connecting lead data to your other business systems.

Both of these Facebook messaging ad options are genuine engagement unicorns with amazing ROI that stands out in a sea of donkeys. Give them a try today.

Larry Kim is the CEO of MobileMonkey, an integrated web chat, SMS, and Facebook Messenger bot platform for marketing and customer service. He's also the founder of WordStream, Inc., the leading provider of Google Ads, Facebook Ads, and keyword tools used by over a million marketers worldwide.

# Chapter 20

# The Anatomy of a Facebook Retargeting Campaign

You learned about Retargeting way back in Chapter 3. We've emphasized it's best for an advertiser to start with a Retargeting Campaign to warm traffic (visitors who've been to your website). This is why we taught this to you so early in the book, even before you learned about Facebook Campaigns, Ad Sets, and Ads.

In this chapter, you are going to see the anatomy of a Retargeting ad and we challenge you to find a way to model this ad for something in your business.

By following along how we constructed this campaign, we know you will be successful creating and publishing your own Retargeting campaign!

## THE STRUCTURE OF A RETARGETING CAMPAIGN

The general structure of a basic Retargeting Campaign is shown in Figure 20–1 on page 240.

## RETARGETING USERS WHO VISIT YOUR WEBSITE

In the Seniors in Service example, we send people to a landing page about volunteering, as seen in Figure 20–2 on page 240. It has links to specific ways

**FIGURE 20–1.** General Structure of a Retargeting Campaign

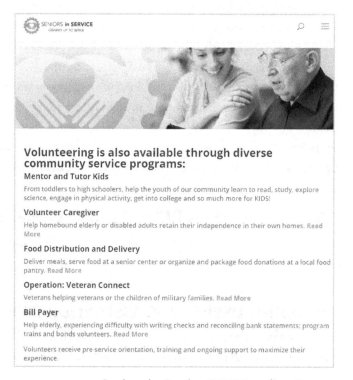

**FIGURE 20–2.** Seniors in Service RSVP Landing Page

they can volunteer. One of those is the Volunteer Caregiver program where they visit and provide friendship and possibly assist with chores for a home-bound elderly person.

When someone engages with the ad and indicates they are interested in general volunteering, the next step is to tell them about this particular program.

Here's how we accomplished this.

First, we created an audience of everyone who visited the landing page both from our initial prospecting ad and other traffic sources. Not only can we retarget the people we paid to reach our landing page, we are also able to retarget those who landed on our page from other paid sources like Google Ads or even those who found us through a search or referral from a friend.

We also exclude a page that talks about the Volunteer Caregiver program that we're going to send these people to. If they have already seen the page, then we're not going to pay to send them there again. The setup is shown in Figure 20–3.

Next, we created an audience of people who have already visited the page about being a Volunteer Caregiver as seen in Figure 20–4 on page 242. This way, we don't waste ad spend and annoy people who have already visited the page.

Then we created a Reach Campaign to show our ads to as many people that viewed the original landing page as possible. Note that they were originally driven there by a Traffic Campaign, so they have already proven they will click on our ads.

If you have a lot of traffic to your site, and the audience of people in the seven-day period is over 1,000 people, you should optimize for Traffic or Conversion rather than Reach. Use the Traffic Objective if you do not have a specific offer or action they can take on the page. Use the Conversion Objective when you have a measurable action they can take.

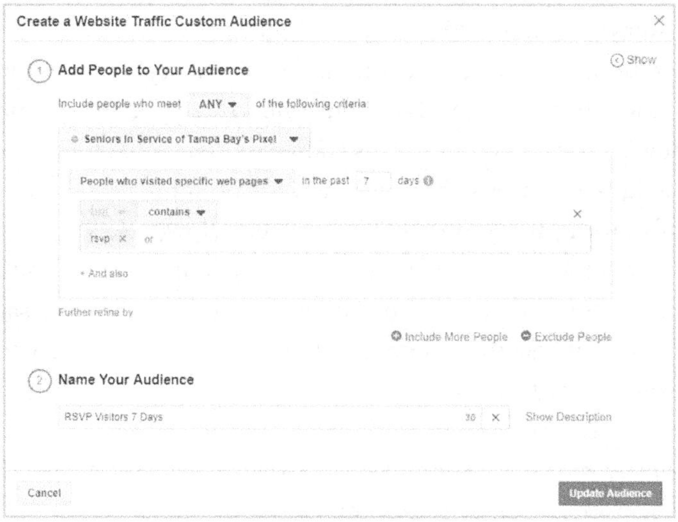

**FIGURE 20–3.** RSVP Landing Page Visitor Audience Creation

**FIGURE 20–4.** Volunteer Caregiver Landing Page Visitor Audience Creation

Next, we defined our audience as the visitors of the main RSVP volunteering page and we excluded the people who already visited the caregiver page where we'll send the traffic. We also excluded existing volunteers since we have a list of them, as shown in Figure 20–5 on page 243.

Then we applied the same geographical and age restrictions as our Prospecting Ad since not all of the page's traffic comes from our Facebook Ads.

For placements, we chose only the Facebook and Instagram feeds and deselected everything else. These are still the best-performing placements and we're still getting an understanding of how everything works before we try more exotic and less-performing placements, as shown in Figure 20–6 on page 243.

For optimization, you need to define a frequency cap for the Reach Campaign. Remember, the more urgently you want someone to see your ad, the more impressions you want to show each day. An example is shown in Figure 20–7 on page 244.

People often have questions about frequency. You want people to see your ads, but the downside of showing an ad too often is it will get a lower click-through rate and cost more per impression. It also annoys frequent Facebook users. We've found it's a balance of wanting people to see your ad and not hammering them with the same ad over and over again. We recommend a frequency cap of two impressions per day for this audience of landing page visitors within the last seven days.

Next we created the ad shown in Figure 20–8 on page 244. It used a shortcut by taking some copy from the new landing page to use as part of the ad. Doing that is efficient and it helps the ad and the landing page's messages match.

When you're done creating the ad, don't forget to publish your changes.

**FIGURE 20–5.** Audience Geographic and Demographic Restrictions

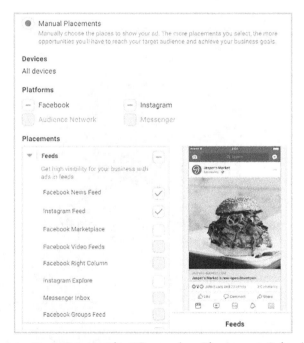

**FIGURE 20–6.** Retargeting Campaign Placement Selection

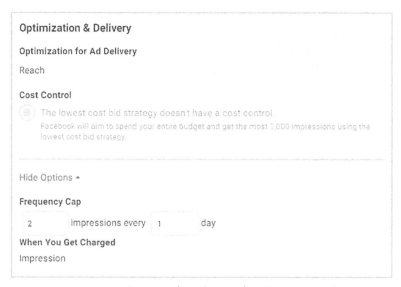

**FIGURE 20–7.** Retargeting Campaign Frequency Cap

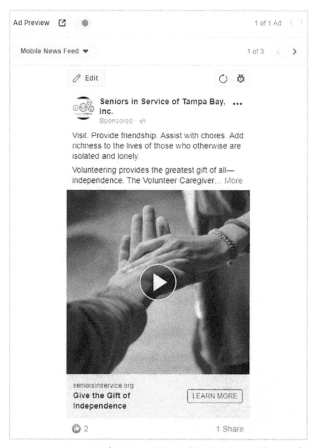

**FIGURE 20–8.** Volunteer Caregiver Retargeting Ad

## RETARGETING USERS WHO ENGAGE WITH YOUR VIDEO AD

When someone visits a landing page from a Traffic Campaign, that is a very good sign of their interest. However, you can also target people who don't visit your landing page but rather show serious engagement with a video ad by watching most of it all the way through.

Getting back to our Seniors in Service example, here's how we did that:

Inside our Reach/Retargeting Campaign, we created a second ad set. Instead of calling it 7 Day Visitors, we call it 7 Day Prospecting Video (RSVP) Viewers 75%.

We created two new audiences for this ad set.

The first is one called 7 Day Prospecting Video (RSVP) Viewers 75%. Its source is Video and it targets people who viewed at least 75 percent of our prospecting video from the ad in the last seven days. See Figure 20–9.

Next, we created a new audience called Three Second Viewers Caregiver Retargeting.

Once both audiences were created, we moved the Three Second Viewers to the Exclusion list. We use this to prevent the Retargeting ad from showing again to someone who watched three seconds of this video and took no action.

We don't want to annoy these users and we don't want to waste money on people who are not interested in our content. By the way, this is an advantage you'll have over big companies that have large budgets who will ignore this detail!

We applied demographic restrictions and chose the News Feed placements again.

Here we targeted the audience of 75 percent Video Viewers. We excluded our audience of volunteers, people who visited our initial landing page and RSVP within seven days, and Three Second Viewers. You can see the whole setup in Figure 20–10 on page 246.

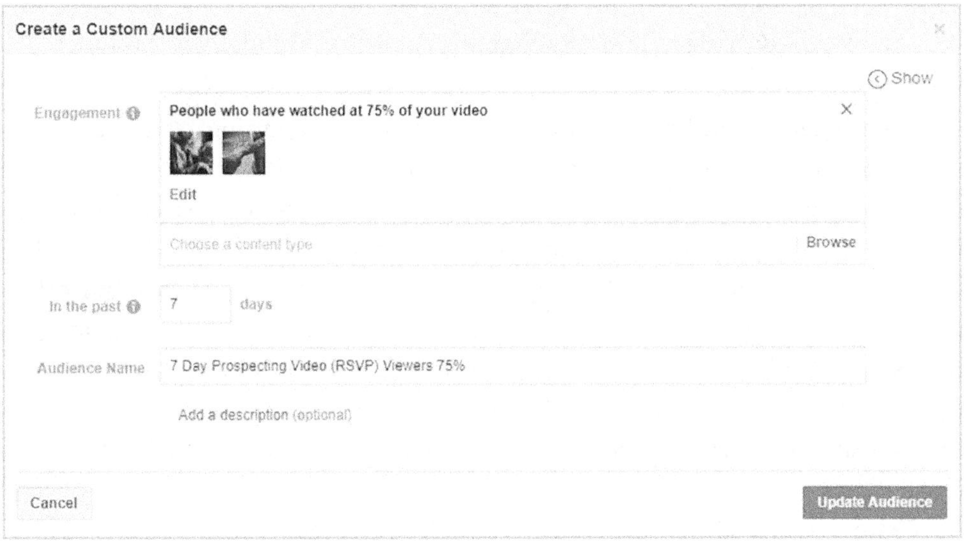

**FIGURE 20–9.** 75-Percent Video Viewer Retargeting Audience

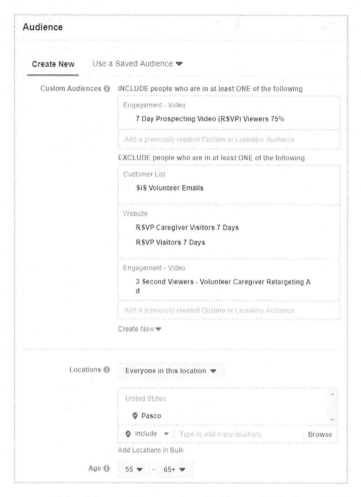

**FIGURE 20–10.** Video Viewer Retargeting Audience Includes and Excludes

For optimization and delivery, we chose a frequency of one impression every day.

We chose a lower amount of impressions (one vs. two a day) than the landing page visitor example in the previous section because this audience is less engaged. They only viewed our prospecting video compared to the landing page visitors who viewed some of the video and clicked to the landing page. We used the same ad as in our other Ad Set for the landing page visitors. You can easily copy your ad from the Landing Page Visitors to the Video Viewers by finding the ad inside Ads Manager, then clicking the Duplicate button on it as shown in Figure 20–11 on page 247. Then choose Existing Campaign and unselect the existing ad group of Landing Page Visitors and choose the Video Viewers.

The final step, as always, is to click the Publish Changes button.

**FIGURE 20–11.** Copy Existing Ad with Engagements

## RETARGETING USERS WHO ABANDON FACEBOOK LEAD FORMS

You can also use Retargeting Campaigns to get Facebook Lead Forms completed.

Some people will open your Lead Forms and not submit them. It could be because they decided not to submit it, but it's more likely they were distracted and forgot. You can create an audience based on people who opened your Lead Form but didn't submit it, as seen in Figure 20–12 on page 248.

Send these people to another ad that asks them to fill out the form or lists additional benefits of filling it out.

## RETARGETING IS NOT JUST FOR PROSPECTING

Keeping with the theme of recency, a recent buyer is most likely to buy from you again. Instead of using a prospecting page as the source of the Retargeting Audience, you can

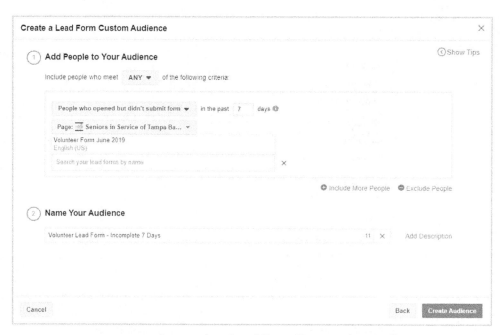

**FIGURE 20–12.** Incomplete Lead Form Retargeting Audience

use your Thank You or Order Complete page and target recent buyers with an upsell or cross-sell campaign. The setup would be the same, but the source audience would only be visitors to the post-sale page. You'll see these strategies in Chapters 21 through 23.

# Chapter 21

# Using Deep Funnel Marketing™ to Make Your Customers See You Everywhere

**D**eep Funnels have been a staple in every campaign we've worked on since 2014. They help us fill appointment calendars for professionals and thought leaders. They help our SaaS and ecommerce clients sell products like checks, clothing, headbands, medical devices, software, training, iPhone apps, supplements, and dirt (yes, dirt). They help our clients land six-figure contracts, fill $2,000 seminar seats, and recruit members for their high-end coaching programs.

The Deep Funnel makes it appear like you are everywhere and you magically appear at the right time with just the right content in the prospect's News Feed. It provides you opportunities to go much deeper into conversation with your prospects. It gives you time to educate before you sell.

In this chapter, you will learn an advertising strategy that correctly assumes all your potential customers are each in a different place in their buying decision process. It's a structure that allows you to present the *right creative* at the *right time* to the *right audience* and moves them towards a buying decision.

## HOW DOES THE DEEP FUNNEL RELATE TO MY BUSINESS?

This is a common problem with people we consult with.

We once had a financial advisor talk with us about how frustrated he was with his website. Not clear on what he meant, we asked him to clarify.

"I get all this traffic, but when they land on my site no one books an appointment to see me in my office!"

Here's what we said: "Are you one of those guys who fell in love at first sight and married your wife a week after you met?"

Confused, he said, "No, I dated my wife for four years in college before we got married."

We said, "How many people with over a million dollars of investable assets are going to leave their current advisor and discuss their concerns with someone they don't know after a single search? Wouldn't it be reasonable for them to check you out a bit before they strike up a conversation? Isn't it possible your wife did a little homework on you before she agreed to dinner?"

He agreed, of course, and understood the point.

We business owners market differently than we act in the real world. Most people don't make complicated, thoughtful decisions in the moment. They need time and information before committing to something complicated or expensive.

I (Bob) wrote about this in my first book, *Big Ticket eCommerce* (self-published, 2007).

The fact is most business owners don't go deep enough with their marketing funnels to properly educate and woo prospects. Too many try to close the deal like it's a Tinder date and move on when all it takes is a little more patience and effort to close a deal.

## THE CUSTOMER AWARENESS TIMELINE AND DEEP FUNNELS

As you learned in Chapter 1, most customers go through five steps of awareness before they decide to purchase anything.

As the customer moves from being Unaware to Most Aware, the less resistance they encounter to doing business with you.

The concept that drives Deep Funnel Marketing is that most advertisers underestimate the depth they have to go to in order to convince somebody to buy from them. Everyone wants to believe their product acts like a simple impulse-buy kitchen gadget. Most advertisers try to move a prospect through all five steps of customer awareness (Unaware, Problem Aware, Solution Aware, Your Solution Aware, The Most Aware) with a single ad. That's very narrow thinking.

In reality, the advertiser who's going to win is the one who acknowledges the depth they need to go to in order to convince the prospect to become a customer. If you understand it, believe in it, and invest in it, you're the one who's going to win all the business. This isn't an 80/20 situation, but more like a 95/5 or even a 99/1 winner-take-all one when you get your advertising aligned to move prospects through all five stages. Five percent of the advertisers will get 95 percent of the sales.

Most people won't have the knowledge or ability to create a Deep Funnel, or they won't have the financial wherewithal to do it. It's very hard to convince a financial planner to invest several thousand dollars over a few months to win a new client *even though that client is worth tens or even hundreds of thousands of dollars to them over their lifetime.*

Most people aren't going to be able to see past spending the first few thousand even though it will pay off 10:1 or even 50:1 over the next ten years. Most planners will look at the cost and not do it. They will go back to their free dinner strategy simply because it costs less up front. They'll revert back to what's easy for them.

## FACEBOOK IS AN INTERRUPTION MEDIA

People do not open the Facebook App to solve problems. Ads that scroll by a user on their desktop or phone are interruptions amongst the pictures of children, re-posted memes, and food selfies.

When prospecting in a Deep Funnel scenario, it's proper to assume that everyone you advertise to is at Unaware on the Customer Awareness Timeline.

Thankfully, there is Retargeting (which you've read a lot about already in this book). The best part of Retargeting is it removes the pressure from you to close sales on the first visit. Most people (in fact, only like .05 percent of people) are not far enough down the Customer Awareness Timeline to make a purchase the first time they see an ad from you.

Retargeting gives you the ability to orient your advertising to each person's timeline and gives you multiple opportunities to carry on a conversation over time and help move that person from Unaware to The Most Aware.

With your ability to retarget, and using the technology provided to you in the Facebook Pixel, you can create very sophisticated deep sequences of ads that show in the person's Facebook News Feed over time. It provides you opportunities to go much deeper into conversation with your prospects. It gives you time to educate before you sell.

## BASIC DEEP FUNNEL MARKETING STRATEGIES FOR TOP OF FUNNEL

There isn't a market we've come across where Deep Funnel didn't produce a boost to customer acquisition in some form or another, whether it be cost, return on ad spend (ROAS), or even just volume of conversions.

Remember the financial advisor client who took four years to court his future wife? Well, we're not going to give you dating advice for finding a future mate, but we are going to show you the best way we know to court your prospects and make it extremely easy for them to get to know, like, and trust you over time.

The following strategies are useful for any business, whether it's an ecommerce business, service business, information business, or local business.

You will use these strategies used for prospecting or ToFu (Top of Funnel). It's for prospects that are Unaware, Problem Aware, or Solution Aware.

The goals are to:

- Capture their attention
- Move them to Problem Aware (if they are Unaware) or
- Move them to Solution Aware (if they are Problem Aware)

You will either capture their attention by driving them from Facebook to an article or blog post on a landing page or showing a 30- to 90-second Facebook Video Ad.

This strategy shown in Figure 21–1 will seem most familiar to you if you've done some digital marketing before. It will involve placing an ad on Facebook and driving interested prospects to your website or Landing Page.

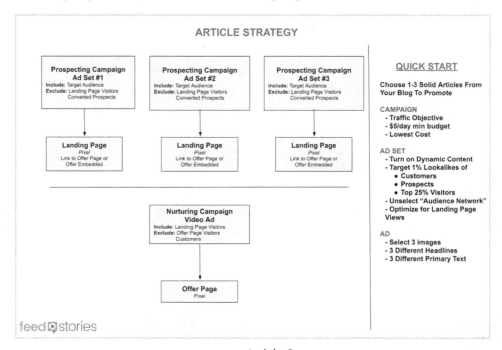

**FIGURE 21–1.** Article Strategy

## LAUNCHING YOUR ARTICLE STRATEGY PROSPECTING CAMPAIGN

The process starts by creating a Facebook Campaign that you will name using one of these words: Prospecting or ToFu. You can choose a Conversion Objective if you are capturing leads or generating sales, but only if you give the Facebook Optimizer enough time and budget to analyze your campaign. Remember, you need to give Facebook about 50 data points during the Learning Phase to reach statistical significance. If you cannot reasonably expect to generate at least 50 conversions in a week, then use the Traffic Objective for your campaign. Then, choose your budget amount.

## CREATING YOUR INITIAL PROSPECTING AD SET

Next, you will create your first Ad Set and choose your target audience. Chapters 5 and 9 taught you all about creating your audiences and setting up your Ad Sets. In the example you'll see shortly, we're using a Custom Audience called Agency Leads which is a list of email addresses we exported from our CRM of agencies we have relationships with.

The first concept of the Deep Funnel is to exclude certain users from seeing your ad unnecessarily. Remember, your Prospecting Campaign is meant to capture the attention of cold traffic and either move the prospect to Problem Aware or Solution Aware. You don't want to show your ads to people who are already in the middle of your funnel.

### Exclude Visitors and Viewers

After reading your ad and visiting your landing page, visitors have moved to the right on the timeline and are now sitting on the Solution Aware portion of the timeline. They are aware of a problem, they are aware of a solution, and now they are also aware of YOU—a provider of a solution to that problem! Therefore, your first Top of Funnel Ad or Prospecting Ad no longer needs to be shown to these visitors. You'd be wasting your money. You will exclude them from seeing your ad again.

You do this first by creating a Website Custom Audience for all visitors to your landing page. Typically, you will create a 30-day Audience as shown in Figure 21–2 on page 254.

Then, use this exclusion in the Audience area of your Ad Set as shown in Figure 21–3 on page 254.

**FIGURE 21–2.** 30-Day Website Visitor Audience

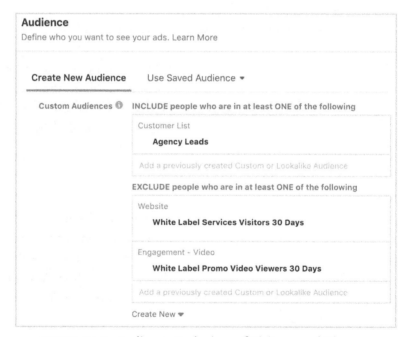

**FIGURE 21–3.** Audience Exclusion of Visitors and Viewers

### Exclude Video Viewers

Note in the example shown previously in Figure 21–3, we also have an exclusion for Video Viewers. We typically prefer to use video for our ads, and there are many reasons to do this as you've already learned. One of the reasons we prefer Video Ads is that you can take an additional signal from the Facebook user if they are interested in you.

So, you'll also create a *second* Video Custom Audience that records users who've watched at least three seconds of the video you are using in your ad. You will use "three seconds" viewers for all Videos Ads that are 15 seconds or less (as shown in Figure 21–4), and "ten seconds" viewers for Video Ads over 15 seconds.

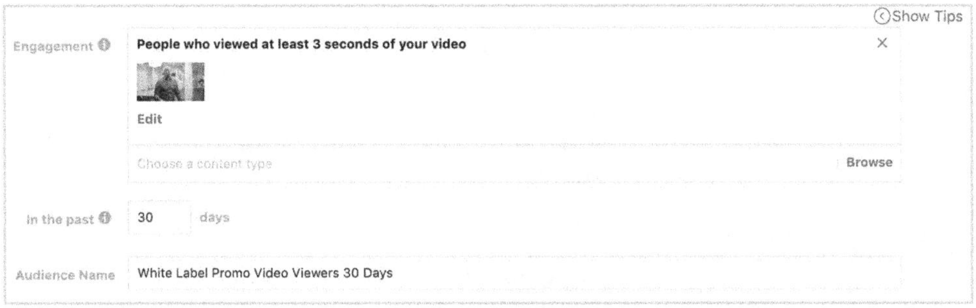

**FIGURE 21–4.** Second Viewers for 30-Days Audience

Three seconds seems short, but for a 15-second ad, that's 20 percent of the video! What you're trying to do is identify people who spent at least 20 to 25 percent of their time on your ad. If they skimmed past it, you'll possibly try and show it to them again if Facebook selects them. However, if they spent at least 20 to 25 percent of their time on your ad, you know they at least had enough time to make a quick decision on it.

If they watched for three or ten seconds but did not visit the landing page, you want to eliminate them from your prospect pool for this ad. You're trying to reach only those users who are most interested in what you're offering. You don't want to waste money by showing this ad continually to the same person who hasn't shown interest in it. You're not totally giving up on them, however. This strategy involves creating three separate ads so you will have a shot at them with your second and third ad.

## Exclude Current Customers

The most important exclusion in your Ad Set within your Prospecting Campaign is your current customers. Create a Customer Custom Audience like we taught you in Chapter 5 and keep it updated. In our example, our customer list is called Infusion Customers as seen in Figure 21–5 on page 256.

A number of CRMs have APIs that can connect to Facebook Custom Audience so that the process can be automated. However, if you don't have this ability, you should schedule a time to upload a new customer list at least once a quarter. If you have much greater sales volume, you may need to do this monthly or even weekly.

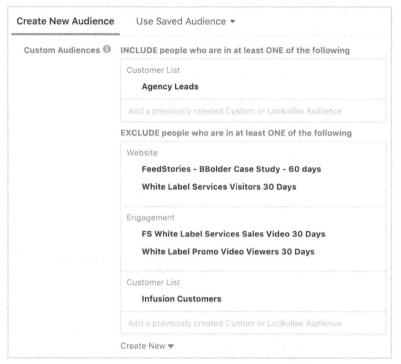

**FIGURE 21–5.** Customer Custom Audience Exclusion Example

### Exclude Custom Audiences

There are two more audiences we are excluding in our example. Feedstories BBolder Case Study 60 Days is a Website Custom Audience (WCA) of people who visited a page they only show to people in their Nurturing Campaign. It's only for people who have taken steps with them to prove they want to see material of this depth. We don't want their Prospecting Ad to show up in the News Feed of someone this far down the path with them.

The second audience, White Label Services Sales Video, is a Video Custom Audience of people who watched 75 percent or more of the Sales Video Ad that shows inside their Nurturing Campaign. Once again, someone seeing this video is already in the Deep Funnel and you don't want them to see a Prospecting Ad.

## CREATING YOUR INITIAL PROSPECTING ADS

Once you've set up your exclusions to create your Ad Set, it's time to create the ad itself using the steps you learned in Chapter 12. Your ad will drive users from Facebook to the article on your landing page. This page could be a blog post, a product page on an ecommerce site, a registration page for an event, or a typical landing page where you offer someone a lead magnet in exchange for their email address.

This landing page will have your pixel installed. By landing on this page, the user has been "cookied" and is now available for you to retarget with more ads, as shown in Figure 21–6.

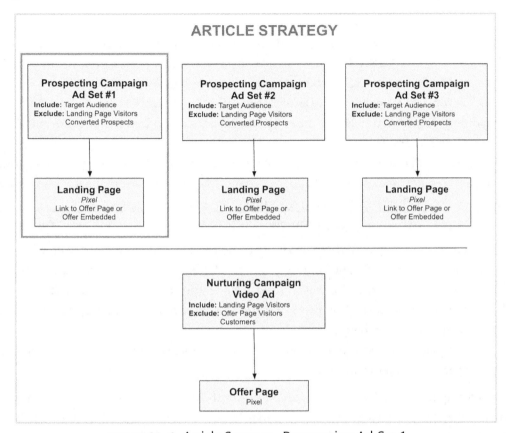

**FIGURE 21–6.** Article Strategy—Prospecting Ad Set 1

At this point, you've just created Ad Set #1 and ad #1 for the Article Strategy. You haven't created #2 or #3 yet.

Start by duplicating Ad Set #1 and create two copies so you have three Ad Sets and each will have one ad associated with it. Make each Ad Set name unique so the three Ad Sets will be completely identical except for the name.

At this point you need to make a decision. Will you use the same landing page for all three ads, or will you use a different landing page for each ad? If your landing page is the same, you can skip this next step.

If you use three different landing pages, then you need to create two additional Website Custom Audiences (WCA). You'll create one for each of those two pages, and you need to change the Exclusion Audience section of each Ad Set so that each one has the WCA that corresponds with the ad.

For example, let's say you have three pages that are named:

- /landing-page-1
- /landing-page-2
- /landing-page-3

You need to create three unique WCAs to track and collect visitors to each of these three pages. In the Ad Set #1, you will have Ad #1 that sends people to /landing-page-1. To ensure you do not send the person to the landing page twice, you will want to add the WCA for landing-page-1 as an audience exclusion to Ad Set #1. You will do the same for landing-page-2's audience as an exclusion Ad Set #2 and landing-page-3's audience as an exclusion for Ad Set #3.

Next, go and modify the Creative for Ad #2 and #3 so that each is unique. We suggest using a different video (or image) and also change the wording to emphasize something different, especially if you are using the same offer and landing page.

Creating three landing pages is more work, but is worth it in many cases, such as:

- *For a service or information business.* By using three unique blog posts you will send them to three different landing pages and have unique creative on each of those ads to promote the blog posts. You can touch on three different subjects.
- *For an ecommerce site.* You can easily promote three of your most popular products to appeal to different interests.
- *For a local business like a restaurant.* You can promote three different menu items or specials to cater to unique tastes.

To help illustrate, let's say you intend to run this campaign for the entire month of June and you've given Facebook a $15 per-day budget. You next need to decide how these three Ad Sets will run: in parallel or in sequence.

The simpler strategy is to allow all three Ad Sets to run in parallel the entire month and let Facebook optimize each Ad Set. All three ads and Ad Sets will have different performance. This is essentially a three-way split test.

The second, and our preferred way, is to schedule these Ad Sets so that only one is active at a time. For this example, we set up a ten-day schedule for each Ad Set, as seen in Figure 21–7 on page 259.

After setting up all three, you'll see that each Ad Set will run for 10 days as shown in Figure 21–8 on page 259. This also happens to be a great strategy for combating ad fatigue on a smaller audience.

## CREATING YOUR ARTICLE STRATEGY NURTURING CAMPAIGN

At this point, you've created your Prospecting Campaign with three Ad Sets and three unique ads. Hopefully you've had some overachievers convert already, but normally

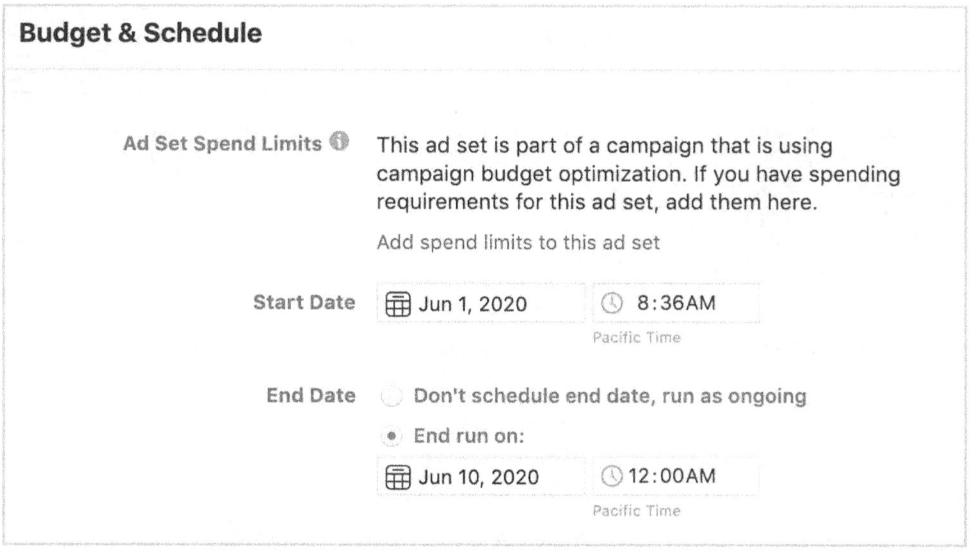

## Budget & Schedule

**Ad Set Spend Limits** ⓘ  This ad set is part of a campaign that is using campaign budget optimization. If you have spending requirements for this ad set, add them here.

Add spend limits to this ad set

**Start Date**  🗓 Jun 1, 2020    🕐 8:36AM

Pacific Time

**End Date**  ○ Don't schedule end date, run as ongoing

● End run on:

🗓 Jun 10, 2020    🕐 12:00AM

Pacific Time

**FIGURE 21–7.** Sample Ten-Day Schedule for Three Ad Sets Per Month

| Ad Set Name | Delivery | Bid Strategy | Budget |
|---|---|---|---|
| Agency Leads - V1 | ○ In Draft | Lowest cost<br>Landing Page... | $10.00<br>Daily |
| Agency Leads - V2 | ○ In Draft | Lowest cost<br>Landing Page... | $10.00<br>Daily |
| Agency Leads - V3 | ○ In Draft | Lowest cost<br>Landing Page... | $10.00<br>Daily |

**FIGURE 21–8.** Ad Sets Per Month

most people will need a push. That's where your Nurturing Campaign takes over, as seen in Figure 21-9 on page 260.

Nurturing Campaigns use the power of Retargeting, your pixel, and Custom Audiences. Prospects at this point are in Mid-to-Deep Funnel and are likely at Your Solution Aware on the Awareness Timeline.

Create your Nurturing Campaign based on your volume of traffic. If you average less than 1,000 visitors per day to your Landing Page, create a new Campaign with a Reach Objective. If you have more than 1,000 visitors per day, create a Conversion Objective Campaign.

As this runs continually, go with a daily budget which, depending on how much traffic you get on a daily basis, should be about two to ten times smaller than your Prospecting Campaign Budget. We suggest starting with a minimum of $5 per day and then adding more budget to ensure you can reach all of the visitors from your Prospecting Campaign.

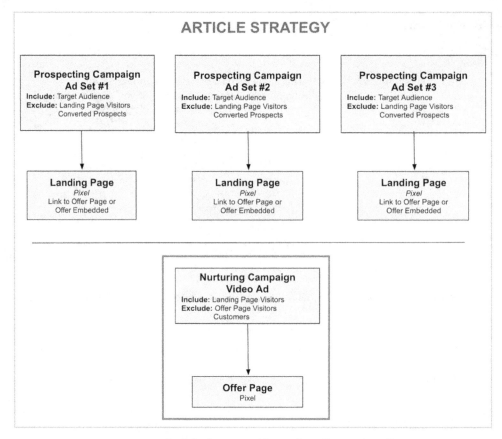

**FIGURE 21–9.** Article Strategy Nurturing Campaign Setup

Next, create your ad and Ad Set like before, but this time, only include the Landing Page Visitors that you generated with your Prospecting Campaign. Exclude people who watched 75 percent more of your Nurturing Video Ad as shown in Figure 21–10 on page 261. The video is this case is a 60-second web commercial that we run in the News Feed.

The Nurturing Ad displays the video and drives visitors to a different landing page (called the Offer Page) that contains the case study.

Your ad in a Nurturing Campaign is typically much deeper in content. We like doing longer-form videos (30 to 90 seconds). This example is a web commercial, but you can do FAQ or explainer videos, testimonials, or demos.

People who have narrowed down their decision to a few providers will need greater depth from you: more education, more information, more incentives, and more personalization. This is where you can move from very shallow storytelling to deeper, more impactful storytelling to convert more prospects into believers of you, your company, and your product.

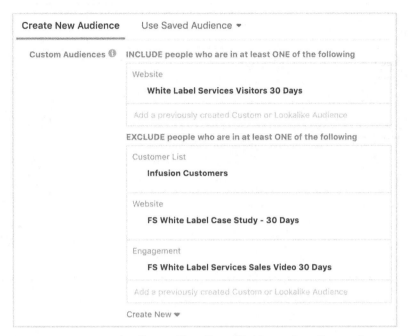

**FIGURE 21–10.** Audience Creation for Nurturing Campaign

One last note: Although the model shows only one Ad Set, that's only for simplicity. The fact is you should have multiple Ad Sets within your Nurturing Campaign. Remember, nurturing isn't prospecting. People who are deeper within your Funnel are looking for reasons to either eliminate you from contention or choose you. Don't get eliminated for lack of information and connection.

The Deep Funnel Marketing Concept gives you strategies to get signals from your audience for who's interested in your products and services. Use the strategies to keep your prospects connected and remind them that you are the only best solution to their problem!

## DEEP FUNNEL MARKETING VIDEO STRATEGY

The Deep Funnel Marketing Video Strategy is unique to Facebook and uses video and a concept of sequential marketing that you often see in email autoresponders.

This also will look similar to what our guest author Jeff Walker teaches in Chapter 24. Jeff is a good friend and brilliant entrepreneur who developed a concept called the Product Launch Formula. We are fortunate that Jeff has a chapter in this book to talk more about how to build anticipation in your audience through video and storytelling.

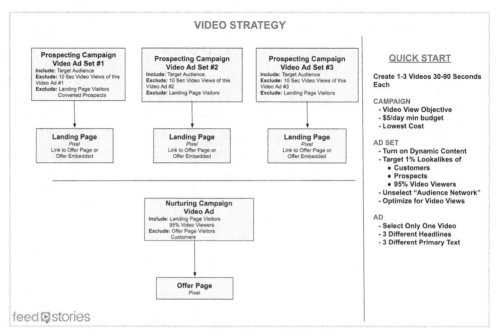

**FIGURE 21–11.** Deep Funnel Video Strategy

The Deep Funnel Marketing Video Strategy is loosely based on this concept, and you'll use video and Video Custom Audiences to deploy it. It's outlined in Figure 21–11.

Similar to the Article Strategy, you're going to create a Prospecting Campaign with three Ad Sets and ads and hopefully drive people to a landing page and offer, but you're taking things a bit slower.

The process starts by creating a Facebook Campaign that includes the word Prospecting in its name. You will choose a Video Views Objective. Then, choose your budget amount before setting up your Ad Set.

## CREATING YOUR INITIAL VIDEO STRATEGY PROSPECTING AD SET

For this strategy, you'll once again target the Custom Audience called Agency Leads. The exclusions are the Customer Custom Audience, 30-Day Visitors to the Landing Page, and 10 Second Video Viewers of the first video in the sequence. This video is 40 seconds long, so you want to use a ten-second view to eliminate anyone from seeing this ad again if they watched 25 percent of this Video Ad, as shown in Figure 21–12 on page 263.

## CREATING YOUR INITIAL VIDEO STRATEGY PROSPECTING AD

Next, create your first Video Ad.

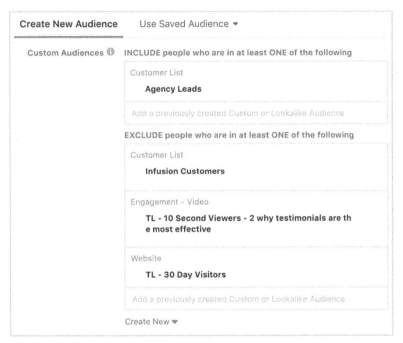

**FIGURE 21–12.** Video Prospecting Audience and Exclusions

Your ad will still have a URL that drives users from Facebook to your landing page, but it's not the primary focus. Instead, this strategy is to build up a Video View Custom Audience of people who watched 75 percent or more of the video.

These people are staying tuned in for at least 75 percent of your video and are giving you a signal that they are interested in your content. These are the people you're going to focus on in the next step.

Note that to get even more targeted prospects, you can use 95 percent as your threshold. Use 95 percent if you are getting tens and hundreds of thousands of views per day and have enough users watching the entire video to build up a sizable audience quickly. Stick with 75 percent when you are starting off with a lower budget.

This Audience of users who watched Video #1 for more than 75 percent of the way through and did not visit the landing page will be passed on to Video Ad #2 for the next video in the sequence.

## Alternative Strategy

You can also run a version of this strategy where you only run a video and choose to not place a URL in the ad. This strategy can be used to build up anticipation for the next video, especially if you tease that fact in your copy and/or video in Ad #1. You would only allow them to visit your landing page after they've seen Video Ad #3.

Whichever way you choose to run this will be effective. We prefer the alternative strategy when the videos are particularly compelling and have a definite sequence that will hold the user's attention and desire for seeing the next video. We prefer the primary strategy when each video can stand alone. Take a look at the video strategy in Figure 21–13.

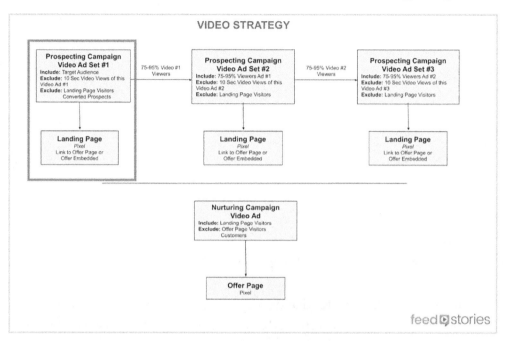

**FIGURE 21-13.** Deep Funnel Video Strategy Prospecting Ad Set 1

## CREATING YOUR NEXT TWO VIDEO STRATEGY PROSPECTING ADS AND AD SETS

At this point you've just created Ad Set #1 and Ad #1 for the Video Strategy.

Again, start by duplicating Ad Set #1 and create two copies so you have three Ad Sets, and each will have one ad associated with it. Give each Ad Set a unique name.

Now, edit Ad Set #2. Your target audience is now a 75-percent (or 95-percent) Video View Custom Audience of the video you promoted with Video Ad #1.

You will exclude customers and landing page visitors as before, but now since you will be promoting a different video in Ad #2, you will create a ten-second audience of that video and add that here, as shown in Figure 21–14 on page 265.

Next, edit Ad Set #3.

Your new target audience is now a 75-percent (or 95-percent) Video View Custom Audience of the video you promoted with Video Ad #2.

Continue to exclude customers and landing Page visitors as before. Create a ten-second audience of your video from Video Ad #2 and add that here, as you can see in Figure 21–15.

Create New Audience
Use Saved Audience
Custom Audiences
INCLUDE people who are in at least ONE of the following
Engagement
TL - 75% Viewers - 2 why testimonials are the most effective
Add a previously created Custom or Lookalike Audience
EXCLUDE people who are in at least ONE of the following
Customer List
Infusion Customers
Website
TL - 30 Day Visitors
Engagement
TL - 10 Second Viewers - 3 written vs video testim onial
Add a previously created Custom or Lookalike Audience
Create New

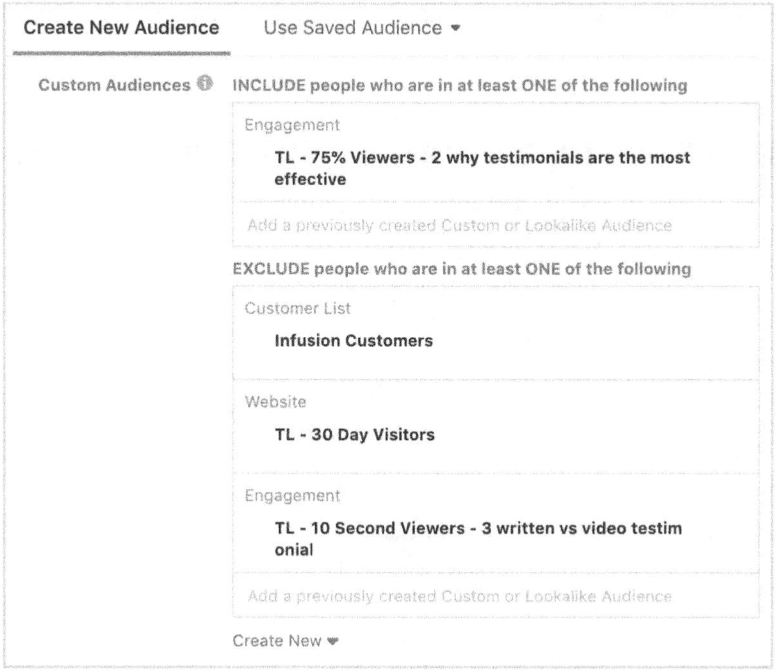

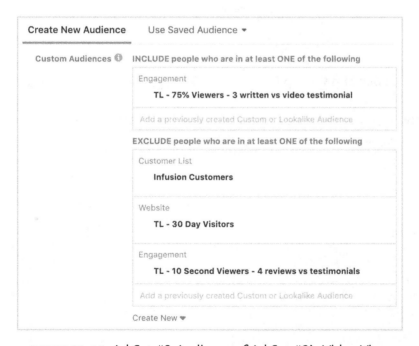

**FIGURE 21–14.** Ad Set #2 Audience of Ad Set #1's Video Viewers

Create New Audience
Use Saved Audience
Custom Audiences
INCLUDE people who are in at least ONE of the following
Engagement
TL - 75% Viewers - 3 written vs video testimonial
Add a previously created Custom or Lookalike Audience
EXCLUDE people who are in at least ONE of the following
Customer List
Infusion Customers
Website
TL - 30 Day Visitors
Engagement
TL - 10 Second Viewers - 4 reviews vs testimonials
Add a previously created Custom or Lookalike Audience
Create New

**FIGURE 21–15.** Ad Set #3 Audience of Ad Set #2's Video Viewers

Last, modify Video Ad #2 by putting your second video and creative in place. Do the same for Video Ad #3.

## CREATING YOUR VIDEO STRATEGY NURTURING CAMPAIGN

At this point, you've created your Prospecting Campaign with three Ad Sets (in sequence) and three unique Video Ads.

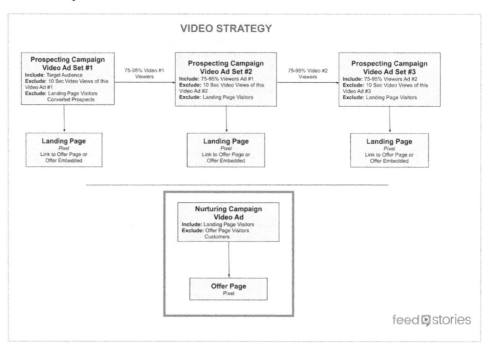

**FIGURE 21–16.** Deep Funnel Video Strategy Nurturing Campaign

To create your Nurturing Campaign (shown in Figure 21–16), refer back to the Article Strategy section above and follow the same steps.

# Chapter 22

# Advanced Deep Funnel Marketing™ Strategies

I n the previous chapter, you learned landing page and video prospecting strategies. In this chapter, we're going to build on those concepts and start making more detailed and complex Deep Funnels to nurture your prospects.

Figure 22–1 on page 268 is the complete diagram we hand out to our coaching students. This is highly detailed and likely a bit overwhelming, so we encourage you to download and print out the PDF version of this on our Resources page at www.PerryMarshall.com/fbtools on 11-by-17 tabloid paper to get the full effect.

For all these examples, we show four ad/Ad Sets. Deep Funnels can be as simple as one ad/Ad Set or as complex as 50 or more. The point is you create what you need to properly nurture your prospects according to your sales timeline.

## NURTURING CAMPAIGNS AREN'T JUST FOR RETARGETING FACEBOOK TRAFFIC

The first thing to note is that with Retargeting capability, you can market on Facebook even if you don't initially drive traffic from Facebook Ads. If you are a heavy Google Ads user, have great organic presence in the search

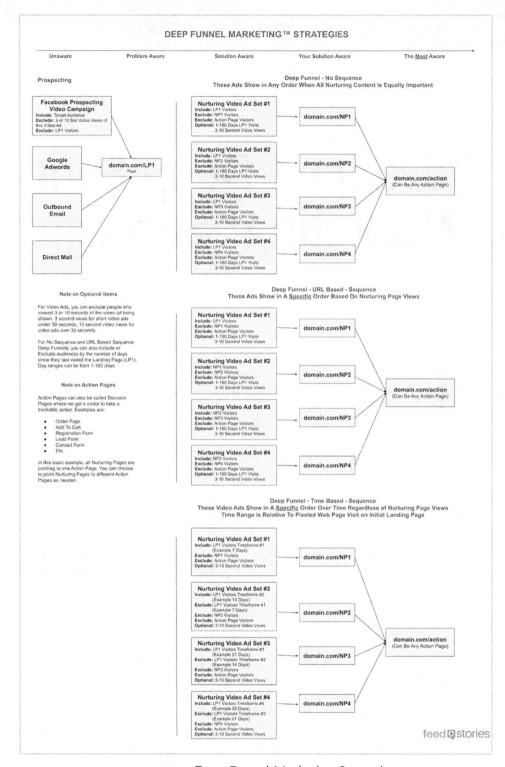

**FIGURE 22–1.** Deep Funnel Marketing Strategies

engines, advertise on radio or TV, send out direct mail, or place ads on billboards, you can nurture on Facebook using ads.

## AD CONTENT IN YOUR DEEP FUNNEL

Your ads in a Nurturing Campaign are typically much deeper in terms of content: more education, more information, more incentives, more personalization. This is where you move into more impactful storytelling to convert more prospects into believers of you, your company, and your product.

Some examples of ads and videos you will include in a Nurturing Campaign are:

- *Testimonials*. Video testimonials like those provided by Feedstories via Testimonials.live are ways for customers to let prospects know how you and your business changed their life
- *Case Studies*. These are expanded testimonials with much more detail about what problem a customer was having and how your business solved it.
- *Product Demos*. If you have a product, a demo video of your item in action helps prospects understand how your product will work for them. This is highly effective for SaaS companies who demo their software and for goods that solve problems. We've seen great ones for products like snoring devices, travel cases, automotive accessories, teeth whitening products, gardening tools, home appliances, exercise equipment, and many more.
- *Frequently-Asked Questions*. Answering the top questions prospects always ask is a great way to educate prospects and resolve objections to buying from you.
- *Explainers*. These help give the prospect confidence in you that you are the right person to help them. Using these can allow a thought leader, service provider, or CEO to demonstrate personal or corporate expertise to a prospect.
- *Benefits*. These are specific highlights of the main benefits of the products and services you sell that help the prospects know the most important aspects of your offer to them.
- *Sales Video*. At Feedstories, we call them Feedmericals™ or Web Commercials. This is an extended pitch that encompasses all parts of a typical sales presentation: headline, benefits, proof, guarantees, testimonials, offer, call to action, and more. These videos are usually one to three minutes.
- *Lead Magnets*. Lead magnets are things like discounts, offers, information, tools, downloadable content, and more that you offer to prospects in exchange for their information. Your ad might highlight the benefits and features of the lead magnet.
- *Discounts*. These are typically reserved for later parts of the funnel, as we typically don't want our clients to lead with discounts and train their customers to only

buy when discounts are offered. However, they work well when they are specific and generous.

■ *Humor or Emotion*. Some ads are given to evoke a response and get shared. These ads make people laugh or cry. A mighty powerful strategy if played right, or a car wreck if they are played wrong. Sometimes people won't get your humor and it will have the opposite effect on them. If people think you are manipulating them with an emotional video, it has the same effect. Only use these types of ads with firms that understand how these are produced.

These are just a few ways to be creative and communicate with your prospects. We've also collected some actual examples for you to study, and they are available in the Resources page at www.PerryMarshall.com/fbtools.

## WEBSITE ASSETS FOR YOUR DEEP FUNNEL

To properly execute a Nurture Campaign, you should have already set up four additional landing pages that we call Nurturing Pages 1 through 4. You also want an Action Page.

Action Pages can also be called Decision Pages where you get a visitor to take a trackable action. Examples are:

■ Order Page
■ Add To Cart
■ Registration Form
■ Lead Form
■ Contact Form

In the examples, all Nurturing Pages are pointing to one Action Page, but you can choose to point Nurturing Pages to different Action Pages as needed.

If you are just beginning, you can create a single Nurturing Page and a single Action Page, but four Nurturing Pages works much better to convert prospects.

## SETTING UP DEEP FUNNEL NURTURING AUDIENCES

Start by setting up four new audiences to exclude visitors to each of the four Nurturing Pages. All of these examples are using 30-day audiences, but you can choose any duration from one to 180 days. See Figure 22–2 on page 271.

The number of days you choose will be based on your sales process.

Use 7-day windows for simple, non-expensive products.

Use 30-day windows for service and information businesses.

Use 30- to 90-day windows for businesses that have high-cost, complex products and services.

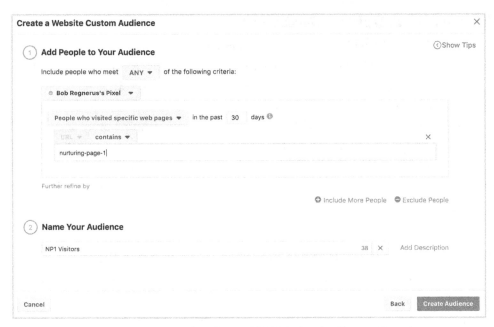

**FIGURE 22–2.** Nurturing Page #1 Website Audience Creation

Then do the same setup for Nurturing Pages 2 through 4. See Figure 22–3 for an example.

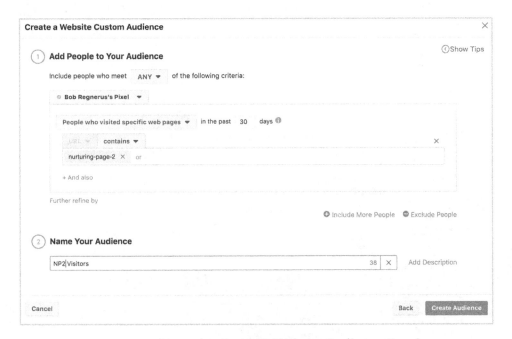

**FIGURE 22–3.** Nurturing Page #2 Website Audience Creation

## SETTING UP A DEEP FUNNEL NURTURING CAMPAIGN

Create your Deep Funnel Nurturing Campaign based on your volume of traffic. If you average fewer than 1,000 visitors per day to your landing page, create a new campaign with a Reach Objective. If you have more than 1,000 visitors per day, create a Conversion Objective Campaign.

As this runs continually, go with a daily budget, and, depending on how much traffic you get on a daily basis, this budget should be about two to ten times smaller than your Prospecting Campaign Budget. We suggest starting with a minimum of $5 per day and then add more budget to ensure you can reach all of the visitors from your Prospecting Campaign.

## SETTING UP DEEP FUNNEL AD SETS, NO SEQUENCE

This type of Deep Funnel Nurturing Campaign is perfect for when you want to show ads that can be viewed in any order as seen in Figure 22–4.

You can begin by creating your four Ad Sets. First, start with Nurturing Video Ad Set #1.

You are going to only target people who landed on your landing page (LP1 Visitors). You will continue to exclude customers and people who landed on your Action Page

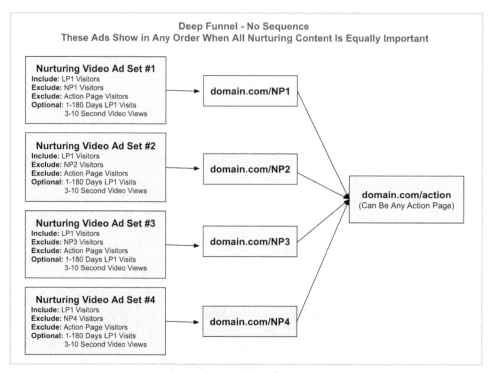

**FIGURE 22–4.** Deep Funnel—No Sequence

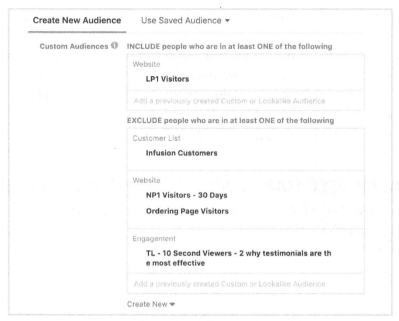

**FIGURE 22–5.** Deep Funnel Nurturing Ad Set #1

(Ordering Page Visitors). Finally, you'll exclude anyone who watched your Video Ad #1 for ten seconds or more, as seen in Figure 22–5.

Next you will set up Nurturing Video Ad Sets #2 through 4, which you can see in Figure 22–6.

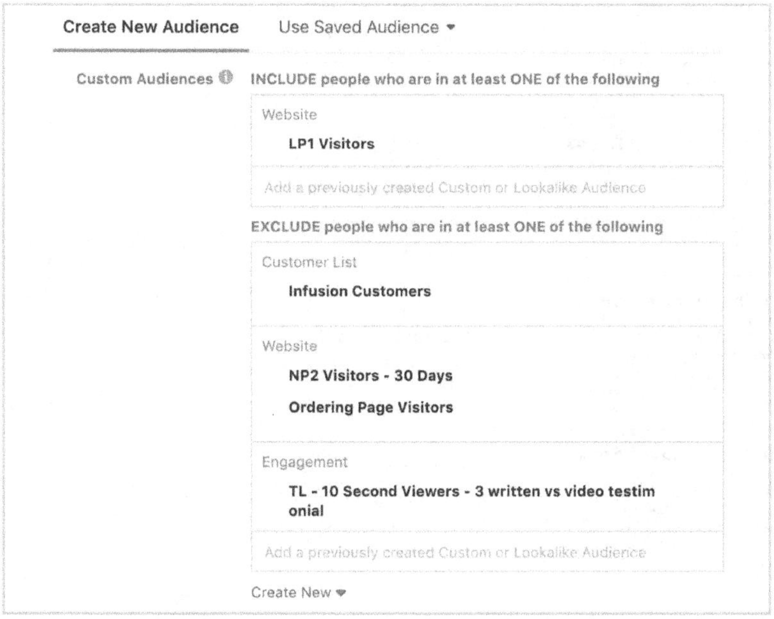

**FIGURE 22–6.** Deep Funnel Nurturing Ad Set #2

Since this is a non-sequenced Nurturing Campaign, each Ad Set has the same target audience.

The only difference is that you will now exclude visitors to Nurturing Page #2 and anyone who watched ten seconds or more of your Nurturing Video Ad #2.

You will repeat this for Ad Set #3 through 4 (changing the two audiences as you did in Ad Set #2).

Be sure to set up each of your Video Ads and choose Publish.

## SETTING UP DEEP FUNNEL AD SETS: URL-BASED SEQUENCE

This type of Deep Funnel Nurturing Campaign is perfect for when you want to show ads that are best viewed in a specific order, as shown in Figure 22–7.

Start with Nurturing Video Ad Set #1.

As with a No Sequence Campaign, you are going to only target people that landed on your landing page (LP1 Visitors). You will continue to exclude customers and people who landed on your Action Page (Ordering Page Visitors). Finally, you'll exclude anyone who watched your Video Ad #1 for ten seconds or more. See Figure 22–8 on page 275.

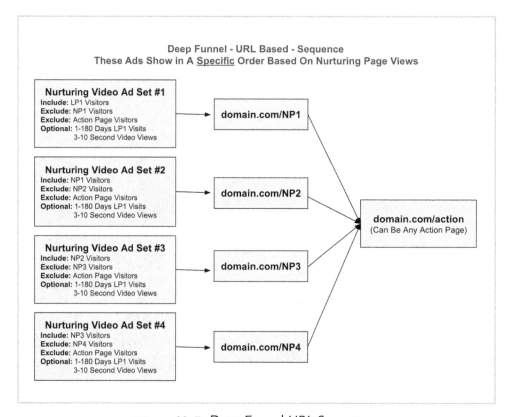

**FIGURE 22–7.** Deep Funnel URL Sequence

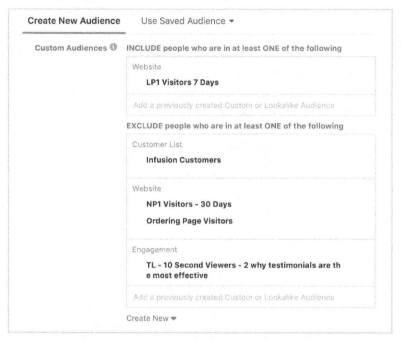

**FIGURE 22–8.** Deep Funnel Time Sequence Ad Set #1

Next you will set up Nurturing Video Ad Set #2 as in Figure 22–9.

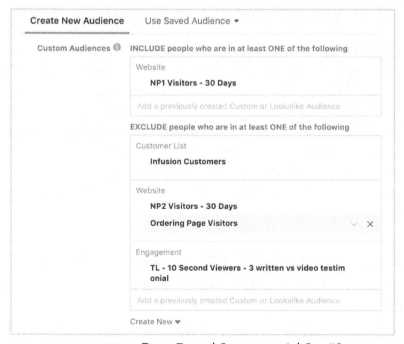

**FIGURE 22–9.** Deep Funnel Sequence, Ad Set #2

Note with a Sequence-Based Campaign, you only target visitors who landed on your Nurturing Page #1. You will exclude people who have already visited Nurturing Page #2 and anyone who watched 10 seconds or more of your Nurturing Video Ad #2. Next, set up Nurturing Video Ad Set #3, which you can see in Figure 22–10.

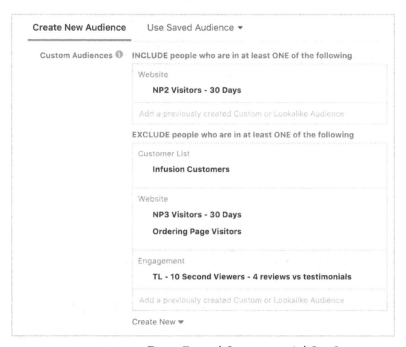

**FIGURE 22–10.** Deep Funnel Sequence, Ad Set 3

This time you'll only target visitors to Nurturing Page #2 and exclude people that landed on Nurturing Page #3 and watched more than ten seconds of the Nurturing Video #3.

Last, set up Nurturing Video Ad Set #4. You've probably picked up the formula by now. Only target visitors to Nurturing Page #3 and exclude people that landed on Nurturing Page #4 and watched more than ten seconds of Nurturing Video #4 ( Figure 22–11 on page 277).

Be sure to set up each of your Video Ads and publish.

Once you've set up a URL-Based Sequence Nurturing Campaign, you've effectively walked your prospect from Ad #1 to Ad #4—if they need that much nurturing. Remember, the prospect can jump off at any point and take the action you desire.

## SETTING UP DEEP FUNNEL: TIME-BASED SEQUENCE

This type of Deep Funnel Nurturing Campaign is perfect for when you want to show ads in a specific order over time regardless of Nurturing Page views.

As shown in Figure 22–12, the time range is relative to the user's last visit to your landing page.

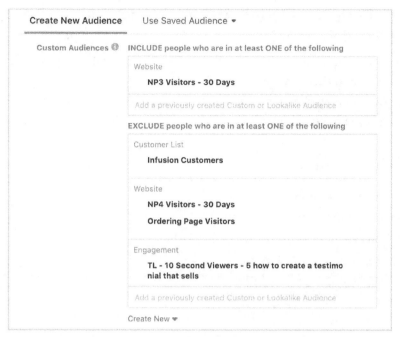

**FIGURE 22–11.** Deep Funnel Sequence, Ad Set 4

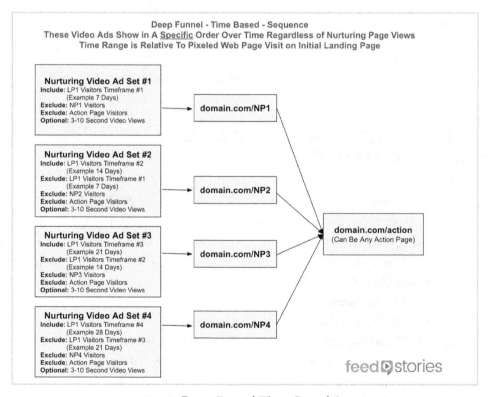

**FIGURE 22–12.** Deep Funnel Time-Based Sequence

## SETTING UP DEEP FUNNEL AUDIENCES FOR A TIME-BASED SEQUENCE

For a time-based sequence as shown in Figure 22–12, you will set up your landing page audiences relative to their last visit to the landing page.

Figure 22–13 shows the first of four audiences set up based on a 7, 14, 21, and 28-day last visit. Simply change the number of days for each audience you create.

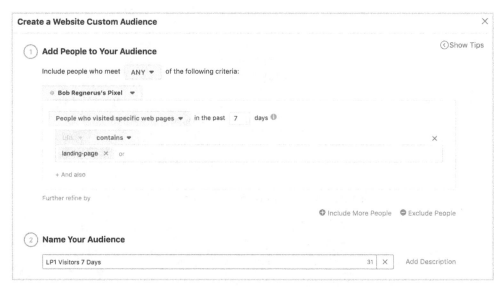

**FIGURE 22–13.** Landing Page Seven-Day Website Custom Audience

## SETTING UP DEEP FUNNEL AD SETS FOR A TIME-BASED SEQUENCE

Create your four Ad Sets as follows:

Start with Nurturing Video Ad Set #1 as shown in Figure 22–14 on page 279.

You are only going to target people who landed on your landing page within the last seven days. As always, exclude customers and people who landed on your Action Page (Ordering Page Visitors). Exclude anyone who watched your Video Ad #1 for ten seconds or more and who landed on your Nurturing Page #1.

Next, the setup for Nurturing Video Ad Set #2 is shown in Figure 22–15 on page 279.

The main difference is that now you're targeting people who have visited within 14 days, but you will exclude anyone who visited within the last seven days. This effectively only sets up your target as people that have visited eight to 14 days ago. As in previous setups, exclude visitors to Nurturing Page #2 and anyone who watched ten seconds or more of your Nurturing Video Ad #2.

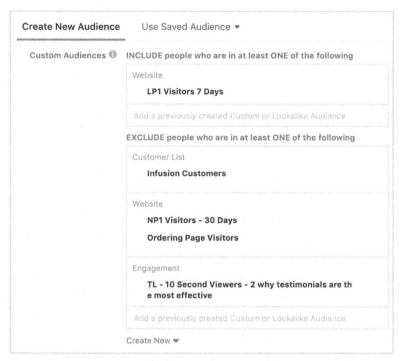

**FIGURE 22–14.** Deep Funnel Time Sequence Ad Set One to Seven Days

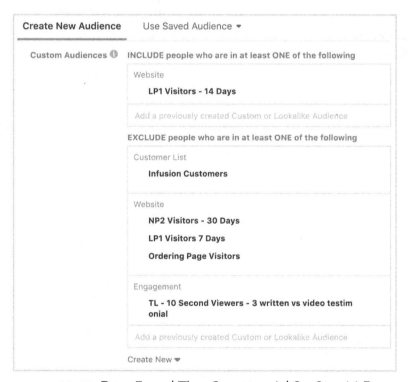

**FIGURE 22–15.** Deep Funnel Time Sequence Ad Set 2 to 14 Days

Then, set up Nurturing Video Ad Set #3. In this Ad Set, target people who have visited within 21 days, but exclude anyone who visited within the last 14 days. This targets people that visited 15 to 21 days ago.

As in previous setups, exclude visitors to Nurturing Page #3 and anyone who watched 10 seconds or more of your Nurturing Video Ad #3.

Last, for Nurturing Video Ad Set #4, target people who have visited within 28 days, but exclude anyone who visited within the last 21 days. This targets people that visited 22 to 28 days ago.

As in previous setups, exclude visitors to Nurturing Page #4 and anyone who watched 10 seconds or more of your Nurturing Video Ad #4. Your ads within a sequence like this should get increasingly more powerful in terms of offers. Like the other sequences, once a prospect responds to the action you want them to take, they are removed from the sequence.

You will find those most interested will take action on Ad #1, then more will take action on Ad #2 and Ad #3, and Ad #4 becomes your final offer. You'll want to give them the best offer you have, such as a large discount.

You should not waste your best offer on Ad #1. Let the hyper-responders take action on an offer that is more profitable to you.

You can follow up with a Testimonial or strong Explainer in Ad #2 and Ad #3, and then follow up with a powerful guarantee and/or discount in Ad #4.

In the next chapter, we're going to switch gears a bit and talk about strategies for getting your campaigns launched quickly.

# Chapter 23

# Blueprints and Strategies to Help You Launch Campaigns Quickly

In 2010, my business partner and I (Bob) got invited to the headquarters of Stansberry Research (a division of Agora Publishing) to meet with their team and teach them about what we were doing with video.

All along, all I could think was, "How did we get this gig?"

Just a few years prior to that meeting, we had a 20-something client who was running a small internet information business while cutting his teeth as a copywriter. He managed to land a dream internship at Stansberry Research and left his side hustle to focus on that opportunity.

Fast forward to the summer of 2010. We got a call from this past client who said he'd been watching some of the things we'd been doing with video sales letters. He asked if we'd be interested in sharing our strategies with them because he shared one of our videos for a different project with the head of Stansberry, who loved it.

I got on the phone with them and quoted the biggest number I could think of without my voice cracking under the anxiety. $25,000 for a single day of consulting. To my surprise, they didn't even counteroffer.

I was thrilled and terrified! My partner and I then got on a plane and spent several hours at their mansion in Baltimore and shared our video and follow-up strategy.

I know we made an impact because within a matter of a few weeks, across the internet came a video sales letter called *The End of America*. We have a link to a copy of the video in the Resource section at www.PerryMarshall.com/fbtools. This promotion ran for months, and it's rumored that this single promotion generated more sales and revenue for Stansberry Research than they ever had. Some people even call this one of the most famous direct marketing campaigns in history.

We take no credit for this success, but it does show what a very powerful offer in the hands of one of the most talented copywriters on the planet using a very simple strategy can do.

We hope you can get a slice of that success and more by rolling one of the simple strategies we teach you below with powerful offers and creative like Stansberry did.

In this chapter, you will study our blueprints for getting campaigns launched quickly. You will also get a peek into many strategies we use for clients to help them get traffic and sales.

Many of the campaign blueprints and strategies you see here are based on what you've learned so far in this book. Your challenge is to study, adapt, and deploy for your business.

## PROSPECTING STRATEGIES FOR COLD AUDIENCES

Cold audiences are Facebook users who do not know about you. They are usually in the Unaware or Problem Aware phase of the Customer Awareness Timeline (see Chapter 1). The audiences you typically target are:

1. Lookalike Audiences
2. Detailed targeting of interests and behaviors
3. Imported lists in the form of a Custom Audience

Your job is to make them aware of you and the problem you solve.

These are four great ways to prospect to a cold audience:

1. Send traffic to a landing page to collect leads or sales using the Conversion Campaign Objective.
2. Collect leads inside Facebook using the Lead Generation Campaign Objective.
3. Send traffic to a landing page without an offer using the Traffic Campaign Objective.
4. Build a Video Custom Audience of interested users using the Video Campaign Objective.

Let's explore each of these.

### Send Traffic to a Landing Page to Collect Leads or Sales

Use this when your main goal is to get leads or sales.

Typically, only someone in an ecommerce business with a fairly inexpensive or simple product will try and get a sale right away. Most other businesses will generate leads to do more follow-up either by salespeople or automated marketing methods.

Your landing page needs to have a trackable event that Facebook can optimize for. Typically, this is some sort of form the prospect will fill out to register for something (white paper, webinar, newsletter, etc.).

### Collect Leads Inside Facebook

Use this when your main goal is to get leads and you don't need the user to leave Facebook.

You can use this objective when you are testing a new idea. Because users don't need to leave Facebook with this objective, you don't need a landing page. This is a great time and money saver to quickly test new offers without the hassle of getting a landing page done.

This works best when your offer is simple, straightforward, and doesn't require a lot of salesmanship or explanation to move the user to fill out the lead form.

You may find this strategy gets you a better cost-per-lead (CPL) compared to a landing page because the user's path to completion is much simpler. They never leave Facebook, and some of the information on your form is pre-filled, such as their name, email, and phone number.

### Send Traffic to a Landing Page without an Offer

Use this when your main goal is to drive people away from Facebook and get impressions on your landing page.

This strategy works well for businesses who have advertising on their website and charge their clients based on impressions. This is also a useful strategy if you have a lower budget and traffic and cannot get Facebook the 50 conversions per week needed to optimize your campaign.

### Building a Video Custom Audience of Interested Users

Use this when your main goal is to inexpensively find interested prospects from large audiences (usually 2 to 20 million).

You can use this objective when you have a good 30- to 90-second video that speaks to the best prospects and users don't need to leave Facebook. So, once again, you don't need a landing page.

This is a great, inexpensive way to build an audience compared to the other objectives we've covered. This audience becomes your target audience for your Nurturing Strategy.

## CAMPAIGN STRATEGIES FOR SPECIFIC OBJECTIVES

The following campaign strategies are useful for specific objectives and situations that you have for your business.

### 100-Page Likes Strategy

*Campaign Objective*: Page Likes Campaign

*Used By:* Any Facebook Advertiser

*Use*: To jump-start a new Facebook Page and get at least 100 Page likes. We've found a new Page with very few likes creates skepticism for your audience. Having at least 100 likes is a good strategy to give your Page some legitimacy and social proof.

*Target Audience*: The larger the audience, the less expensive your likes will be. Unlike in the early days of Facebook Advertising, you're not building an audience of people to be on your Page and see all your organic posts. Very few fans or people who like your Page will see your posts. All you're doing is getting your Page some legitimacy, so if you expand your audience to more than just the United States, that will save you a lot of money. If you have a Seed Audience (an existing list, a Website Custom Audience, or Video Custom Audience) to create a Lookalike Audience with (see Chapter 5), you should use a 5-percent (even 10-percent) Lookalike Audience here. If you don't have a Seed Audience, use Detailed Targeting and have your audience be at least 5 million people.

*Ad Creative Example (Figure 23–1 on page 285):* Page like ads are very basic. You can use your logo or another image to start, but you can also use a video. DO NOT ask people to like your Page in your ad copy. Instead, give them your mission or reason why you exist. If they feel like your Page interests them, they will click the thumbs-up on the ad and become a follower/fan of your Page.

### Education Strategy

*Campaign Objective*: Traffic, Conversion, or Video Views Objective

*Used By*:
- Coaches/consultants/thought leaders/training
- Service businesses: personal, home, B2B
- Information/digital product/affiliate marketing/lead generation

FIGURE 23–1. 100 Page Likes Sample Ad

- SAAS
- Ecommerce
- Subscription
- Nonprofit/charities

*Use*: To demonstrate your expertise in a subject area and teach prospects something they don't already know. The goal is to build an audience that will convert to an opt-in or sale later.

*Target Audiences*:

- Cold Audiences (Prospecting: Lookalikes, Detailed Targeting)
- Warm Audiences (Nurturing: Website/Video/App Custom Audiences)
- Custom Lists (customers, prospects, mailing lists)
- Connections (fans of your Page, users of your app)

*Ad Creative Example (Figure 23–2):* Provide the user a video or send them to an article on your blog. Use the Video or Landing Page or Article Strategy as detailed in Chapter 21.

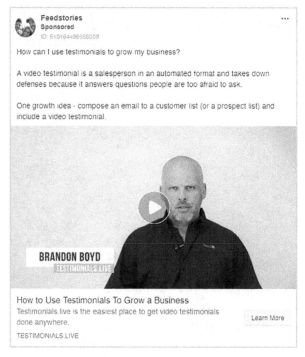

**FIGURE 23–2.** Education Sample Ad

## Awareness Strategy

*Campaign Objective:* Post Engagement or Video Views Objective.

*Used By:*
- Local brick-and-mortar businesses
- Service businesses: personal, home, B2B
- Experiential/hospitality/travel
- Entertainment
- Nonprofit/charities

*Use:* To inform your Audience about something they may not be aware of and to maintain a connection, create engagement, or set up another strategy.

*Target Audiences:*
- Cold Audiences (Prospecting: Lookalikes, Detailed Targeting)
- Warm Audiences (Nurturing: Website/Video/App Custom Audiences)
- Custom Lists (customers, prospects, mailing lists)
- Connections (fans of your Page, users of your app)

*Ad Creative Example (Figure 23–3):* Show the user a video or a thumb-stopping image to get their attention. A good example is, "It's National French Fry Day." It's simply informing a user and bringing an idea to the top of their mind.

**FIGURE 23–3.** Awareness Sample Ad

## Event Strategy

*Campaign Objective*: Event Objective (for a Facebook Event) or Conversion Objective (for all other events).

*Used By:* Any Facebook Advertiser

*Use*: To invite your Audience to an online or offline event. The first type is a Facebook event so you can get information about the event, RSVP, get comments, ask questions, and have people share the event. This is perfect for virtual or local live events. The second are live online events that typically are webinars. These have a lead form or landing page that allows someone to register for the event. Use the Conversion Objective with a successful registration as the Conversion Event.

*Target Audiences*:
- Cold Audiences (Prospecting: Lookalikes, Detailed Targeting)
- Warm Audiences (Nurturing: Website/Video/App Custom Audiences)
- Custom Lists (customers, prospects, mailing lists)
- Connections (fans of your Page, users of your app)

*Ad Creative Example (Figure 23–4 on page 288):* Show the user a video or a thumb-stopping image to get their attention. Use good copy to get them to take action on your ad.

**FIGURE 23–4.** Event Sample Ad

### Single Product Ecommerce Strategy

*Campaign Objective*: Conversion Objective

*Used By*:

- Coaches/consultants/thought leaders/training
- Information/digital product/affiliate marketing/lead generation
- SAAS
- Ecommerce
- Subscription

*Use*: This is for a business that has only one product or a tightly related product line. This can also be used as the sales process for one of your products if you have a larger catalog. The most popular products or lead products from an ecommerce store could use this to promote that single product. Many brands use a loss-leader product to introduce their brand to prospects with this strategy.

This is not a multistep process. It's great for lower-priced items under $100. It can be a physical or digital product. Remember your Deep Funnel concepts and be sure to nurture the non-purchasers who initiate checkout or add the product to their shopping cart (the Initiate Checkout and Add-To-Cart standard events), but don't purchase.

*Target Audiences*:

- Cold Audiences (Prospecting: Lookalikes, Detailed Targeting)
- Warm Audiences (Nurturing: Website/Video/App Custom Audiences)
- Custom Lists (customers, prospects, mailing lists)
- Connections (fans of your Page, users of your app)

*Ad Creative Example (Figure 23–5):* Show the user a video or a thumb-stopping image to get their attention. Use good copy to get them to take action on your ad. A popular format is using a product demo video in the ad that drives to a sales page.

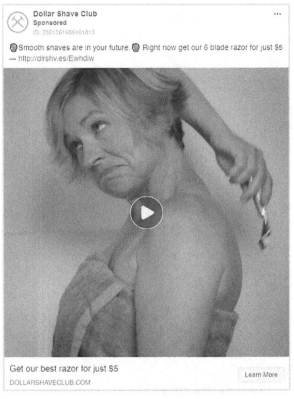

**FIGURE 23–5.** Single Product Sample Ad

## Multi-Product Ecommerce Strategy

*Campaign Objective*: Catalog Sales or Conversion Objective

*Used By*:

- Information/digital product/affiliate marketing/lead generation
- Ecommerce
- Subscription

*Use*: The Multi-Product Ecommerce Strategy is used by businesses with a large catalog of products. Use dynamic product ads to connect your *entire* catalog instead of creating campaigns for every single product line.

*Target Audiences*:

- Cold Audiences (Prospecting: Lookalikes, Detailed Targeting)
- Warm Audiences (Nurturing: Website/Video/App Custom Audiences)
- Custom Lists (customers, prospects, mailing lists)
- Connections (fans of your Page, users of your app)

*Ad Creative Example (Figure 23–6):* Show the user videos and/or thumb-stopping images from your catalog to get their attention.

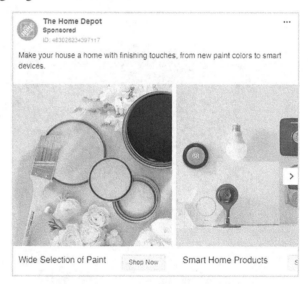

**FIGURE 23–6.** Multiple Product Sample Ad

### List-Building Strategy

*Campaign Objective*: Conversion Objective

*Used By:* Any Facebook Advertiser

*Use*: The List Building Strategy offers users something valuable in exchange for an email address and sometimes more. Ideas of valuable items are:

1. Tools
2. Checklists
3. White Papers
4. Training
5. Quiz or Survey

The strategy is to build a list in another medium so that you can market to them via that medium. It's usually an email list but can also build an address list to market via direct mail. We've also built lists of people in other online platforms. You can use this strategy to build up YouTube subscribers, Twitter followers, LinkedIn connections, and more.

*Target Audiences*:

- Cold Audiences (Prospecting: Lookalikes, Detailed Targeting)
- Warm Audiences (Nurturing: Website/Video/App Custom Audiences)
- Custom Lists (customers, prospects, mailing lists)
- Connections (fans of your Page, users of your app)

*Ad Creative Example (Figure 23–7):* Provide the user a video or send them to an article on your blog. Use the Video or Landing Page or Article Strategy, as detailed in Chapter 21.

**FIGURE 23–7.** List-Building Sample Ad

### Facebook Messenger Strategy

*Campaign Objective*: Messages Objective

*Used By:* Any Facebook Advertiser

*Use*: The Facebook Messenger Strategy allows you to engage in one-on-one conversations with prospects and customers. This is useful for FAQs and answering common objections. The advantage of Messenger over email is you get a higher response-and-read rate vs. emails that get blocked or filtered. Messenger Bots (if you create them) allow you to create smart, contextual responses to common questions, and you can easily create conversational trees to allow a person to self-select a conversation path or journey like a traditional phone tree ("Press 1 for sales. Press 2 for Support.").

*Target Audiences*:
- Warm Audiences (Nurturing: Website/Video/App Custom Audiences)
- Custom Lists (Customers, Prospects, Mailing Lists)

*Ad Creative Example (Figure 23–8):* Show the user a video or a thumb-stopping image to get their attention. Use good copy to get them to click the Send Message button on your ad.

**FIGURE 23–8.** Facebook Messenger Sample Ad

### Contest Strategy

*Campaign Objective*: Conversion or Page Likes Objective

*Used By:* Any Facebook Advertiser

*Use*: The Contest Strategy can either be a sweepstakes or a contest. The only difference is a sweepstakes winner is chosen randomly and a content winner is chosen by judges. A prospect will exchange their contact info in exchange for an entry to win.

When using this to prospect, it is a great way to generate a LOT of cheap leads or Page likes. However, be aware that people who enter contests or sweepstakes are not necessarily buyers. It's difficult to turn sweepstakes entries into high-end buyers. Think about the difficulty and cost it takes for timeshare companies to turn free weekends into actual sales. The people doing the selling are high-end closers.

However, running contests to your Warm Audiences, especially existing customers, works great. We've used this with ecommerce clients. For instance, Bolder Band Headbands would run monthly contests for its customers to submit pictures of themselves working out or doing active things wearing their products. Winners were chosen every month and given free products. We used the submitted images in future ads.

*Target Audiences*:

- Cold Audiences (Prospecting: Lookalikes, Detailed Targeting)
- Warm Audiences (Nurturing: Website/Video/App Custom Audiences)
- Custom Lists (customers, prospects, mailing lists)
- Connections (fans of your Page, users of your app)

*Ad Creative Example (Figure 23–9):* Show the user a video or a thumb-stopping image to get their attention. Use good copy to get them to click the call-to-action button on your ad.

**FIGURE 23–9.** Contest Sample Ad

### Proof Strategy

*Campaign Objective*: Reach, Message, or Video View Objective

*Used By:* Any Facebook Advertiser

*Use*: The Proof Strategy sends prospects to a case study, testimonial, or experience article. The goal is to give a prospect more depth into a product or service. This is a smart strategy because your customers are talking about their experience with you rather than you talking about yourself. This is very similar to the Educational Strategy, except it's not used for cold traffic. Proof is always introduced after you introduce the product.

This is for nurturing prospects who have engaged with Prospecting Campaigns and allows them to go deeper with your business.

*Target Audiences*:

- Warm Audiences (Nurturing: Website/Video/App Custom Audiences)
- Custom Lists (customers, prospects, mailing lists)

*Ad Creative Example (Figure 23–10):* We prefer to use a video directly in the News Feed. That way, prospects don't have to click through to your site. The example below is a testimonial from Perry for Bob's company, Feedstories.

**FIGURE 23–10.** Proof Sample Ad

### App Install Strategy

*Campaign Objective*: Conversion Objective with App Install Event

*Used By:* Any Facebook Advertiser

*Use*: These ads run on mobile devices only and drive users from the ad to the App Store (Apple devices) or Google Play Store (Android devices). The advantage of sending someone directly to either store is they have fewer steps to take before installing the app. It's only a tap away vs. reading the website and then going to the App Store.

The disadvantage of sending visitors directly to the App Store is you can't retarget people who didn't install because there's no way to put a pixel on the App Store page. Non-installers can be nurtured with an Educational Strategy and a Proof Strategy to get them to install.

For most Advertisers, it makes most sense to drive users directly to the App Store by using a video ad so that you can nurture the 75 percent or more video viewers and exclude those who installed your app.

*Target Audiences*:

- Cold Audiences (Prospecting: Lookalikes, Detailed Targeting)
- Warm Audiences (Nurturing: Website/Video/App Custom Audiences)
- Custom Lists (customers, prospects, mailing lists)
- Connections (fans of your Page, users of your app)

*Ad Creative Example (Figure 23–11):* Show the user a demo video or a thumb-stopping image to get their attention. Use good copy to get them to click an Install App or Download Now button on your ad.

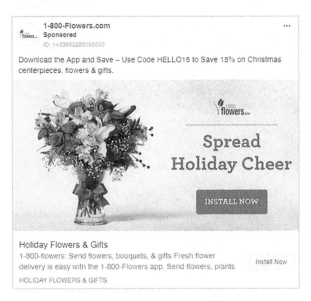

**FIGURE 23–11.** App Install Sample Ad

### Discount Strategy

*Campaign Objective*: Conversion or Reach Objective

*Used By:* Any Facebook Advertiser with something to sell

*Use*: Discounting is a Nurturing Strategy. It doesn't make sense to offer a discount before you introduce your business to a prospect. You should use a Conversion Objective if you have a large audience, or a Reach Objective if you have a smaller audience or want to treat everyone equally. This is a percentage, dollars off, or free shipping offer that sends people back to your sales page.

*Target Audiences*:

- Warm Audiences (Nurturing: Website/Video/App Custom Audiences)
- Custom Lists (customers, prospects, mailing lists)

*Ad Creative Example (Figure 23–12):* Show the user a demo video or a thumb-stopping image to get their attention. Use good copy to get them to click your call-to-action button.

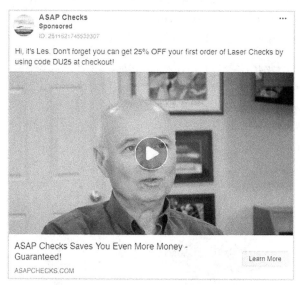

**FIGURE 23–12.** Discount Sample Ad

### Free Trial or Low-Price Initial Offer Strategy

*Campaign Objective*: Conversion Objective

*Used By*:

- Service businesses: personal, home, B2B
- Information/digital product/affiliate marketing/lead generation

- SAAS
- Ecommerce
- Subscription
- Experiential/hospitality/travel

*Use*: Free trials or discounted, low-price, initial-time-period offers are primarily used by companies offering subscription products. This strategy can be used for both prospecting and nurturing. A prospect purchases your product for a deep discount or a free trial that rolls into a paid subscription program or service.

*Target Audiences*:
- Cold Audiences (Prospecting: Lookalikes, Detailed Targeting)
- Warm Audiences (Nurturing: Website/Video/App Custom Audiences)
- Custom Lists (customers, prospects, mailing lists)
- Connections (fans of your Page, users of your app)

*Ad Creative Example (Figure 23–13):* Show the user a demo video or a thumb-stopping image to get their attention. Use good copy to get them to click your call-to-action button and visit your sales page.

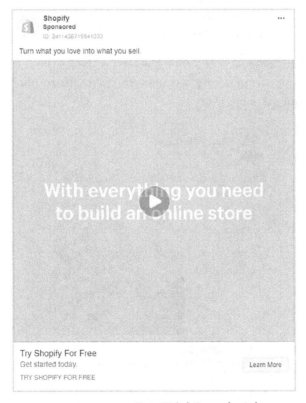

**FIGURE 23–13.** Free Trial Sample Ad

### Free Product Plus Shipping Strategy

*Campaign Objective*: Conversion Objective

*Used By*:

- Coaches/consultants/thought leaders/training
- Information/digital product/affiliate marketing/lead generation
- SAAS
- Ecommerce
- Subscription

*Use*: The Free Product Plus Shipping Strategy gives away the product and charges only for shipping. This is incredibly popular with physical books and supplements. Shipping is usually under $10. It's another way of presenting the Free Trial Strategy, but it usually gets a more committed buyer because they've paid some small amount of money. It can be used for both prospecting and nurturing.

*Target Audiences*:

- Cold Audiences (Prospecting: Lookalikes, Detailed Targeting)
- Warm Audiences (Nurturing: Website/Video/App Custom Audiences)
- Custom Lists (customers, prospects, mailing lists)
- Connections (fans of your Page, users of your app)

*Ad Creative Example (Figure 23–14):* Show the user a demo video or a thumb-stopping image to get their attention. Use good copy to get them to click your call-to-action button and visit your sales page.

**FIGURE 23–14.** Free Plus Shipping

## Walk-In Strategy

*Campaign Objective*: Conversion Objective

*Used By*:

- Service businesses: personal, home, business
- Local brick and mortar
- Experiential/hospitality/travel
- Entertainment
- Nonprofit/charities

*Use*: This is especially for a brick-and-mortar business to get customers to walk in. Also used by businesses when they are at a remote location and want to drive people to where they are located. Use the Event Strategy, Awareness Strategy, Discount Strategy, Contest Strategy, or Life Event Strategy to give them a reason to come in.

*Target Audiences*:

- Cold Audiences (Prospecting: Lookalikes, Detailed Targeting)
- Warm Audiences (Nurturing: Website/Video/App Custom Audiences)
- Custom Lists (customers, prospects, mailing lists)
- Connections (fans of your Page, users of your app)

Use location-based targeting to target people when they are close to your place of business or even inside your four walls! You can target an area as small as one-mile radius and as large as 50 miles. You can also use multiple areas at once and also multiple excludes.

*Ad Creative Example #1 (Figure 23–15):* Say you run a Chicago hot dog stand within walking distance of Guaranteed Rate Field where the Chicago White Sox play their home

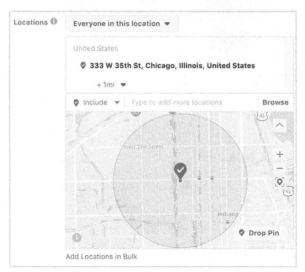

**FIGURE 23–15.** Walk-In Strategy Targeting Location, 1 Mile

baseball games. You can plug in your address and do a one-mile radius around your restaurant, or in this case, we drew the circle around the address of the ballpark.

We have also used the Walk-In Strategy for driving customers to booths at trade shows and increasing attendance at conference breakout sessions for speakers.

*Ad Creative Example #2 (Figure 23–16):* Show the user a demo video or a thumb-stopping image to get their attention. Use good copy to get them to click your call-to-action button and visit your place of business.

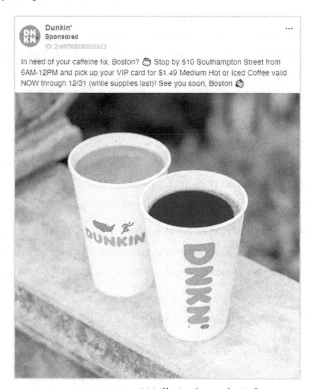

**FIGURE 23–16.** Walk-In Sample Ad

### Thank-You Strategy

*Campaign Objective*: Reach Objective

*Used By:* Any Facebook Advertiser

*Use*: The Thank-You Strategy is a post-purchase strategy to collect testimonials and positive reviews, get feedback, and generally get goodwill.

*Target Audiences*:

- Customers
- Fans

*Ad Creative Example (Figure 23–17):* You can thank people for liking your Page or follow up with buyers. Kohl's runs this ad to people who made a purchase and reminds them to spend their Kohl's cash.

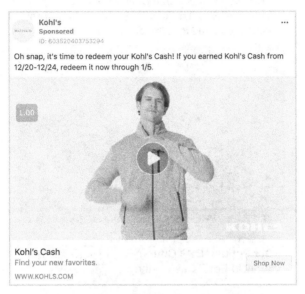

**FIGURE 23–17.** Thank-You Sample Ad

## Upsell/Cross-Sell Strategy

*Campaign Objective*: Reach Objective

*Used By:* Any Facebook Advertiser with something to sell

*Use*: Use for increasing margin. Target anyone who purchased and offer a complimentary product for a limited time of one to three days after their purchase.

*Target Audience*:
- Customers

*Ad Creative Example (Figure 23–18 on page 302):* Create an offer just like you would with other strategies. Use an image or video to get their attention and use good copy to move them to click your Shop Now or Learn More button.

## Reactivation Strategy

*Campaign Objective*: Video Views, Reach, or Conversion Objective

*Used By:* Any Facebook Advertiser

*Use*: The Reactivation Strategy is used to bring back previous customers who haven't bought in a while. If you know the average length between purchases, anyone who hasn't

**FIGURE 23–18.** Upsell/Cross-Sell Sample Ad

purchased in twice that amount needs to be reactivated. It's also used for warming up cold prospects, setting up the launch of a new product, and nurturing leads that have gone cold.

*Target Audiences*:

- Warm Audiences that have gone cold (Nurturing: Website/Video/App Custom Audiences)
- Custom Lists (Customers, Prospects)
- Connections (fans of your Page, users of your app)

*Ad Creative Example (Figure 23–19 on page 303):* Create an offer just like you would with other strategies. Use an image or video to get their attention and use good copy to move them to click your Shop Now or Learn More button.

### Ad Engagement and Social Proof Strategy

*Used By:* Any Facebook Advertiser

*Campaign Objective*: Post Engagement Objective

*Use*: This is an advanced two-step strategy to build up an ad's social proof (likes, comments, video views, and shares). The first step is to use a Post Engagement Objective

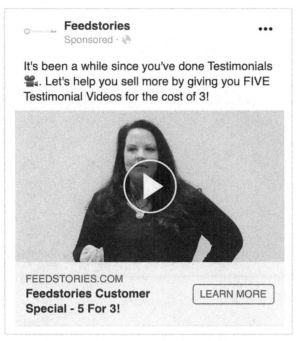

**FIGURE 23–19.** Reactivation Strategy

with a large audience to get as many post reactions and engagements at the least expensive cost. Post engagement gets Facebook to find people who especially like to engage and share posts. This allows you to "season" an ad and get it ready to show to your true Prospecting Audience.

If an ad has no engagement, the feeling is similar in the user's mind to going to a restaurant at dinner time when it should be busy and only seeing one other table filled. It just doesn't feel right and they wonder if they've made a bad choice.

You're not trying to get leads or sales at this point (but you'll take them). You're trying to get inexpensive engagement.

*Target Audiences*:

- Cold Audiences (Prospecting: Lookalikes, Detailed Targeting)
- Warm Audiences (Nurturing: Website/Video/App Custom Audiences)
- Custom Lists (customers, prospects, mailing lists)
- Connections (fans of your Page, users of your app)

*Ad Creative Example (Figure 23–20 on page 304):* Notice how much activity is on this ad. Even getting 1 percent of this activity is a good start to an ad vs. none at all.

Once you have enough engagement, then you will use that same ad in your Prospecting Campaign. All the engagements will follow that ad.

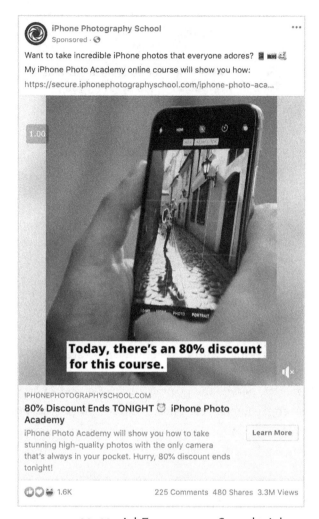

**FIGURE 23–20.** Ad Engagement Sample Ad

When you create your ad, instead of the default Create Ad, click on Use Existing Post. You can choose the Post from the dropdown list, or you can enter the Post ID manually like in Figure 23–21 on page 305.

## SPECIFIC AUDIENCE STRATEGIES

Advertisers can use these specific audience strategies in addition to those we taught in previous chapters.

### *Life Events Strategy*

*Used By*:

- Service businesses: personal, home, B2B

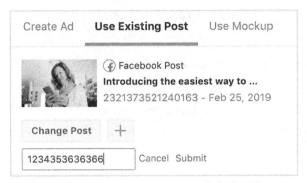

**FIGURE 23-21.** How to Use an Existing Post

- Ecommerce
- Local brick and mortar
- Experiential/hospitality/travel
- Entertainment

*Use*: This is an audience strategy that works in conjunction with any other strategy in this chapter. These life events use Facebook's built-in targeting to drive special offers to people in the timeframe of one of these events, plus people closely related to those having one of these events. You can target life events to individuals who:

- Are away from family
- Are away from hometown
- Started a new job
- Entered a new relationship
- Are newly engaged
- Are newly married
- Recently moved
- Have an upcoming anniversary
- Have an upcoming birthday

You can also target Facebook friends of people who have these events so you can target people with friends who have birthdays, anniversaries, etc.

This should get your creative juices flowing!

If you offer services to brides, Facebook lets you know everyone who updates their status to engaged. If you offer unique, gift-type products, you can target people who have Friends who have become engaged, gotten married, moved, or have had birthdays. Local hotels can target couples with anniversaries and offer romantic getaway packages.

Restaurants can target locals (or their friends) on their birthday with special offers or free food. Pizza places or furniture stores can target recent movers with new neighbor offers.

This works especially well if you are a local business because your audience is limited in size, and you can run this continuously as Facebook will keep your audience fresh.

This is also a nice strategy for a national business to use with their prospect and customer lists.

*Ad Creative Example (Figure 23–22):* Show the user a demo video or a thumb-stopping image to get their attention. Use good copy to get them to click your call-to-action button and visit your website.

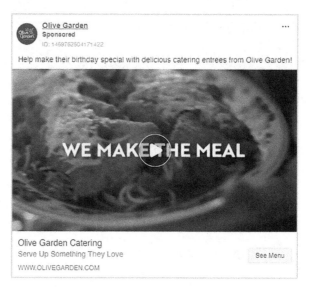

**FIGURE 23–22.** Birthday Life Event Sample Ad

### Friends of People Who Like My Page Strategy

*Used By:* Any Facebook Advertiser

*Use*: This is an audience strategy that works in conjunction with any other strategy in this chapter. The big benefit of this strategy is it gives your ads social proof and an implied endorsement from a prospect's Facebook friends. Above, the ad has a friend's name liking the page. You choose this targeting option under Connections at the Ad Set level. See Figure 23–23 on page 307.

*Ad Creative Example (Figure 23–24 on page 307):* Notice the top of the ad: Susan Kruger Likes Positive Parenting Solutions.

We hope this chapter gives you insights on the best strategies to use and where they will help you be most successful. Refer back to this chapter often as you are getting more experienced with Facebook Ads, but also when you need new ideas to generate sales and leads.

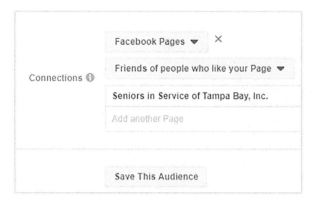

**FIGURE 23–23.** Friends of People Who Like Your Page

**FIGURE 23–24.** Social Proof from a Friend Sample Ad

# Chapter 24

# The Product Launch Formula and Facebook

## Guest Author Jeff Walker

Imagine your current business humming right along, having an average month and an average year. You've got your normal day-to-day struggles and triumphs, trials, tribulations, and small wins of your regular business days. And then in the midst of business as usual, you have a promotion where you do more sales in that one week than you usually do in an entire year.

That would be an amazing week, wouldn't it?

Now, that might sound completely preposterous, but stick with me for a little bit, because what I'm going to show you comes from experience. Of course, I can't guarantee that type of a result for you (as a matter of fact, I can't guarantee anything for you), but that's the type of result I've seen many times.

It's what I call a launch. This chapter is about your next (or your first) launch. And the digital world gives you some unique advantages that allow even the smallest businesses to create amazing launches.

The reality is that if you're in business today, whether you're just starting out or you've got a well-established business, you always need to be launching. It could be a new product, service, or simply a new bundle of the things you're already offering. But the market we're in constantly demands something new, and a launch is the way you bring your new offers to market.

Now just to be clear, none of what I'm about to tell you is theory; it's all been proven over and over by myself and thousands of my clients. Let me explain.

I'm Jeff Walker, and I started my first online business in 1996. It was extremely humble and started from a homemade desk in my basement when I was a stay-at-home dad taking care of a five-year-old son and three-year-old daughter. I'd been a corporate failure who was desperate to try and help support the family. I started off publishing an email newsletter about the stock market and grew my business from there. Since there weren't any online marketing experts at the time, I had to figure out marketing and selling online by myself.

To shorten a long story, I got very good at launching new offers. My first launch did $1,650 (which was an incredible amount of money to me at the time). Within a few years, my launches were in the tens of thousands of dollars, and then the hundreds of thousands. I don't want to make this sound like it was easy or it happened overnight, but my launches eventually grew into the millions of dollars. I've actually had million-dollar days (i.e., sales of over a million dollars in a single day), and even million-dollar hours. All of this out of my home office with a very small team, and very high-margin products.

In 2005, I codified my strategies into what I call the Product Launch Formula (PLF). I've taught my system to tens of thousands of clients, and they've collectively done over a billion dollars in product launches.

OK, that's my quick intro to let you know that everything I'm about to share with you is proven in the real world. These strategies and tactics have been used in almost every market, niche, country, and language you can imagine.

In this chapter, I'm going to give you a whirlwind quick introduction to the Product Launch Formula, and then show you how to use Facebook to launch using both your warm audience and Custom Audiences to reach cold traffic (i.e., new prospects who don't know you). I would love to regale you with case studies and amazing launch stories, but there's not space for that here, so I'm just going to stick with the core formula.

## ANTICIPATION (AND TURNING YOUR MARKETING INTO AN EVENT)

When Hollywood releases a new blockbuster film, they don't just drop it into theaters on a random Tuesday. They build up to the release with trailers, ads, and celebrity interviews on all the talk shows. For the bigger films, this campaign might start a year in advance. It's all designed to build up anticipation so that people are lining up to see the film. And Hollywood isn't alone; many other industries do a great job with their launch campaigns. For example, Apple has been masterful with their launches for a long time (although they've lost some firepower in recent years).

The common strategy for all these launches is based on building the anticipation for the release. In other words, turning the launch (and the marketing for it) into an event. And even though we don't have huge ad budgets, the online world means people with our types of small business can do the same thing with our promotions.

We live in a noisy world. You're trying to build your business in a noisy marketplace. This is a book about using Facebook to build your business. The thing is, Facebook is one of the most perfect distraction mechanisms ever built. The people running Facebook have hired the brightest minds in behavioral science to create an addictive environment that will keep their users scrolling and clicking around their walled garden.

Now don't get me wrong. There's amazing business-building power on Facebook, but understand that by the very design of Facebook, you're going to be fighting a very strong current. And one of the best ways to do that is by turning your marketing into an event. That's the very essence of the PLF.

The word I like to use is "anticipation," which is a very powerful mental trigger that grabs and holds people's attention. Basically, you turn your marketing into a multi-part story that delivers real value while it leads into your offer.

Let's unpack it a bit because it's simpler than it sounds.

Before you actually launch your offer and start taking orders, you put together a series of pre-launch content (PLC). Your PLC can take any form you like, but these days the most effective (and generally the easiest to create) is video content. Again, you can do all of this via text or even audio, but for the rest of this chapter I'm going to assume that you're using video for your pre-launch.

In a typical launch you'll have three pieces of PLC, and there's a formula to follow for that content. Your first PLC is what we call the "opportunity" or the "journey" video. Your second PLC is called the "transformation" video, and the third is the "ownership" video. We'll break these down in a minute, but here are a few important things to remember about your pre-launch content:

- You need to deliver real value in your PLC. This isn't about creating a long sales video and splitting it into three parts. The best PLC teaches and inspires, and if you do that well enough your pre-launch will actually get shared and will develop its own word-of-mouth traffic.
- Each piece of pre-launch content can stand alone, but it's also part of a larger storyline, similar to the best serial TV shows. Each show can stand alone, but there's a through line across the episodes. Your pre-launch should do the same.
- Your pre-launch should take people down what I call the Problem-Solution Path (PSP). You introduce a series of problems that your typical prospect might face, and then offer real solutions during your pre-launch. As you do this, you deliver

real value and build trust, which drives the conversions when you actually make your offer.

## PRE-LAUNCH CONTENT #1: THE OPPORTUNITY

At the end of the day, your product or service is going to make your client's life better. It's either going to take away some type of pain or deliver some type of pleasure. Your first piece of PLC is about the opportunity for their lives to be better. If you're teaching people how to sing or lower their golf score, first they need to understand (and believe) that they actually can sing better or golf better. If you're selling a roofing service, they have to believe that they can get their roof repaired in a painless and cost-effective way. The first piece of PLC shows this can happen; it's showing the possibility of a brighter future.

Launches always perform better if you can get your prospects to consume this first piece of PLC, so it's worth putting in some extra effort to get them to watch this video.

If you're primarily launching to your warm audience, you will use every means at your disposal to drive people to your pre-launch content. Email has been a primary tool for this for years, and it will continue to be. But these days we have additional means—and Facebook Ads are another primary tool to drive people to your video.

If you're launching to a cold audience, or if you want to use your launch to build your audience, this is an ideal time to use Lookalike Audiences on Facebook. Your video is pure value, so it's ideal for starting to build that relationship with people who don't know you yet.

Remember, at this point you're not trying to make the sale. This first video is setting up the eventual sale. This might sound counterintuitive, but this process has been proven over literally thousands of tests.

## PRE-LAUNCH CONTENT #2: TRANSFORMATION

Your first video was about the opportunity, and now your second piece of PLC takes that to the next level and shows how that opportunity will actually work in your prospect's life. It's about the transformation in your prospect's life—how their life will change once they have your solution.

This second piece of pre-launch is generally the one with the most latitude, but it's all about making it real for your prospect. The first video is about the possibility, and this second one is about that possibility actually happening in your prospect's life. In this video, I often like to show case studies of past clients to demonstrate how they've had real-life results.

In this second video, I also like to do some teaching that helps the prospect find exactly how my solution will fit into their life. For example, when I'm in a launch for my high-end coaching program, we'll teach about the three primary types of launches and help my viewer figure out which of those three is the best fit for their business.

In this second piece of PLC, it's important to start the video with a recap of the opportunity from the first video. Do this quickly. Remember that your viewers will be a mix of people who have seen your first video, and some who are new to your pre-launch. So, your recap of the opportunity needs to be short enough to not bore the people who saw it the first time, but complete enough for the folks who didn't see the first video.

You should foreshadow the third video at the end of this one. Again, do this quickly with a simple, "In the next video I'm going to show you _____."

As with the first video, you're going to drive your warm audience to this video with every means at your disposal. Use your email list. Use Facebook Ads. And use every other channel that you've got.

When I first started using Facebook Ads for my launches, I would only focus on driving people into PLC1, my first pre-launch video. My thinking was that PLC1 was the start of the journey, and I wanted all my new prospects to see the full story.

Well, that thinking turned out to be flawed. As it turns out, we can never be sure that people will see all of our pre-launch. Testing showed that lots of people coming into the middle of the process will get pulled into the launch excitement and end up buying.

## PRE-LAUNCH CONTENT #3: OWNERSHIP

Your third pre-launch video is all about ownership: getting your prospect to take ownership over the change in their life that your product or service will provide. It's also about them eventually owning your product or service, and this video will often give an overall map of what it's like to be one of your clients.

As with your second video, you need to start with a short recap of the opportunity. You can (and should) encourage people to also go back and watch your first two videos.

Again, you're not actually selling in this video. At this point, you've taken people through two videos that hopefully have changed the way they think about their life. In the third video, I like to think of it as time to show how all this will *actually* fit into their lives.

Even though you're not overtly selling, at some point later in the video you need to create a soft landing for your next video, where you will actually be making your offer. I like to think of this as the pivot to the sale. It doesn't have to be lengthy or complicated— just a simple closing will do. Something like this will work: "I hope you've enjoyed these training videos, and I hope you put all of this to work in your life. If you're interested in taking this any further, watch my next video where I tell you about my new [product or service] that I'm going to be launching in a few days."

As with the first two videos, you're going to put this video in front of your warm audience. And if you're really doing things right, at this point you'll likely have people asking you to just take their credit card already—they're ready to buy. That's anticipation at work.

Note that you can still be sending cold traffic into this video by using Lookalike Audiences.

## LAUNCH DAY (AND THE OPEN CART)

So far this launch process might sound like a big exercise in deferred gratification (and it is), but this is where it all comes together. Your launch day is the beginning of what I call the "Open Cart" period. As the name implies, this is when you open up your shopping cart and start taking orders. This is a very specific shift in your launch, as you move from your pre-launch phase into launch. Your prospects can still go watch your pre-launch content, but your focus now is on making sales.

If you think back to the beginning of this chapter, I mentioned Hollywood's big movie releases as an example of building to a launch. The thing that every movie release has is a definite release date, and you need the same. You need a specific start to your actual launch, which is your launch day. You've put in a lot of work by this point, and this is the happy day you actually start taking orders. This is when you start sending all your people to your sales page via email, Facebook Ads, and every other channel you've got.

Now there's something else you need (when I discovered this, it nearly quadrupled the sales in my launches), and that's a definitive end to your launch. You need a hard deadline at the end of your launch when your special launch offer is no longer available.

The very simple language I like to use with my students is, "Something bad needs to happen if they don't buy before the end of the launch."

What you're doing here is activating another mental trigger: scarcity. This is one of the most powerful triggers there is because nothing moves people like a deadline. In most launches you will see 50 percent of your sales come in during the last day of the Open Cart. That's the power of the deadline.

There are three primary ways to create that deadline:

1. Some or all of the bonuses go away, and your prospects have to purchase by the deadline to get the bonuses.
2. The price goes up. Your people have to buy before the end of the launch to get your special pricing.
3. The offer is no longer available. You close down the order process completely. If your prospects don't buy before the deadline, they can't get in.

Note that you can combine more than one of those options. They're listed in general order of their power, and the most powerful is closing the offer down completely.

Of course, the specifics of your business might mean that you are limited in how you use those scarcity elements. For instance, you might have an ongoing service with only one offer and if you pull the offer completely off the market, then you'll be dead in the water. I get it—every business is different. But the reality is that I have yet to see a business that couldn't build one of those scarcity elements into their launch.

I generally recommend that your Open Cart period last between five and seven days. If you go much longer, you'll end up in something of a beg-a-thon, which is always horrible positioning. You could go shorter than five days, but I wouldn't do that until you've built up some experience. Five days gives you time to course-correct in case anything goes wrong.

I also like to publish additional content during the Open Cart, which may be case studies, a product tour, or an additional short piece of content that is self-contained and gives you a chance to talk about your offer. A typical Open Cart publishing schedule would look like:

- Day 1: We're Open!
- Day 2: Case Studies
- Day 3: Short Content Piece or Product Tour
- Day 4: Closing Tomorrow!
- Day 5: Closing Today!

During Open Cart, you'll want to email your list every day. This is why longer Open Cart periods are not recommended—because you'll run out of things to say, and the excitement will wane.

This is also the time to step up your Facebook game and evolve your message during Open Cart. Early in your cart week, you'll be pushing people into the offer. Later in cart week, you'll be focusing on the scarcity of your cart close. And you'll also want to target people who've already seen your sales page differently from the people who haven't seen it yet. The same idea applies with people who have made it to your order page or who have abandoned a partially filled out shopping cart. They should get targeted messaging in your Facebook Ads.

## YOUR POST-LAUNCH SEQUENCE

When you follow this process, you should end up with a bunch of new and very engaged clients. This is the time to focus on them and make sure they have a great experience and get amazing results. That's what will build your business in the long run.

It's also important to remember the people who went through your launch process and did not buy. No matter how powerful this process, the vast majority of your prospects won't buy from you in the first launch. HOWEVER, they are going to be super-engaged with you. This process will build the warmest, most engaged following you can imagine. By delivering the content you did throughout your pre-launch, people are going to fall in love with you.

So, don't make the mistake of letting those good vibes fade away. It's amazing how often people build up a warm relationship with their followers, and then let it fade away. Don't do this.

Be sure to create a post-launch engagement strategy. This is as simple as a regular publishing schedule where you continue to deliver value to the people that didn't buy. At a minimum, publish one cornerstone piece of content each week for them. This strategy will pay off in a huge way during your next launch.

## THE LAUNCH CONVERSATION

One of the most powerful parts of this process is what I call the *launch conversation*. By that I mean this isn't a one-way broadcast of videos, emails, and ads. You want to create and engage in a conversation with your prospects. They'll tell you what's landing and what isn't. The great thing about this process is that you'll have time to adapt your positioning, copy, and even your offer. Facebook is fantastic for this because there is commenting built in for everything you publish. Be sure to engage in those comments and encourage the conversation. Listen to your prospects; they will tell you how they want to be sold and what they want to buy.

## YOUR LAUNCH

This was a bullet-fast introduction to launching. At its core, this is an incredibly powerful way to stand apart from the noise in your niche, deliver huge value in the market, and make a lot of sales.

There is definitely a significant amount of work in pulling a launch together, but the results can be truly outsized. In addition to the sales you make, you will build your following and greatly increase your positioning in the market.

Just remember that you're delivering value and building connection first. Don't rush to the sale. The sales will be there, but during that pre-launch you're in the romance phase. Engage in the launch conversation and listen to what the market is telling you.

Then when it's time to shift to Open Cart, make your offer and focus on closing sales. Remember that half or more of your sales will likely come in the last 24 hours.

And don't forget about your Post-Launch Sequence both for your new customers and the prospects that haven't bought from you yet.

Jeff Walker is the author of the #1 New York Times bestseller *LAUNCH*. He teaches people how to launch online courses, products, services, and brands online. His Product Launch Formula transformed the online marketing world from the day it was released in 2005 . . . and Jeff and PLF have never slowed down. Now all these years later, the Product Launch Formula brand is the gold standard in the online entrepreneurial training market. Jeff's students and clients have done over a BILLION dollars in launches in hundreds of niches and markets . . . and dozens of countries around the world. Learn more at JeffWalker.com.

# Chapter 25

# Choosing the Best Facebook Funnel for You

## Guest Author David Nadler

A few years ago, I was working with a client who had it all pretty well together. They had a great, proven product that had already sold over six figures. They had a well-groomed, if slightly stale email list. They were well funded and had a founder-owner who was a great writer and great on video. They had just put together a new launch of their existing product and brought us in to run their Facebook Ads. We all had very high hopes and expectations. Given all the assets we had in place, the launch should have been a grand slam, but the first few weeks were a depressing failure. Within about 14 days, we had spent thousands on Facebook Ads and had precious few sales to show for it. Everything inside the Facebook account was perfect; the problem was outside the Facebook account. They were using a video series funnel when they really needed a challenge or webinar funnel. You can avoid this by matching your business situation to the six conversion funnels best suited for capitalizing on Facebook traffic.

As we covered in Chapter 1, having a sales funnel in place is the best way to connect the dots between *spending* money on your Facebook Ads to *making* money on the backend. In order to make money, you need an effective sales funnel in place, one where your prospects land when they click through your ads and that incubates people through the sales process, warming up your prospects until they are ready to make a buying decision. Funnels use web pages, emails, video, written site content, SMS messages, and more to educate, inform, and win over your prospects.

In this chapter, you will learn the six types of funnels that work best with Facebook Ads. Since sales funnels can be customized to fit your business and marketing goals, there are almost an infinite number of variations. This chapter will give you a snapshot of the most fundamental, most effective strategies in funnel building for Facebook Ads so that you are able to start with proven strategies that will convert your clicks into customers.

## THE LEAD MAGNET FUNNEL

A lead magnet is a bite-sized piece of information that you offer someone in exchange for their email address. A Lead Magnet Funnel is made up of a landing page that offers the lead magnet, a Thank-You page that delivers the lead magnet, and an email autoresponder integration.

Lead Magnet Funnels work best when they are focused on solving a very specific problem in a short period of time. Great lead magnets are brief, to the point, and are highly targeted at one pain point with which your prospective customer is struggling. The specific benefit of the lead magnet should be expressed within the landing page for maximum impact. The lead magnet should whet the appetite of the consumer but not attempt to sell them anything.

A lead magnet can be presented in various forms. They most typically are delivered as ebooks, case studies, checklists, toolkits, audio, or video files. A good rule of thumb is that a prospect should be able to consume the lead magnet in ten minutes or less.

Figure 25–1 on page 321 is a Lead Magnet Funnel Map.

Lead Magnet Funnels are effective for virtually every type of business. Because the purpose of this funnel is to generate new leads, anyone can benefit from having it in place.

It is important to note that a Lead Magnet Funnel is a lead-generation tool, not a sales device. The purpose of the funnel is *not* to make sales. This type of funnel is used for the beginning of the customer awareness journey rather than the end. The funnel, coupled with your Facebook Ads, will bring users into your business who may not know anything about you or your products. After you have collected their email exchange for the ultra-specific content you delivered, you have the opportunity to grow your relationship with them and market directly via email.

### Lead Magnet Funnel Pros and Cons

*Pros:* One reason Lead Magnet Funnels are so popular and effective is they are relatively inexpensive to develop and maintain. Because the funnel consists of a bite-sized

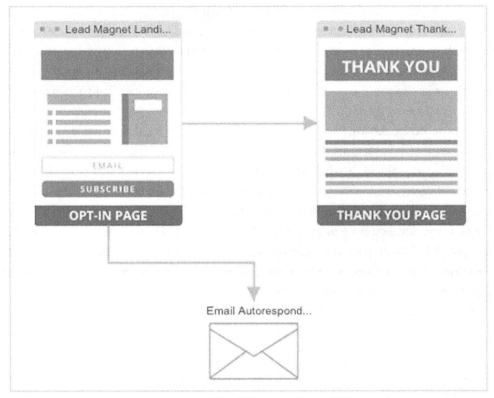

**FIGURE 25–1.** Lead Magnet Funnel Map

piece of very specific content, it can be developed at a low cost and does not require a significant investment in design and development. In addition, Lead Magnet Funnels don't require a high level of technical skill to implement.

*Cons.* Certain content formats can potentially make it difficult to update a Lead Magnet Funnel. For example, highly produced videos or designed documents can be time consuming and expensive to update.

Here's what you need:

- The lead magnet (PDF, video, audio, etc.)
- Landing page
- Thank-You page
- Follow-up email series

## THE MINI COURSE FUNNEL

The Mini Course Funnel is a series of emails in an autoresponder that is delivered to users who opt in to receive in-depth information on a certain subject. The most common mini course autoresponders are approximately five to 21 days long.

This type of funnel allows you to deliver content through your email service provider directly to your contacts. Setting it up as an autoresponder is important because it starts the day the person opts in, and consequently they don't miss any of the content you are sending out in your mini course. The emails in your autoresponder or email sequence are set up with delay timers so that the content is broken up and fed to users in a way that makes sense to them.

As a marketer, getting people to read your emails from the start creates significant value. This means that the user will not have to keep a folder of various course downloads they need to dig through when they want to read your course content. Having the content delivered in an email means easy access and higher consumption rates.

Important to note: This type of funnel can also be *combined* with the Lead Magnet Funnel. For example, a lead magnet might be a five-page PDF with "Nine Tips for Better Facebook Ads." After your leads download the initial PDF, you can follow up with a mini course. You could deliver nine emails, one per day, breaking down the overall lead magnet into smaller pieces and delivering them independently.

Figure 25–2 is the Mini Course Funnel Map.

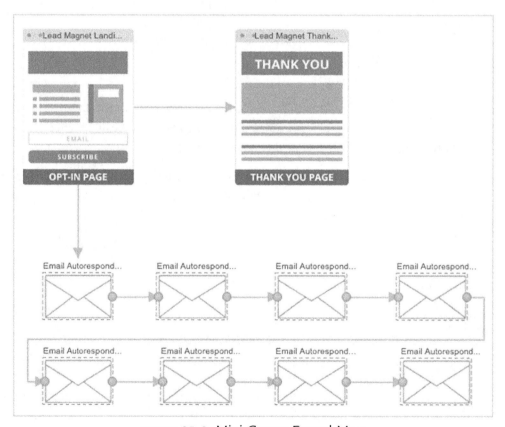

**FIGURE 25–2.** Mini Course Funnel Map

The Mini Course Funnel is designed for the sole purpose of lead generation. Any business that wants to generate leads will benefit greatly from having this type of funnel in place. Similar to the Lead Magnet Funnel, the mini course is not typically used for closing sales.

The Mini Course Funnel targets customers toward the beginning of the customer awareness timeline. Those who opt in for a mini course or series of informative emails are, as a rule, going to be just learning about you or the products you offer.

By opting into your mini course, they are figuratively raising their hand and letting you know that they would like more material and information regarding what you can do for them. Mini courses are a great way to nurture these new leads and get them prepared to eventually buy something from you.

### Mini Course Funnel Pros and Cons

*Pros.* One of the great things about the Mini Course Funnel is that, along with the Lead Magnet Funnel, it has low development and maintenance costs. As long as you have an email service provider that has autoresponder capabilities (Mailchimp, Drip, ConvertKit, Infusionsoft, Active Campaign, etc.), you already have the tool you need in order to deliver this type of funnel.

Because there are no heavy graphic design or development needs, simple landing pages and web forms can be created with a page builder software. The real work for this funnel lies within the email copy and setting up the autoresponder. Once the emails are written, you could have this funnel up and running in a single day.

*Cons.* Along with other lead generation-focused funnels, the Mini Course Funnel is not the most effective for actively closing sales. However, if your end goal is to make sales, it is possible to follow up with contacts who have opted into your mini course with additional marketing.

Here's what you need:

- Landing page
- Thank-You page
- Follow-up email series

## THE FREE-PLUS-SHIPPING FUNNEL

The Free-Plus-Shipping Funnel is a great way to sell books and is how this funnel is most commonly used. You can use it as a way of giving away your book and having users just pay for shipping and handling in order to receive it. It's simply a different way of positioning the sale. Instead of selling a book for $7.99, you can say, "I'm giving away my book for free. All you have to do is pay shipping and handling." The goal is to not lose money on the transaction while growing your list, your authority, and your credibility.

It is used typically for people who have a "calling card" book (those who are not primarily concerned with book sales, but instead want to generate sales of other products when people read their book). The purpose of the book is to establish credibility and authority in a specific market space. Figure 25–3 shows the Free Plus Shipping Funnel Map.

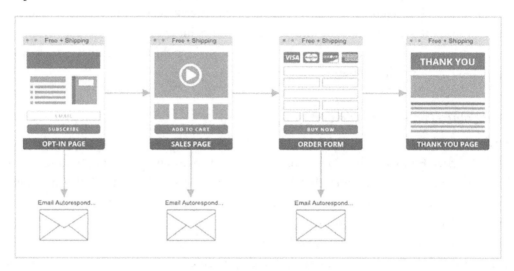

**FIGURE 25–3.** Free Plus Shipping Funnel Map

This type of offer is great for anybody who has published a book. The important thing to note here is that the sole purpose is not to *sell* the book, but to build authority and credibility. It is using the book to generate leads for people who are interested in your business, products, or services. It is meant for the purpose of using your book to liquidate the cost of traffic.

The Free-Plus-Shipping Funnel is not for someone looking to turn a quick profit in book revenues or simply sell more books. It is better suited for positioning yourself as an authority in a market and generating new leads to grow your business.

### Free-Plus-Shipping Funnel Pros and Cons

*Pros.* With a Free-Plus-Shipping Funnel, you can often find many new readers of your book at a net zero cost. This means that after you pay for the book cost, advertising, shipping, and any other costs and you add up everything you make from your shipping and handling fees, order bumps, and one-time offers, you'll end up not making any money, but not losing any, either. While this may not seem like a big benefit at first, many people love the idea of getting their calling card book into the hands of ideal prospects at a net-zero cost.

The Free-Plus-Shipping Funnel is one of the few funnels that allows (and requires) physical fulfillment, meaning someone will need to ship a physical product. Whether you do this yourself or have it completed by a fulfillment house, you are able to use the product fulfillment to provide other physical products or promotions in the same package. This is very difficult, if not impossible to do with other book distribution channels.

*Cons.* The development and maintenance of a Free-Plus-Shipping Funnel is more complex than the Lead Magnet and Mini Course Funnels. This is because you are now able to have varying follow-up email sequences based on the actions the users perform on your landing page. For example, you will have a list of users who complete the first step of the two-step opt-in, but not the second. You will also have a list for those who complete both steps of the two-step opt-in. You may even have a separate list for users who opted into both steps but didn't purchase the order bump on your order form. This would mean you now have three separate email sequences to set up. Because of the additional follow-up sequences, the Free-Plus-Shipping Funnel is more complex than the other funnels.

With this funnel, you are typically going to be working with a fulfillment house which also increases the complexity of the funnel. This means that you should be prepared to connect your system with someone else's system in order to create a smooth fulfillment and shipping process.

Here's what you need:

- Landing page
- Order bump or one-click upsell
- One-click upsell sales page
- Thank-You page
- Multiple email sequences
- Additional fulfillment options

If you decide to go the fulfillment house center route, they will house all of the product for you and handle shipping to the purchasers of the book. With this option, you will need to connect your systems to the fulfillment centers so that they receive notifications each time the book is purchased and they know where to send them.

Depending on the volume of books you anticipate shipping, you may want to consider ordering the books yourself and handling the shipping. This is a great alternative for those who are looking to customize their packages to customers by inserting other information like sales letters, special offers, etc.

This type of funnel is highly adaptable if the product you are selling is already finished and ready to go, namely a book that is already published.

## THE ASSESSMENT OR QUIZ FUNNEL

There is a unique psychology behind why people enjoy taking online assessments and quizzes. People like to self-diagnose and discover their own results for many different kinds of things, whether it's a personality test or knowledge-based questionnaire. Because people innately enjoy doing them, assessments and quizzes are very valuable.

Many people use the term "quiz" and "assessment" interchangeably and believe they are the same thing. They are distinctly different. Here's how:

A *quiz* is primarily used for general lead generation no matter the industry. A user can answer a series of questions and then fill out their name and email address to receive the results of the quiz.

An *assessment* is more likely to be industry specific and feeds the answers of users back into the system so that you can serve them exactly what they need based on their results. The results page is customized, and it lets users know how they rank against others who have completed the assessment.

Both quizzes and assessments collect customized information about your prospects. For more sophisticated marketing, you can use what you learn about them to deliver what they want or need from you. They make for great segmentation tools and they can help you distinguish the core differentiating factors about the people coming onto your list.

If your business has multiple avatars and you want to have the ability to communicate to all of them differently, an assessment is the ideal choice. Users interact with the assessment questions and generate their own unique results. Those results are placed in your database and give you the opportunity to segment and create different communications based on those results. Figure 25–4 on page 327 shows the Quiz and Assessment Funnel Map.

Quizzes and assessments are great lead-generation tools. If you're offering a non-complex, low-dollar offer, a quiz might be good for lead gen because the segmentation wouldn't be needed. If you sell a more complex product, the segmentation that an Assessment Funnel provides will allow you to communicate differently with each avatar.

### Assessment Funnel Pros and Cons

*Pros.* Assessments are extremely valuable for collecting custom information about each potential client and storing it along with their contact record in your database. When an assessment is used properly, you will know how each contact compares to the average contact in your database, which is powerful for many types of marketing.

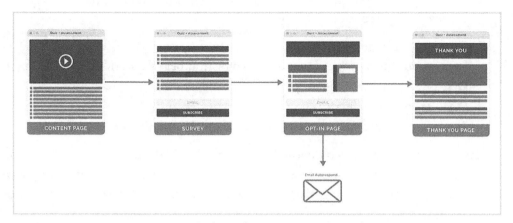

**FIGURE 25–4.** Quiz and Assessment Funnel Map

When you've captured all this information, you can see the power of the assessment. You know where they are strong and weak compared to other people in an industry so you can serve them exactly the way they need to be served. It's good for you as a business because you're offering the best thing for them, and it's good for the consumer because they're being offered exactly what they need.

*Cons.* The technical intensity for building an assessment is high because you will need to pass a lot of custom variables into your database. The Assessment Funnel is not easy to adapt for the same reason. If you want to change or add a question, it can be technically complicated due to the communication between the assessment platform and your database.

The development intensity is high because the value of the results comes from comparison to an existing, assessed population. Time is required to survey a sample and then create a standardized set of results so that new participants can compare themselves to the average.

## Quiz Funnel Pros and Cons

*Pros.* Quizzes are popular with users since they are often brief. Plus, they are great lead-generation tools. Compared to a full Assessment Funnel, they are also relatively fast and easy to set up.

The technical intensity for building a Quiz Funnel (and not an assessment) is low because you will most likely be using a quiz building software (SurveyGizmo, LeadQuizzes, etc.) which is easy to navigate and put together for simple lead generation. Additionally, the maintenance of this type of funnel is going to be relatively low because it's pretty much plug-and-play and will live in its existing form.

*Cons.* Quizzes are more difficult to set up than a simple written lead magnet or an email mini course.

Here's what you need for a quiz:

- Quiz landing page
- Internal quiz pages (number determined by number of questions on your quiz)
- Dynamic Thank-You page
- Email follow-up sequence
- Some form of integration between quiz Thank You and your CRM

Up to this point, you haven't needed an integration. Customers have simply entered their email and gone directly into your CRM. Now at this point with a quiz, people are going to be taking the quiz on a platform that is not your CRM, so custom integration will be needed.

Here's what you need for an assessment:

- Assessment landing page
- Internal questions pages
- Custom form to collect email address and other pieces of information that weren't identified in the assessment. These will include segmentation questions that allow you to segment your respondents. Examples could include business size, years in the industry, income goals, or position in the company.
- Dynamic Thank-You page
- Customized email follow-up sequences that match up your avatars, the products you have available for sale, and user results.

## THE CHALLENGE FUNNEL

The Challenge Funnel is a full funnel, meaning it works for both lead generation and making sales. This is a great solution for selling a high-priced offer on the backend of the actual challenge content you will be delivering. Some examples of programs to sell with a Challenge Funnel include coaching programs, consulting, digital products, and software. Using a Challenge Funnel allows you to have a gateway product for your core offering that lets you warm up your prospects before pitching them your higher-priced flagship offering.

A Challenge Funnel works by inviting people into a fairly short (typically between 5 and 30 days) training series. During this training series, many things will occur:

You charge a relatively low dollar amount for the actual challenge itself. This micro-commitment gets users into the challenge group so that you can use the duration of the challenge to set the stage for pitching a higher ticket product at the end.

You overdeliver on the challenge content and communicate with your customers to build rapport. Building relationships with these users is essential as you are setting the stage to sell a higher ticket offer.

You deliver the training each day through a live group coaching call, typically done over video meeting or webinar.

You create a place where customers can communicate with you and other users. This is commonly hosted as a private Facebook group.

You take people through a training process during that 5- to 30-day challenge.

The goal of the challenge is to give someone a taste of who you are as a trainer and leader in your industry. In order for this to be successful, you must help your customers achieve a big success in a short period of time. By getting the participant's micro commitment at a lower dollar, you are lowering their risk on your core offer of perhaps hundreds or thousands of dollars.

The Challenge Funnel is so powerful because it gives the trainer live, face-to-face time with their best prospects. If you can get someone to commit $27 or $97 and show up for five live training sessions, that's five sessions you, the expert, has to build a rapport with your potential clients.

For all the funnels we have mentioned previously in this book, the content is most likely going to be pre-determined and pre-recorded. This means that there is less opportunity to personally interact with prospects and really get to know them. The unique thing about the Challenge Funnel is that there are numerous times where you can meet with your prospects face-to-face to build trust and get to know them as individuals. This also gives you the opportunity to customize your content as you go.

Figure 25–5 is the Challenge Funnel Map.

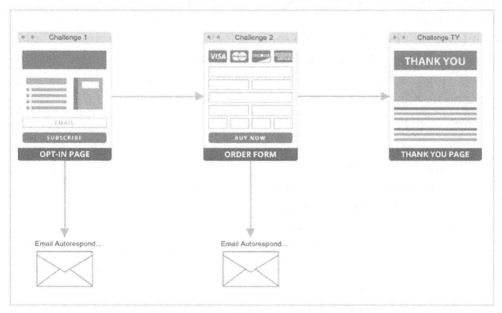

**FIGURE 25–5.** Challenge Funnel Map

This type of offer works best for selling a high-end training program—typically an expert space. This funnel works well in expert marketing because there is a natural extension from a short, content-based challenge into a core offering of coaching, higher-end training programs, and more. Challenges work for both lead generation and for making sales.

### Challenge Funnel Pros and Cons

*Pros.* Challenges are excellent lead gen and closing funnels in part because they put the expert in direct, live contact with consumers. The Challenge Funnel offers more face-to-face time with prospects than any other funnel option.

Additionally, because the challenge is run live, it is one of the few funnels that allows you to adjust your messaging and sales pitch from challenge to challenge.

The development intensity for the Challenge Funnel is moderate because there are several technical integrations based on the segmented email sequences.

*Cons.* The Challenge Funnel includes a number of live events so many elements of the Challenge Funnel cannot be automated.

Also, because the Challenge Funnel is a live event, it has manual processes that need to be built out and managed throughout the challenge. This is unique from the rest of the funnels because there needs to be someone managing the entire process, from the project planning and setup all the way through the live content delivery. This includes the live video calls, inviting users into the private group, posting welcome messages, and more.

Adaptability for this type of funnel is high. The reason for this is if you are running a Challenge Funnel monthly or quarterly, you will be adjusting the training content based on how it performs in previous funnels. Other funnels have content that is set in stone.

Here's what you need:

- Opt-in page
- Challenge sales page
- A private group, often hosted on Facebook
- A series of live webinars/conference calls
- Product on the backend to sell, so a sales page or application
- Three email sequences (opt-in but no buy, challenge purchasers, product purchasers)
- Challenge content
- Admin process for the challenge

## THE ON-DEMAND WEBINAR FUNNEL

The great thing about an On-Demand Webinar Funnel is that it has a lot of the benefits of a live event like a webinar, but it is simulated. You get the benefits of having a live webinar, yet you also have automation working in your favor.

One of the primary benefits business owners love is that they don't have to do the webinar over and over. The webinar is developed as a recording and can then run automatically.

There is also a significant benefit to the audience in that they don't have to wait for the live event to occur. With an automated webinar, you can offer more flexibility. You can run it multiple times a day so prospects can consume the content shortly after they click instead of waiting for the live event, which could be up to a week or more.

It works well with Facebook Ads because if you get someone to click on your ad and they like your stuff, you just got them excited and you can deliver an automated webinar to them instantly.

Webinars are typically used in markets and for products where consumers need time to make a buying decision. You're giving them the information they need to make this buying decision. An automated webinar allows for the best way to deliver that information.

Figure 25–6 is the On-Demand Webinar Funnel Map.

These work to sell mid- and high-priced items. You're going to see things being sold by webinar that are most often $1,000 to $3,000, but they can also be used to sell $3,000 to $10,000+ products. It can be lower, but if the price drops too far below $1,000, consumers are not usually willing to invest the time in a webinar to make a buying decision.

Current best practice recommends that if the price point of the offering goes over $2,000, then the results will be best if the Webinar Funnel drives people to an application

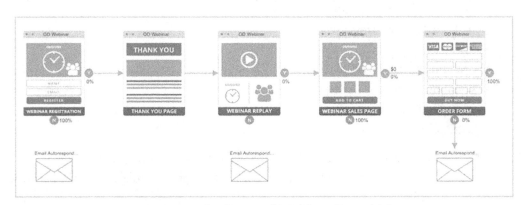

**FIGURE 25–6.** On-Demand Webinar Funnel Map

or sales call instead of directly to a sales page. It's important to get qualified leads on your sales calls, and the webinar qualifies them.

### On-Demand Webinar Funnel Pros and Cons

*Pros.* One great thing about the On-Demand Webinar Funnel is that the ongoing maintenance intensity is low. Unlike the Live Webinar Funnel, once you have your on-demand webinar set up, you don't have to reset it week after week. With an automated webinar, all of your funnel elements become dynamic so you don't have to reset anything. It can run 365 days a year without any maintenance.

*Cons.* One of the drawbacks of the On-Demand Webinar Funnel is that because it's a higher intensity setup and highly automated, changes are more difficult to make. Because it's running all the time, it is harder to make individual tweaks as you go. This type of funnel makes most sense for businesses that have their sales and promotional messaging crystallized. If an organization is still testing and learning what hooks and closes work best, it might be better to select one of the more adaptable funnels.

The technical skill intensity for this funnel is mid to high because there are a lot of small but important pieces that have to be connected the right way for this funnel to work effectively. You are trying to simulate the experience of a live event and there are certain components that aren't going to happen. Therefore, all of the pieces need to be dialed in and perfect to make up for that.

Here's what you need:

- Webinar registration page
- Webinar Tank-You Page
- Webinar recording
- Special software that automates your webinar
- WebinarJam/Everwebinar
- StealthSeminar
- ClickFunnels (we DO NOT like this for webinars)
- Webinar reminder emails
- Follow-up sales emails
- Sales page/order form/application

If selling direct from webinar, sending someone to sales page or order form.

The call to action may be to fill out an application or schedule service for booking a consultation call.

# HOW TO QUICKLY CHOOSE A FUNNEL

Figure 25-7 is a conversion funnel matrix that covers, in simple visual terms, the elements discussed in this chapter. It shows the six different funnels that work best with Facebook traffic. It shows, at a glance, the important high-level considerations when choosing a funnel. The matrix includes Offer Type, Traffic Type, Development/ Maintenance Intensity and Adaptability, Lead Gen vs. Sales Funnel, and Required Tech Skills.

It can be used to quickly and effectively narrow down funnel options and help select the funnel most likely to generate fantastic results for you by converting more of your Facebook Ads clicks into subscribers and buyers.

**CONVERSION FUNNEL MATRIX**

| | Low Ticket Offer (0-250) | Mid Ticket Offer (250-2000) | High Ticket Offer (2000+) | Affiliate Traffic | Paid Traffic | Organic Traffic | Email Traffic | Development Intensity | Maintenance Intensity | Adaptability | Lead Gen Focused | Sales Focused | "Full Funnel" | Tech Skills |
|---|---|---|---|---|---|---|---|---|---|---|---|---|---|---|
| On Demand Webinar Funnel | | • | • | • | • | • | • | MID | LOW | LOW | • | • | • | MID |
| Challenge Funnel | | • | • | • | • | • | • | MID | HIGH | HIGH | • | • | • | MID |
| Assessment (Quiz) Funnel | • | | | • | • | • | • | HIGH | LOW | LOW | • | | | HIGH |
| Mini Course Funnel | • | | | | • | • | | LOW | LOW | HIGH | • | | | LOW |
| Lead Magnet Funnel | • | | | | • | • | | LOW | LOW | HIGH | • | | | LOW |
| Free + Shipping Funnel | • | | | | • | • | • | MID | MID | HIGH | • | | | MID |

**FIGURE 25-7.** Funnel Selection Matrix

David Nadler is the owner of Automate & Convert, a digital marketing agency specializing in client acquisition for experts offering high-end coaching and training products. Over the past five years, he honed his ability to help business owners and entrepreneurs drive profitability by building and optimizing automated sales funnels that convert. David can be reached at automateandconvert.com.

# Chapter 26

# Boosting Posts and Unicorns

## Guest Author Dennis Yu

If you actively post content on your Facebook page, you will find that out of every several dozen posts, there will be one post that stands out because it has exponential engagement and reach over the others. These I like to call "unicorns."

I recommend going "all-in" on unicorns by putting ad dollars behind your unicorn posts. You do this by clicking the Boost Post button on the post from your Page. I teach my clients to just do a $1 per day for seven days and you will get even more engagement for very little investment.

Figure 26–1 on page 336 is an example unicorn, identified by one of many triggers, such as an engagement rate greater than 10 percent.

Sometimes, content is almost a unicorn, but you've boosted to the wrong audience. The audience won't be the same for every post. Sometimes for us, the right audience has fans of *Social Media Marketing World, Digital Marketer*, or whatever audience is most relevant.

In this case, from the hustle nature of the article—and that it's 2:23 A.M., and I'm still working—I chose Gary Vaynerchuk fans.

I spent $98.86 to drive 2,703 likes, which works out to 3.6 cents a like. This is not great, but not terrible for this type of boost.

The numbers do not account for secondary effects, however. If your friend shares your post and their friend likes it, it won't be counted. Your

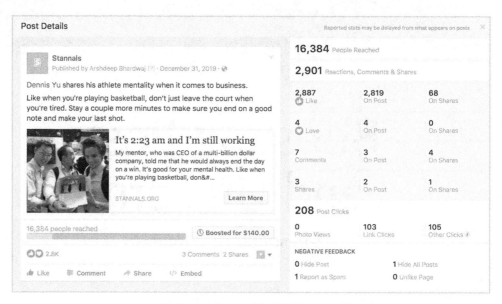

**FIGURE 26–1.** Unicorn Post with 18-Percent Engagement

numbers are actually better than your results say they are. A share is worth 13 times more than a like on Facebook. A like is a dead end when one person enjoys your post, and it stops there. A share multiplies your numbers when a person promotes your post to everyone they are connected with and extends your reach.

## GET THE RESULTS

Now I have some social proof, which means not only is there high engagement, but also that it's the right fans. So, it's time to switch-boost to a media inception audience to create a unicorn baby. See Figure 26–2 on page 337.

Let's break this down:

*Switch-boost.* I originally boosted to a broader interest or behavioral target. I want not only high engagement for cheap to stimulate the algorithm love on this post, but I also want to create social proof. So, I'm switching the audience of the boosted post to an influencer audience.

*Media inception audience.* The influencer audience I've switched to is a media workplace audience. I'm targeting all the people who work at *CNN*, *The Wall Street Journal*, and so forth—not people who read these publications.

If they find the content compelling and newsworthy (viral counts as newsworthy), then they may write about it or share my post. And when we get coverage by these outlets, we share their posts and boost again to media inception targets, creating "unicorn babies."

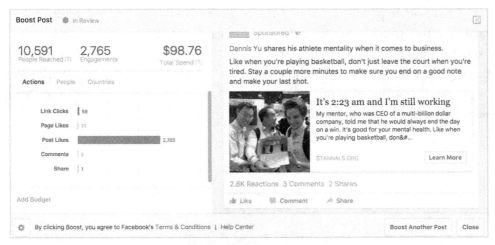

**FIGURE 26–2.** Three-Cent Likes

*Unicorn baby.* Once I've got one unicorn, I want to create many variants, which we call unicorn babies. We can create these babies by switching the audience of the boost or even duplicating the Ad Set, so we're running against two at the same time. We can create derivative (similar or related) pieces of content, to replicate the effect of the initial unicorn.

Got these three components (switch-boost, media inception audience, and unicorn baby), and how they fit together? Great! Let's dive into the mechanics.

Figure 26–3 is the boosted post after I switch-boosted to the media inception audience:

Notice I created a *saved* audience called Mega Media Inception? It's one I reuse often. Even though I can create one of these audiences straight from the boosted post in just ten minutes, I prefer to keep things clean.

**FIGURE 26–3.** Media Inception Audience

If I have other people managing the account, they must use the audiences we've already created, which eliminates the mess most people have. There's no law against switch-boosting multiple times to test or take advantage of current events. For example, let's say I'm speaking at Social Media Marketing World in a couple weeks. Then I would take a few older boosted posts and switch to *Social Media Examiner* fans for a couple weeks. See Figure 26–4.

**FIGURE 26–4.** Media Inception Saved Audience

## SWITCH-BOOST

When I switch-boost, the post keeps all the existing social proof it's built up over time. So, I get this rolling snowball effect that I can redirect wherever I want.

If we don't have something we're currently promoting—a book, event, product, or sale—we'll keep it on the media inception audience.

If the post is amazing, we'll duplicate the Ad Set in Ads Manager so that I might keep it going at a dollar a day against social media marketers and then whatever audience I'm currently using in the boosted post itself.

Yes, you get only one audience at a time when you boost from the timeline of the page, but there's no law against choosing page post engagement from Ads Manager so I can run multiple audiences against this post.

I happen to be lazy and like to avoid having to go to the Ads Manager. I spend 90 percent of my time in the page's timeline and the Insights tab where I can see organic and paid stats together.

Ads Manager doesn't show organic data, so if your post is going viral you might miss it if you aren't looking elsewhere.

And most of what we do in tuning ads is trying different audience combos for posts, as opposed to creating tons of new posts. We believe in quality instead of quantity—a key distinction between ROI-driven social marketers and the "just post X times per day" social marketers. Larry Kim and I believe in spending the bulk of our time cultivating winners (unicorns), rather than trying to coax donkeys to fly.

## GREATEST HITS

You've listened to your favorite song more than once in your lifetime. Just like music, create a "greatest hits" that lists your most successful posts. Boosting isn't a one-time action. If something worked well in the past, it is going to work in the future. Imagine what would happen if the greatest bands sang a song once and then moved on?

After all, if you have your greatest hits, why not keep playing them over and over (plus creating similar versions) instead of trying to make new stuff from scratch over and over again?

Unless you like self-inflicted punishment, you should be looking at what's done well over the last 24 months and switch-boosting. It's so much less effort to boost a winner (as long as the content is evergreen) than trying a moonshot each day.

When you've finally assembled a herd of unicorns, you have a pretty good idea of what's working in your business, which allows you to:

- *Boost articles you have on third-party publications.* The more guest articles, quotes, and mentions you get, the more items to boost.
- *Track your articles, quotes, and mentions in your content library.* A simple Google sheet lets you track which content bits you can link to in new articles, sprinkle in marketing content, and use for boosting.
- *Set up triggers for conversion parts of your funnel.* You can switch-boost to remarketing audiences. If you're in B2B lead gen or have a product/service with a lengthy consideration phase, some high authority mentions can increase your conversion rate. The pros know that increasing conversion rates is less about tweaking button color and more about persuading the user by overcoming various objections.

Boosting to third-party publications is usually more powerful than boosting to your own site.

I wrote an article for Stannals, which is a community of young entrepreneurs, perfect for this content. Another article I wrote about developing people belongs better on Influencive, so I put it there and promoted the Influencive link from my public figure page. See Figure 26–5 on page 340.

**FIGURE 26-5.** Boosting to Third-Party Publications

## CONTENT LIBRARY

Track your articles, quotes, and mentions in your content library—you don't need a fancy tool. Figure 26-6 is our content library, shared out with our internal and extended team.

We have tabs for the several thousands of articles we've written, a list of publications we write for, mentions, pictures with influencers, and so forth. Then anyone who is writing an article knows what they can link to, what images they can handily insert, and who we can reach out to for quotes.

We do this not for SEO purposes but because we know that eager readers will want to dig further if they like our articles. And that's why we're OK with spending our ad

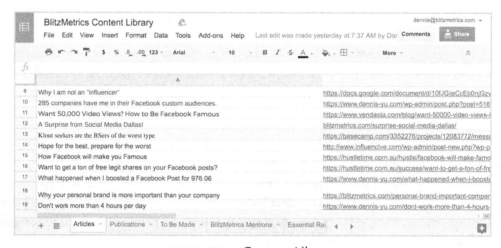

**FIGURE 26-6.** Content Library

dollars to send people to someone else's site, since if the article is good, they'll eventually follow links back to our paid courses.

## FUNNEL

Set up triggers for conversion parts of your funnel—a truly powerful funnel has many sequences, which are if/then statements.

Many Facebook Advertisers confuse sophisticated with being complicated:

- *Complicated* is having tons of remarketing (custom), lookalike, and interest/behavior audiences being used in a ton of Ad Sets.
- *Sophisticated* is having most of your campaigns being driven by remarketing, instead of static demographic and interest targets. The graphic in Figure 26-7, which we call the Bow Tie Formula, is an example of a sophisticated strategy.

When you develop relationships over many touches, you have more opportunities to build value in the funnel, which increases the LTV of the user and allows you to spend more time on acquiring leads.

Having a "value, value, value, offer" strategy also generates goodwill with the community. It doesn't look or feel like selling—more like a trusted friend that you've known for years who is making a recommendation based on what they know about your needs. So, when we think like journalists, our articles have authority, allowing us to share our expertise on high-profile sites. And that's where we create unicorn babies that we amplify via switch-boosting to media inception targets.

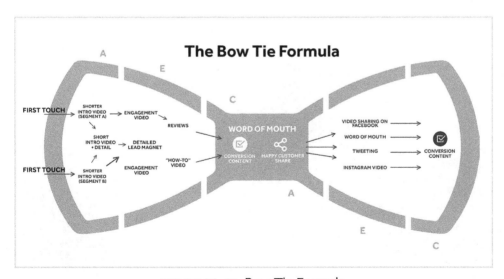

**FIGURE 26–67.** Bow Tie Formula

Remember, not every boost is going to become a unicorn. Measure organically first; then stack worthy posts on top of each other by boosting each of them for a dollar a day over seven days. Compare their reach and engagement. Put more spending against your winners. Once you have your business goal selected, you need to find the content that matches up with it. Choose a target when you boost the post. Then watch how Goals Content Targeting will lead you to success on Facebook.

Dennis Yu is the Chief Executive Officer of BlitzMetrics, a digital marketing company that partners with schools to train young adults. Dennis's program centers around mentorship, helping students grow their expertise to manage social campaigns for enterprise clients like the Golden State Warriors, Nike, and Rosetta Stone. He's an internationally recognized lecturer in Facebook Marketing and has spoken in 17 countries spanning five continents, including keynotes at L2E, Gultaggen, and Marketo Summit. Learn more at BlitzMetrics.com.

# Chapter 27

# Keeping Track of Your Money and Results

A t the end of the day, all business is tracked and reported by the bank account. Money goes out to Facebook Ads. Money comes in from sales. Too many business owners judge by how they *feel* about their marketing. Savvy business owners use all available tracking and reporting not just to know if it's making any money, but also to optimize their ads.

In this chapter, you're going to learn how to track the results of your advertising on Facebook. You will learn some basic terms that might be new to you, but then learn how those terms relate to evaluating your campaign performance.

Lastly, the sheer number of things you can measure are overwhelming. In this chapter you'll also learn the 80/20 of reporting and what is most important for you to focus on.

## COMMON ADVERTISING TERMS

First, let's go over a few quick terms and definitions:

- *Reach.* Unique people who saw your ads.
- *Impressions.* Total number of times the ad was shown.
- *Frequency.* Average number of times a person was shown your ad.

- *Cost per Result*. How much was spent on your Campaign Objective divided by the number of positive results.
- *Link Clicks*. Clicks from an ad that lead to other places (Landing Page, Facebook Page).
- *Clickthrough Rate (CTR)*. Impressions divided by Clicks (under 1 percent usually means something is wrong).
- *Return On Ad Spend (ROAS)*. What percentage of your ad budget comes back in sales. For example, if you spend $100 on ads and get $200 in sales, your ROAS is 200 percent.
- *Lifetime Customer Value (LTCV or LTV)*. Average amount a customer is worth to your business. For example, if you have been in business five years, have total revenue over those five years of $1,000,000 and have generated 10,000 customers, then your LTCV is $100 (1,000,000 divided by 10,000).
- *Cost per Thousand Impressions (CPM)*. Tells you how much it really costs to show the ad (a standard ad measurement for over 100 years). CPM is affected by your budget, performance of your ad, and size of audience. Smaller audiences give you a higher CPM. Facebook charges more for the privilege of showing your ad to a small audience.

Placement is another major factor in your CPM. The more responsive placements have a higher CPM because there's more competition for the higher quality placements like the News Feeds. The lower quality, less engaged placements like the Audience Network are much, much lower priced.

However, high CPM doesn't always mean your ads are expensive. Low CPM doesn't always mean your ads are cheap. Ultimately, it's a measurement of relative cost, but you are more concerned about Cost per Result than most other stats.

## HOW TO VIEW REPORTING

You've already seen reports, but now you're going to make sense of them. It's that giant grid of numbers when you open up Ads Manager. The first thing you want to do is choose a date range that makes sense. If you're just starting out, choose Lifetime from the drop down in the top right corner of Ads Manager as shown in Figure 27–1 on page 345.

Once you've chosen a date range, you'll see a grid of campaigns and their results. At the top of the grid are dropdowns for Columns, Breakdown, and Reports. Columns allow you to turn on and off the columns of data that appear and to reorder them. Breakdown lets you add more rows of data. An example you'll see of a Breakdown is by date. Reports allow you to create very specific reports that can be used at any time. They aren't actually needed for day-to-day reporting.

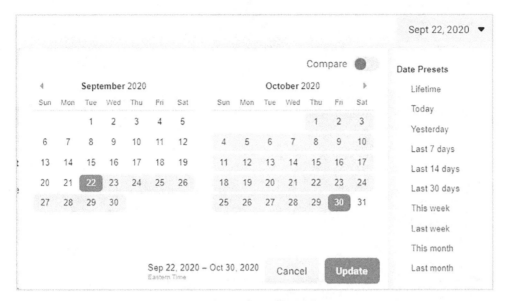

**FIGURE 27-1.** Choosing a Date

In addition to the default sets of columns, you can customize which columns show and in what order. You will usually take the Performance and Clicks report and slightly modify that. You can customize any set of columns by choosing Customize Columns from the bottom of the Columns dropdown as shown in Figure 27-2 on page 346.

Once you have the columns the way you like, check the box in the bottom left-hand corner labeled Save as preset. That way you can quickly get back to your favorite set of columns and quickly work with the data.

If you're not sure what a metric is, you can hover over it and you'll get a short description of what it means.

There are over 120 different columns of data for you and over 540 if you count all of the standard conversion events. That might be overwhelming, but only a few things are important to you in the beginning.

The first is your ad spend under the Amount Spent column.

Next are your Results. The type of result will vary by Campaign (Land Page Views, Reach, Leads, etc.). Facebook does the math for you and gives you a Cost per Result. Those are the most important columns. You can find them under the default column view of Performance.

Once you understand those, the next columns that are important are Reach, Frequency, CTR, and CPM. Reach and Frequency tell you how many people saw your ad. CTR is the clickthrough rate of your ad. It gives you an idea of how relevant your ad is to your audience. Finally, CPM tells you how much you're paying per 1,000 impressions and gives you a guide of what to expect.

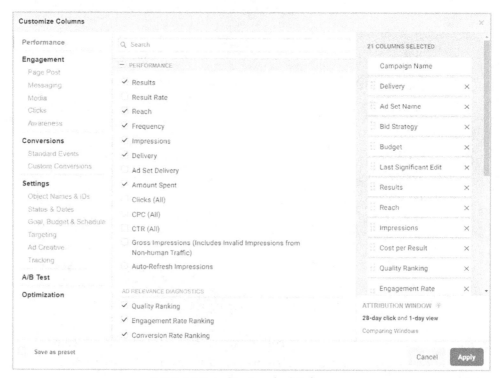

**FIGURE 27–2.** Customize Columns

You can look at reports at three levels. The Campaign, which gives you an overview of everything in it (all Ad Sets and all ads). Then Ad Set, which gives you more detailed view of the same numbers, and the Ad Level with the most specific data. All three levels can show you the same columns of data with more and more specific results.

The default column sets help show relevant columns for different types of campaigns. For example, the Engagement Column Set shows Reactions, Comments, Saves, Shares, and Page Likes from your ad. Those metrics only make sense if you're running a Post Engagement or Page Likes Campaign.

The Video Engagement Column Set shows data related to videos in ads. It only makes sense for ads with videos and at the ad level. It shows Impressions, Two-Second Video Views, Three-Second Video Views, Ten-Second Video Views, and ThruPlays (15+ second plays). It also shows Video Watches at 25 percent, 50 percent, 75 percent, 95 percent, and 100 percent (the entire video). As you can see, many times you switch from Ad to Campaign view and back to end up switching Column Sets to make sense of your data.

## THE BREAKDOWN DROPDOWN

The Breakdown Dropdown adds more rows of data by breaking up a line into smaller parts. The first use you'll have for this is to break down by Time as shown in Figure 27–3. It's useful to see patterns in how ads performed. Although it's interesting to break down a report by day, it's usually too small of a time frame to act on.

**FIGURE 27–3.** Breakdown Dropdown

Now you've seen how to slice and dice your data. When you're looking at a report, the first question you should ask yourself is, "Does this make sense? Based on what I know and what I assume to be true, does this jive?"

Next is, "Do I see anything I can act on?"

For example, you might notice that males never click or males never convert on your ads. Then it might make sense to eliminate males from your audience. Perhaps there's an age group that responds below your expectations such as 65+ or 13-to-18-year-olds don't convert.

You might also see that conversions always trail off at the end of the month. Perhaps you can focus your monthly budget the first three weeks of the month.

You can do a breakdown by Platform and Device. This gives you Facebook vs. Instagram as well as each placement. You'll find some placements significantly outperform others. That allows you to turn off the poor performers and create new optimized campaigns for the high performers. For example, you might notice your ads convert well on Facebook but not Instagram. You likely have to change up your creative on Instagram.

This is just the surface of what reporting and tracking can reveal to you.

## REPORTING IN ADS

Once you have at least 500 impressions, you can start to see your ranking compared to other ads with the same optimization goal which competed for the same audience. No two audiences are exactly the same, so all of these rankings are estimated.

The Ad Ranking is displayed as:

- Above average (top 45 percent of ads)
- Average (middle 35 to 55 percent of ads)
- Below average (bottom 35 percent of ads)
- Below average (bottom 20 percent of ads)
- Below average (bottom 10 percent of ads)

*Quality Ranking* measures an ad's perceived quality. It measures the post-click experience (landing page time on page and bounce rate) and the number of times your ad was hidden or reported and automatic assessments of clickbait, engagement bait, and other negative experiences that violate Facebook's Community Standards and Advertising Policies.

*Engagement Rate Ranking* measures post reactions, comments, shares, clicks, and interactions with your ad such as expanding an image or video to full screen. Facebook claims asking for likes and comments does not improve your ad's performance.

*Conversion Rate Ranking* measures how well your ad contributes to a conversion.

Both Engagement and Conversion rate ranking don't work with the optimization goals of ad recall lift, impressions, reach, and custom conversions because they don't make sense.

It's important to remember that no matter what your Ad Rankings, you're the final judge and *Cost per Result* is usually the most important metric. All of these rankings will help you understand where you might improve compared to the competition. Yet, the biggest metric to consider is, "Are you getting a cost per result that's reasonable for you?"

## OFFLINE EVENT REPORTING

You can upload and import events into your reporting if you also do business offline. You can use this to track in-store purchases, phone orders, or anything else that happens in the real world. Many new CRMs and point-of-sale systems link directly to Facebook to import the events.

If you want to import them manually, choose Offline Events under the Events Manager in the top navigation of your Business Manager account. From there, click on Add New Data Source, then Offline Event Set. Give it a name and a useful description. Once you do that, you can upload offline events.

After your offline event set is created, you can upload a CSV file that has info details of the events. Try to include all of the possible identifiers you have to help Facebook match the person in the file to its users. You can include Name, Email, Phone, Location, Age, and IDs. You'll need the time the event occurred, and finally some details of the event like an Order ID, Item Number, Event Name (Complete Registration, Contact, Donate, Lead, Purchase, etc.), and value.

Once you have the events set up, you can see them in your Facebook reporting. Change your Columns to Offline Conversions and you can see the real-world results from your Facebook Ads!

# Chapter 28

# How to Increase Conversions and Decrease Advertising Costs Over Time

Your advertising should get better and better with time. You do this by testing your ads. Testing is like flossing. Every smart advertiser knows they should do it, but very few people actually do. An advertiser of ordinary skill who relentlessly tests eventually beats almost everybody.

In this chapter, you're going to learn a simple methodology for testing your Facebook Ads to ensure your efforts are rewarded. You'll learn how to use the helpful tools Facebook has built into the Ad Manager interface to accomplish this with ease.

## WHAT TESTING CAN DO

Our client, Seniors in Service, wanted to test if they were reaching the right prospects with their Facebook Ads and see if they could get visitors to their website at a lower cost.

Their benchmark was a Traffic Campaign that was generating landing page visits at $1.44 per visitor. Their base audience was all people in Pasco County over the age of 55.

Their test involved loading a list of current volunteers into a Custom Audience on Facebook. Then they created a 10-percent Lookalike Audience from that list and ran the ad again to people in Pasco County over age 55, except that they limited the audience to only those people who were in their 10-percent Lookalike Audience.

The results were remarkable. For the same ad spend as their control, they were now producing landing page visitors at $0.51 each!

We recently ran a test inspired by the author and podcaster, Tim Ferriss. Tim tested the book title for his bestselling book, *The 4-Hour Workweek* (Harmony, 2009).

The story goes like this: The now-famous book title was the second-best headline they tested. The first one was *Drug Dealing for Fun and Profit,* a tongue-in-cheek name for what was essentially a book about outsourcing in a supplement business. Tim's book publisher said, "No way, Jose, we're not using that title." We bet they thought it would make for poor brand marketing.

They bickered back and forth about titles. Finally, Tim went to the court of last resort—real-world testing on real people. He posted book titles as Google Ads, and the phrase "4-Hour Work Week" magically spiked the response. He renamed his book and organized it around that concept. It became a *New York Times* bestseller because of the brand marketing approach used for the title.

So, when Perry began working on a new book, we mimicked that experiment, except this time on Facebook. We spent around $600 on various headlines and sub-headlines. The ultimate winner of the test and the title of Perry's new book is *Multiply by Subtracting: Accomplish More by Doing Less.*

## WHY TEST?

Testing parts of your Marketing Funnel makes them more efficient. The goal of testing is to get more results for the same amount of money or similar results for less money. Testing is like compounded interest. If you double your click-through rate, double your reach, and double your conversion rate, you don't double your results. You multiply it eight times over your original results!

Doubling your results in each step sounds difficult, but it's very common when you're starting out. You get there by breaking down your elements of your ad and systematically measuring, testing, and improving each step. Think about this fact: Even if you only improve 1 percent each day, by the end of a year you'll be 37 times better. Testing allows you to keep making improvements that pay off over time.

## ACHIEVING STATISTICAL SIGNIFICANCE

Imagine you toss a coin ten times and it comes up heads eight of the ten times. You certainly know that's possible, but you also know it should average out to heads only half of your attempts over time. If you had the patience to flip a coin 100 times, you know you would get heads pretty close to 50 times (half the time) vs. 80 times like your first try of 10 flips showed.

Statistical significance is achieved when you have enough results to accurately see the eventual pattern. With a coin, you know there are only two possible results. With an advertising test, you don't know which variation will win because there are multiple variables that affect the results.

In testing ads, you'll often find that just like your streak of eight heads, it's common for one part of the test to take an early lead, but then lose the overall test once enough results are produced.

Facebook recommends at least a four-day test for the most reliable results. If you aren't sure, start with seven days. In general, your test should run for at least one day. Normally it's not necessary to run a test longer than 30 days. Tests shorter than one day usually don't yield legitimately winning Ad Sets.

Facebook will suggest a budget for your test. You can ignore it until you create all the parts of your test. Then come back and adjust the date to at least four, but probably seven days. (Human behavior runs on a weekly cycle. Ads that win on weekdays don't necessarily win on weekends.) Then adjust your budget until you get an Estimated Test Power over 80 percent. An *Estimated Test Power* is Facebook's estimate of what it takes to determine a winner. The higher the number, the more likely it will find a winning result given your budget and time constraints. The more money you can use for the test, the quicker you can get a valid result.

## WHAT SHOULD YOU TEST?

Spend most of your testing efforts on visual elements like videos and images. Once you find a set of optimal imagery, then you can test the primary text, then start testing headlines, and finally the call-to-action buttons.

As our friend Dave Bullock says, "Test the forest, then the trees, then the branches, then the leaves." We frequently see people who test the color of a button rather than testing a completely different offer. In order to achieve the most success quickly, you have to test things that matter first, then worry about the smaller items.

True split tests simply did not exist within Facebook just a few years ago. However, Facebook currently has three ways you can test ads. We imagine they will produce even more ways as the platform develops. We'll walk through each of them.

## SETTING UP DYNAMIC CREATIVE TESTS

Facebook allows you to quickly test multiple elements of your ad creative with the Dynamic Creative feature. Facebook quickly selects which elements it thinks will do best based on past performance with the elements you choose and your audience criteria.

Since Facebook can pull results from all of the ads that have ever run on their platform, they have a very good idea of what works. You can leverage this data by letting Facebook choose the best elements and run them automatically for you.

Dynamic Creative tests all the major elements of an ad including the visual and call-to-action buttons. It works similar to Multiple Text Options where you add multiple options and Facebook chooses the ones it thinks best for each user. You can customize five parts of your ad for over 6000 possible combinations:

1. Headline (limit 5)
2. Images and/or Videos (limit 10)
3. Primary Text (limit 5)
4. Description (limit 5)
5. CTA Buttons (limit 5)

If you only have a few visual assets, this is a great way to test those.

Interestingly, to enable Dynamic Creative for your ad, you have to go to the Ad Set for the ad first and turn the feature on before the Dynamic Creative options become available.

Dynamic Creative will not work with asset customization where you edit your creative per placement, so you may only want to limit your testing it to a few placements that use the same creative style.

### How to Set Up Dynamic Creative Testing

To set up Dynamic Creative tests, toggle ON the switch for Dynamic Creative in your Ad Set.

Then go into your ad and you'll see one small difference under the media section. Instead of allowing you to use a single image or video, now you can upload up to ten, as shown in Figure 28–1 on page 355.

### Reporting on Dynamic Creative

You can see which elements got the most results by using the Breakdown feature of your ad reports like in Figures 28–2 on page 355 and 28–3 on page 356.

## SETTING UP MULTIPLE TEXT OPTION TESTS

The Multiple Text Option feature lets you test up to five different text versions for your ad's primary text, headline, and description for a single image or video. That's 125 totally

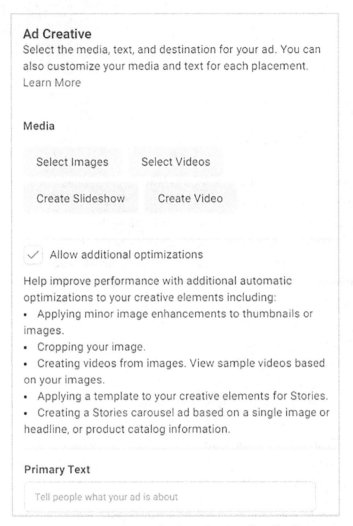

**FIGURE 28–1.** Dynamic Creative Media Choice

**FIGURE 28–2.** Breakdown by Dynamic Creative Asset

**FIGURE 28–3.** Dynamic Creative Test Results

different possible combinations! It's a great way to get started if you don't know what phrases and benefits will get results.

Once you add multiple text options, Facebook will show users the combination it thinks they will most likely respond to, based on what they know about the user's past behavior. Facebook knows which people are penny pinchers and respond to a discount, vs. someone who usually clicks on an ad that talks about speed.

The only thing to watch out for when using Multiple Text Options is that all your primary text and headline options have to make sense no matter what combination Facebook chooses. For example, if one of your headlines says, "Buy One, Get One Free" but then one of your primary text options says, "Everything 50 percent off," it wouldn't make sense to run them together.

You have to keep competing ideas in the same field. In this example, it makes sense to put all the discounts in the headline and leave the primary text for the benefits and not discounts. That way, Facebook can mix and match discounts with benefits for each viewer and still make sense of your ad. If you can only think of a few variations, use the headline because it has more effect on the ad.

### How to Set Up Multiple Text Options

When you create an ad, you have the link to Add Another Option below your Primary Text and Headline prompts, as seen in Figure 28–4 on page 357.

Once you add multiple text options, you can preview them by clicking View More Variations at the top of your ad preview, as shown in Figure 28–5 on page 358.

Everything will be reported as one ad. This is a quick and easy way to get started testing parts of your creative. It saves you from creating different ads to display different headlines and primary text to the same audience.

## PERFORMING A/B SPLIT TESTING

A/B split testing is a process that compares two campaigns that are identical except for one variable. To test that variable, Facebook will serve equal impressions to two unique

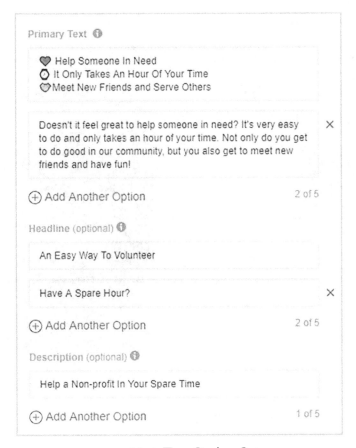

**FIGURE 28–4.** Text Option Setup

versions of your campaign with that one variable as the difference. Facebook will allow you to change more than one variable, but it is strongly recommended to only test one thing at a time.

So far, we've only talked about testing ads. In addition, Facebook also allows you to test placements and audiences with an A/B split test.

You can set up an A/B split test when you create a new campaign or set one up for an existing active Ad Set or ad.

## How to Create a Split Test of Your Creative

When you have a campaign with good results, you want to leave it alone. If you follow these steps to create a new split test, you'll create two new campaigns and leave the winning campaign undisturbed to keep running. First, select the ad you want to test and click the A/B Test button above the list of ads, as shown in Figure 28-6 on page 358.

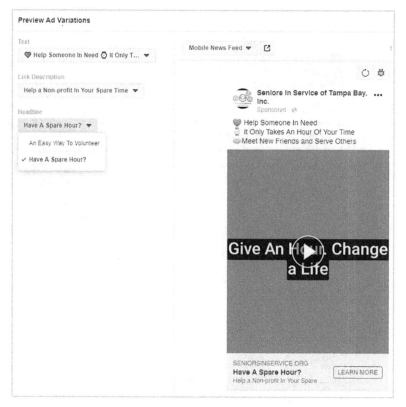

**FIGURE 28-5.** Multiple Text Option Preview

**FIGURE 28-6.** A/B Split Test Button

A new window will pop up asking you what variable you'd like to test. Choose Image, Video, or Ad Text. Once you select the creative element to test, a window will show up to allow you to update the creative element, as seen in Figure 28-7 on page 359. Your original ad is called the control. The new ad to test is called the variant.

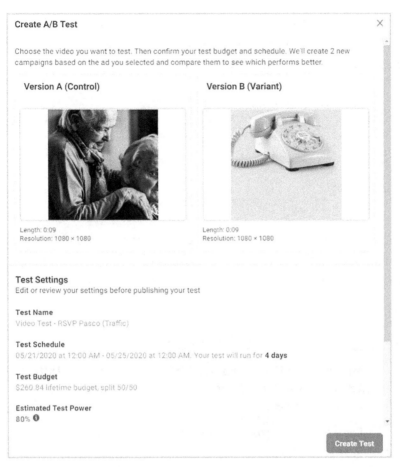

**FIGURE 28–7.** Create Variant

You'll see a recommended schedule. You can leave it at the recommended length or make it one week to avoid any day of week fluctuations. The Test Budget is listed. That is the amount of money Facebook thinks is needed to get a relevant result. The Estimated Test Power is Facebook's estimate of how likely the test will show a clear winner. The closer it is to 100 percent, the more likely a statistically significant winner will be found. However, the closer it is to 100 percent, the more budget is needed for the test.

Once you click Create Test, the campaigns will be created, and the new ad will be submitted for review. Once the ads run for their scheduled time frame, you can see if there is a clear winner.

As Facebook responds to more requests for testing functionality, both the Ad Set and ad split testing will get more variables to test. Please see the Resources at www.PerryMarshall.com/fbtools for updated info.

### Reviewing Split Testing Results

Once you have A/B tests running, you can see the results in the Experiments part of the top navigation, as shown in Figure 28–8.

**FIGURE 28–8.** Split Test Results

You can see that Facebook signifies an Ad Set in split test by placing a flask icon next to it. Once a winner is determined, you will see a golden badge. Here's what you see when you mouse over the badge in Figure 28–9.

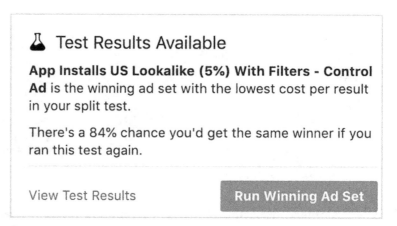

**FIGURE 28–9.** Split Test Results Badge

You can run the winning Ad Set right from there, or you can view the test result detail and see how it looks graphically as seen in Figure 28–10 on page 361.

Now you can confidently test your new ads without disturbing your existing campaign. In the next chapter, we'll dive into some common Facebook Advertising issues and how to troubleshoot them.

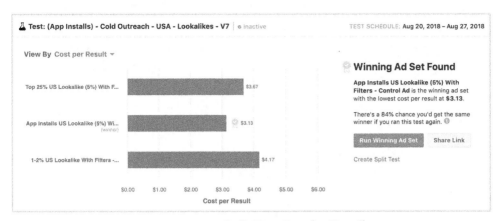

**FIGURE 28–10.** Split Test Results Detail

# Chapter 29

# Troubleshooting Common Facebook Advertising Issues

E very advertiser will have issues with their Facebook campaigns. We are part of several groups of highly experienced advertisers. In these groups, we often share issues we run into that we can't seem to solve. So, if it happens to experienced pros, it will happen to you.

Fortunately, there are some common issues that arise that we can help you with and you'll learn how to address these issues in this chapter.

We've also provided you a way to ask questions and get answers to issues you are having. Visit the Resources section at www.PerryMarshall.com/fbtools to learn about how we can help you.

## WHEN YOU'RE NOT SEEING CONVERSIONS REPORTED

The first common problem you may run into is not seeing results from your ads. This could mean you really have no results, or you simply have a technology problem. Let's start with the technology part. The first thing to check is your system that gets conversions. Check your shopping cart for sales. Check your email autoresponder or CRM for opt-ins or registrations. If you are seeing conversions there, then you know the issue is likely with Facebook technology.

Next, you want to check if you have the *correct* pixel installed on your site. Use the Facebook Pixel Helper Chrome extension and go to your confirmation page where a conversion would be tracked, as shown in Figure 29–1. Then, make sure the extension shows a pixel is on the page, as shown in Figure 29–2. Then match up that Pixel ID with the one in your Pixels Data Source.

**FIGURE 29–1.** Pixel ID in Business Manager

**FIGURE 29–2.** Pixel ID in Pixel Helper

Next, check that the page you consider a conversion is the same page you configured in the Ad Set as a conversion. There is an example in the Ad Set configuration in Figure 29–3 on page 365.

If you're not sure what is counted as a lead, you can go into your Pixel setup, click on the Lead event type, and click Manage, as shown in Figure 29–4 on page 365. That will show you exactly what counts as a Lead.

Once your Facebook setup looks right, now it's time to test the whole process. Go to an ad and preview it as shown in Figure 29–5 on page 366. Choose Preview on

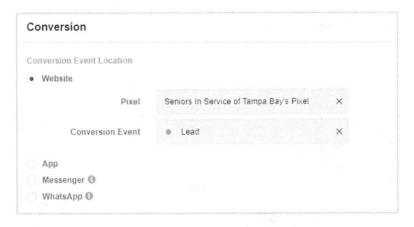

**FIGURE 29–3.** Ad Set Conversion Setup

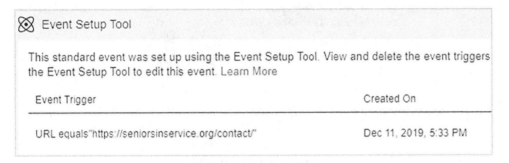

**FIGURE 29–4.** Pixel Event Setup

Device, then Send Notification to Facebook to check your phone to see if you got the ad.

Click on the ad and take the steps needed to convert. See if everything works. Try it again on your desktop and double-check everything with the Pixel Helper Chrome plugin.

If everything above checks out, then your technology is probably working. It's quite possible you don't have any conversions yet. This could simply be because it's too soon. The more likely response is your ad, landing page, and/or offer isn't good enough to get people to convert.

To summarize: If you are seeing conversions in your CRM or shopping cart, then you know it's a pixel issue. If you don't see conversions in your CRM and everything appears to be set up properly on Facebook, then the issue is that you just haven't had a conversion yet.

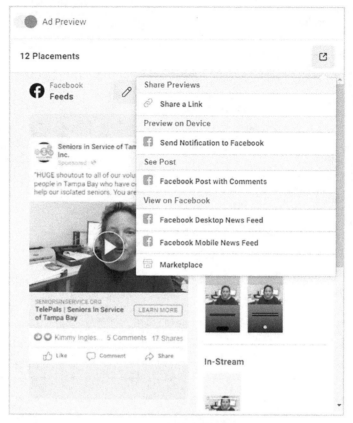

**FIGURE 29-5.** Ad Preview

## WHAT TO DO WHEN YOUR AD PERFORMANCE DECLINES, AKA AD FATIGUE

Ad fatigue happens when an ad that's doing well starts becoming more expensive and getting fewer results. There are two causes of ad fatigue. The first is that your ad has been seen too many times by the same people. The second is you've reached an unresponsive part of your audience. In reality, both of these are at play all the time.

You can monitor ad fatigue in the reporting section of Ad Manager. Look for the Frequency and Cost per Result columns. They're in the Performance and Clicks set of columns. If your Cost per Result is acceptable near the beginning of a campaign, but starts to creep up or even double, then you're most likely dealing with ad fatigue. You may see your frequency start to go up as well when you have a smaller audience.

Figure 29-6 on page 367 shows what ad fatigue looks like as we ran an App Install Campaign to a 1 percent Lookalike Audience of iPhone users only (the total reach of the entire audience was about 1.2 million users in total):

| Ad Name | | | Results | Amount Spent | Reach | Mobile App Installs | Cost per App Install | CPM (Cost per 1,000 Impressions | Frequency | Unique CTR (All) |
|---|---|---|---|---|---|---|---|---|---|---|
| | Fabian – No Trial Mentioned | | 5,011 Mobile Ap... | $14,733.18 | 626,404 | 5,011 | $2.94 | $13.38 | 1.76 | 2.10% |
| | 2018-10-11 – 2018-10-24 | | 1,070 | $2,359.47 | 127,165 | 1,070 | $2.21 | $12.88 | 1.44 | 2.03% |
| | 2018-10-25 – 2018-11-07 | | 1,074 | $2,743.00 | 155,934 | 1,074 | $2.55 | $13.29 | 1.32 | 1.73% |
| | 2018-11-08 – 2018-11-21 | | 1,815 | $5,827.71 | 280,489 | 1,815 | $3.21 | $14.88 | 1.40 | 1.88% |
| | 2018-11-22 – 2018-12-05 | | 1,007 | $3,600.00 | 246,456 | 1,007 | $3.57 | $11.76 | 1.24 | 1.07% |
| | 2018-12-06 – 2018-12-19 | | 45 | $203.00 | 13,926 | 45 | $4.51 | $14.58 | 1.00 | 0.95% |
| > | Results from 1 ad | | 5,011 Mobile App I... | $14,733.18 Total Spent | 626,404 People | 5,011 Total | $2.94 Per Action | $13.38 Per 1,000 Im... | 1.76 Per Person | 2.10% Per Person |

**FIGURE 29–6.** Ad Fatigue (Increasing Cost Per Install)

Note the ramp-up period in October where the Clickthrough Rate (CTR) was over 2 percent and Cost Per App Install is $2.21. Then as we moved forward through November and into December, we were reaching more people, but our Cost Per App Install exceeded $3 and climbed all the way up to $4.51 and CTR fell below 1 percent before we killed the ad. In this case, frequency was not an issue.

We were able to reach just over 50 percent of the entire audience and overall, we were able to run for two months. The Cost Per App Install averaged out to $2.94, which is just under the $3 targeted threshold we agreed on with the client.

Ad fatigue is going to be a factor for anyone advertising to a limited-size audience (even an audience of 1 million can be considered limited when you are spending $15,000 a day). Local businesses are going to run into this because they can only market to those around their location. They don't have the advantage of a national or global audience with plenty of people to reach.

You can visualize your ads responsiveness as a set of concentric circles with the most responsive users in the center and the least responsive to the outer edge as you can see in Figure 29–7 on page 368.

In the Learning Phase of your campaign, Facebook learns what part of your audience is most responsive and shows to those people first. Then it starts showing to people slightly less likely to respond and keeps showing ads to people less and less likely to respond (while simultaneously showing the ad to people who have seen it before).

Given enough time and budget, Facebook will theoretically try to show your ad to every person in the audience you defined. However, there's a law of diminishing returns and it will never truly show to everybody. As your ad is shown to more responsive people more than once, your Ad Frequency increases and it dramatically increases your Cost per Result since fewer conversions take place.

The general rule to follow is that you increase your budget when there's an increased urgency needed for result. If you can afford less urgency, then lowering your budget will help a lot.

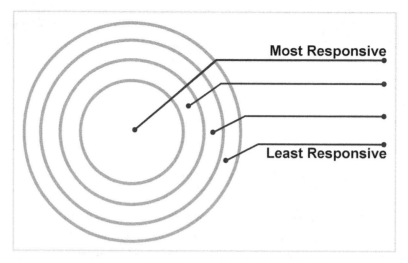

**FIGURE 29–7.** Ad Responsiveness Visualization

In the example in Figure 29–7, our determination was we reached as many of the most responsive members of the audience as we could, and we were now moving to the outer edges for the promotion. Therefore, we stopped the ad and wrote a new offer.

## COMBATTING AD FATIGUE

Budget and audience size determine how quickly your ads fatigue.

You can quickly overwhelm an audience by using too large of a budget for your given audience size. If you are limited to smaller audiences (less than 1 million), no matter how much you increase the budget, you will not get better performance. If your audience is only 100,000 or even 10,000, your likelihood of seeing ad fatigue multiplies significantly.

So, first try to back off the budget. If you have an audience of say 100,000 people and you are spending $100 per day, try to reduce your daily budget by 20 percent every few days until you see the results level off.

Using Lookalike Audiences is also a nice secret way to combat ad fatigue. Facebook tells us that the users within a Lookalike Audience change about 30 percent over a given month. That means in a 1-percent Lookalike Audience in the U.S., about 20,000 new people appear in the audience each day. That's enough to keep your frequency low and combat ad fatigue all on its own.

Increasing the percentage is also a great way to expand your audience. However, remember the Rings of Response and the 10-percent audience will not perform as well as the 1- to 2-percent audience.

We personally have several accounts we manage where we're using Lookalike Audiences with $10/day budgets and they've been running at about the same level of performance for over three years!

Obviously, changing up your creative when ad fatigue sets in is a surefire way to never have ad fatigue, even though that can be cumbersome.

Let's talk about a few more ideas to help you try and limit how many times you have to completely change your ad.

One way is to have multiple ads in your Ad Set. Try using the exact same ad copy but use a different thumbnail for your video or a different still image. The difference can be small. It can be the background color or rearranging the elements in the graphic. However, remember that Facebook will eventually find the ad that works the best and show that one most often. That defeats your ability to use this strategy over time.

Yet another way is to use the Dynamic Creative option and let Facebook mix-and-match elements to keep the ads fresh for your Audience.

Another way we've solved this problem is to run ads on a schedule. Either show the ad on selected days per week or run an ad for two weeks and take a week off to give the Audience a break. A car engine won't last long if you redline the engine, and neither will your ads.

## WHAT TO DO WHEN YOUR CAMPAIGN COSTS ARE TOO HIGH

Costs should always be evaluated in light of your Campaign Objective. It's pointless to fret over click costs when your objective is conversions. So, when evaluating costs, make sure you are optimizing for the proper objective.

Next, you should check your ad's Quality Ranking. These columns are available on the Reporting interface. You can customize your view by adding these columns or by selecting the Performance set of columns, as seen in Figure 29–8. Relevance Score is still being shown to Advertisers, but we've been told this could be eliminated at any time.

| Amount Spent | Link Clicks | CPC (Cost per Link Click) | Website Purchases | Website Purchases Conversion | Relevance Score | Quality Ranking Ad Relevance Di... | CTR (All) | Impressions | CPM (Cost per 1,000 Impressions |
|---|---|---|---|---|---|---|---|---|---|
| $93.91 | 6 | $15.65 | 12 | $1,157.69 | 3 | Below average Bottom 20% of ... | 0.16% | 12,408 | $7.57 |
| $92.74 | 7 | $13.25 | 5 | $346.53 | 2 | Below average Bottom 20% of ... | 0.22% | 7,853 | $11.81 |
| $93.91 | 7 | $13.42 | 3 | $374.91 | — | — | 0.28% | 4,703 | $19.97 |
| $97.19 | 17 | $5.72 | — | $0.00 | 4 | Below average Bottom 35% of ... | 0.27% | 24,159 | $4.02 |
| $378.00 Total Spent | 37 Total | $10.22 Per Action | 20 Total | $1,879.13 Total | | | 0.23% Per Impre... | 49,158 Total | $7.69 Per 1,000 Im... |

**FIGURE 29–8.** Performance Columns—Quality Rankings

Quality Ranking is an estimated score of your ad's perceived quality. Facebook measures quality using feedback on your ads and what happens after they click. Then your ad is ranked against other ads that competed for the same audience.

This is useful, but not entirely scientific. A poor-quality ad often leads to more cost. Remember, you learned in Chapter 8 that the Auction works by showing ads that have the most total value with:

- A higher CTR on your ad than Facebook expects.
- A higher engagement on your ad than Facebook expects.
- A higher bid.

A low-quality ad will have a lower CTR than Facebook expects and/or a lower engagement than Facebook expects. Therefore, to show your ad, Facebook will need to get more budget from you to win an auction. You are getting fewer impressions for more cost, which will drive up your ad costs.

In the example above, you might be alarmed at the high CPC, low CTR, and poor ad quality; however, the only cost you should care about with this set of ads is the Return on Ad Spend (ROAS), which is a phenomenal 5 to 1. The client is making $5 for every dollar they spend!

The next thing to check when your costs are too high is your audience.

Large audiences tend to have lower costs than smaller, restricted audiences. When you give Facebook enough of a sample size to work with, it lowers the CPM and it's more likely that Facebook will find your ideal responders, which always cost less.

Sometimes, though, a large audience isn't the right audience. You may need to evaluate that your audience (no matter the size) is the right fit for the offer you are placing in front of them.

A good offer in front of the wrong audience will lack conversions and drive up CPC and CPS.

Last, you always need to check your offer and landing page. Perhaps everything looks good on Facebook in terms of cost, but your conversions are low and your CPR is high. In this case, you want to put the heat on your offer and landing page and see if there's anything about it that might be off.

If you feel you have the right audience and the right creative, then you need to try testing different offers and test modifications to your landing page. Just make sure you only test one thing at a time so you know what variable is affecting results the most.

## WHAT TO DO WHEN THERE ARE LOW (OR NO) IMPRESSIONS OF YOUR AD

If you are not setting robust impressions of your ad, check three things:

1. Is your audience large enough? If it's below 5,000 people, you might need to expand it. Also check that you haven't inadvertently used an Exclude option with any part of your audience that is preventing it from showing. For example, are you targeting everyone that has bought from you in the past 90 days but excluding visitors to the site in the last 90 days? Don't laugh—it happens to the best of us!

2. Is your budget large enough? You may not have given Facebook enough budget for your ads to compete in the auction. Try to nudge up your budget by 20 percent and see if that helps.

3. Is your ad quality poor? Although this will not prevent an ad from completely showing, a poorly performing ad with a competitive audience will get significantly fewer impressions than an average to above-average ad.

## WHAT TO DO WHEN YOU HAVE AN AD DISAPPROVED

No one likes being called to the principal's office for violating the rules.

Facebook calls you to the principal's office when you do something that violates their advertising policies. You should most definitely review this policy, even if you are in a business that is not "questionable."

We have a link to the most current Advertising Policy on our Resource page at www.PerryMarshall.com/fbtools.

We're sure that most of you intend to follow the rules and are not trying to game the system. So, all of you will have ads disapproved at times for rules that we've unintentionally broken.

Facebook will give you some insight as to why your ad was disapproved and also provide a way for you to easily appeal. Here's an example in Figure 29–9:

**FIGURE 29–9.** Ad Disapproval Reason

This is a typical violation people in the marketing space often see. Sometimes Facebook's bot doesn't understand your intent and you get misclassified. So, in this case, the ad was not promoting what Facebook thought it was. In fact, this ad was pointing out faults with get-rich-quick schemes. Our appeal was approved, and the ad began running.

There are also lists of things you just cannot do on Facebook.

Be sure to review the list of 30+ areas of Prohibited Content in the Ads Policy that you can never promote.

You also cannot discriminate in your targeting audiences, especially for ads dealing with housing, credit, or employment. While you can target audiences to match a product, these are areas Facebook singles out because of federal law.

There are over a dozen areas of restricted content you can use with very specific rules or permission such as alcohol, financial products, social issues, politics, cryptocurrencies, and weight loss.

All forms of over-personalization will trigger a disapproval. Don't imply you know the person by saying something like, "Going bald?" or "Recently divorced?" Facebook is super-targeted, but they don't like you to remind their users of that.

Another form of personalization that triggers a lot of disapproval is the overuse of the word "you." Facebook doesn't like it when you use the word "you" and "your" because it over-personalizes your ad. In copywriting, you are taught to do this. However, on Facebook you need to do the opposite.

Other common reasons your ad might get disapproved:

- *Too much text in your images.* Excessive text in your ad images may trigger this.
- *Your ad copy isn't consistent with the offer on your landing page.* Don't think you can trick Facebook by writing an ad about saving money for college and then sending them to a page about cryptocurrency investments. Their bot technology can sniff this out rather easily.
- *Asking for very personal information in an ad.* Avoid asking about information related to race, sexual orientation, account numbers, health information, and more.
- *Copyright infringements or use of brand logos or names to imply an endorsement.* This especially includes Facebook and Instagram. Also, never abbreviate Facebook in an ad using their stock symbol, FB. In fact, you'd be wise to avoid using the words Facebook or Instagram in any ad because it often triggers a manual review.
- *Non-functioning web pages or non-compliant landing pages.* This happens when your website is temporarily down or if your website is missing things like a privacy policy or uses pop-up windows.
- *Showing before and after photos.* This is another example of a great marketing principle that works in other media but is not allowed on Facebook.

You can often clear up the disapproval by changing the part of your ad that triggered it. Simply make the change and select Publish It.

If you are unable to figure out what the issue is, submit an appeal. If you are still not approved, it's best to chat with Facebook Support and see if they give you any more information.

The best advice is to have the mindset that Facebook reserves the right to determine if they are right. It's their platform and you're trying to use it. It will never help to argue with them. Always keep your composure in your correspondence. Be polite, because the rep on the other side of the chat or email is only following procedures. They can be your advocate if you can clearly and calmly show them how they misunderstand your intentions.

## WHAT TO DO WHEN YOU HAVE ADS STUCK IN REVIEW

Ads typically get approved by Facebook quickly. It won't surprise you to note that they use automated rules and bots to review each part of your ad. They review all the text, review your landing page, and review your images (yes, they have automated image bots)!

It's frustrating to wait more than a couple hours for an ad to be approved and you still see the status of In Review. Ads stuck in review aren't actually stuck. The ads are actually placed in a queue for a human being from Facebook to manually review. Depending on how big the queue has become determines how long you will wait.

There's a few reasons why they might be delaying your ad's approval.

All new accounts must develop trust with Facebook. All new accounts will automatically get their ads placed in manual review. Over time, depending on factors we are not privy to, your account will become trusted and they will allow your ad to be approved by automated means.

Some other reasons your ad will be manually reviewed could be your reputation. Yes, a bad reputation will follow you. Every account has a reputation with Facebook. There are accounts they trust and accounts they don't. New accounts aren't trusted, and neither are accounts that routinely get ads disapproved. This is just like the child who obeys the rules and gets a later curfew than their sibling who pushes the obedience limit with their parents. So, try and be a good advertiser and get a great reputation with Facebook.

Ads will also get stuck in review if the automated bot detects something. It might be a questionable image you use (showing blood, skin, and other things they highly regulate). It might also be a phrase or a single word in your headline or primary text.

If your ad is stuck in review for more than 24 hours (and Facebook is very strict on this), you can submit your ad to be quickly reviewed by using a special form. We've placed a link to that support form on our Resource page at www.PerryMarshall.com/fbtools.

# Chapter 30

# Taking Scary Steps When the Bridge Isn't Yet Visible

There's a very powerful scene in the movie, *Indiana Jones & The Last Crusade*. Indiana has a great chasm to cross and the only way across is a bridge that can only be used after a leap of faith. The bridge is completely invisible. For the bridge to appear, Indiana must step off the cliff and have faith that he will land on solid footing even though it's invisible to the eye.

We all know what happens. Despite his fear, Indiana took that leap!

Indiana is a fictional type of hero who can make a leap of faith like that, but some of the entrepreneurs I know are real heroes, too. I see entrepreneurs making leaps of faith all the time. It's hard-wired into our DNA. I think it's a good exercise to list out all your leaps of faith in the past. Here are some of mine:

- Taking my first basketball coaching gig at age 16.
- Taking a full-time job overnights in college.
- Becoming a parent.
- Leaving a well-paying job and contract gig to start my own company.
- Attending expensive marketing events and joining high-priced mastermind groups before I had the money to justify it.

- Stepping on a stage in front of 300 people for the first time ever and teaching them about generating leads.
- Writing and self-publishing my first book.
- Hiring my full-time employees for the first time.
- Starting a radio show.
- Resurrecting my agency after my failures.

In all these cases when I took the leap, the bridge appeared. I overcame my lack of experience. I got over my anxiety of not feeling qualified. The resources (money) I needed to make some of these things work showed up only after I took the step.

Entrepreneurs are heroes. Who is going to take that leap of faith?

There are people waiting for you to traverse that chasm so they can follow you on their path. They need a hero like you to show them the way. Take that leap and trust the ground under you will be solid footing!

In this book , we've given you the tools to confidently generate traffic from Facebook Ads with enough strategies and advice to help you compete with the biggest advertisers.

Whether you turn this information into success for your own campaigns or apply this toward your career as a paid expert to manage clients' campaigns, you have the tools to succeed.

Speaking of clients, keep this in mind. When you develop the skills and reputation as a master craftsman in the world of customer acquisition, especially focusing on the digital marketing world specializing in channels like Facebook and Instagram, you become very valuable.

There are tons of opportunities to build a consulting business, an agency, or become a digital marketing guru or Facebook Ads specialist inside a fast-growing company. Just go to Upwork and do a few searches to discover all the wanted ads for this in-need position.

If you want to jump into a hot market, build a consulting business, and take control of your own destiny, then we say jump in and do it!

If you would like some help becoming a master craftsman, or if you would like to send some of your team members or employees through our more advanced training programs, workshops, or video courses, then we'd love to help you. Visit www.PerryMarshall.com/fbtools to learn more.

And if you want to take what you learned from this book and start pounding the pavement on your own, then we encourage you to do that, too. Just get started, baby!

# Major Facebook Ad Updates that Experienced Advertisers Need to Know

A
s with most things, the internet and technology change and evolve quickly. Facebook has changed quite a bit since the third version of this book was published in 2017.

Certainly, the Facebook News Feed and app looks (and functions) differently today. For our purposes, let's focus on what changes impact advertisers the most.

If you're currently advertising on Facebook, you probably try to keep track of what's new in Facebook Ads. In this appendix, we'll explain some of the most important changes that Facebook Advertisers need to know.

Let's start by looking at what we feel are the most critical changes in three main areas.

## PRIVACY, TRANSPARENCY, AND TARGETING

The major changes in privacy, transparency, and targeting include:

- Transparency of political, social, and election ads
- Ad transparency for Facebook users
- Financial and health claims
- Targeting restrictions
- Removal of third-party partners

- Restrictions on housing, credit, and employment ads
- Removal or restriction of other targeting options

Regulations and restrictions need to be implemented when a few rogue advertisers cannot police themselves. There are always loopholes and ambiguities in new systems. Facebook was still fairly green as an advertising medium even three years ago. There were many opportunities for advertisers to grab power, influence, and profit at the expense of the user.

Many of the new Advertising policies are reactions (and arguably over-reactions) to issues that Facebook became aware of through whistle blowers and government agencies.

The biggest scandal occurred in March of 2018 when the story broke about political data firm Cambridge Analytica admitting to collecting data on 87 million Facebook users. The data had enough details to create profiles of the users with their location so the firm could create more effective political ads to sway voters. The scandal eventually led to Mark Zuckerberg testifying in front of the U.S. Congress.

This one event is the single most impactful change to Facebook's advertising platform since the advent of the News Feed ad and Retargeting Pixel. It has changed everything for Facebook and for us advertisers. It removed many powerful targeting options and protected users' privacy from third party apps.

Let's dig into these changes a bit more.

## TRANSPARENCY OF POLITICAL, SOCIAL, AND ELECTION ADS

In addition to the data scandal, there have been all kinds of reports and accusations that implicate the Russian government for using Facebook Ads to influence the 2016 U.S. presidential election. Users were deceived by advertisements that appeared to them as news, but instead were political ads with an agenda. For this reason, Facebook has added several restrictions to be able to run ads within these categories.

Restrictions and regulations vary by country, but in the United States, any advertisers running ads about social issues, elections, or politics are required to complete an authorization process where Facebook verifies your personal identity.

Then, when you run ads in these categories, you have to disclose the name of the person or entity that paid for the ad, plus your ads will be stored in the Facebook Ad Library for up to seven years.

To learn more, visit Facebook's help section: https://www.facebook.com/business/help and search for "Political Ads."

### Ad Transparency for Facebook Users

All ads now have a level of transparency. First, all ads are marked as sponsored in some way. Secondly, every user has the ability to click Why Am I Seeing This Ad? on every ad they see, plus view an Ad Library for that advertiser by visiting their Facebook Page and clicking the Page Transparency link.

Users also have the ability to see what personal data advertisers have access to, plus see which advertisers have uploaded their name and demographic data to Custom Audiences. You can see this for yourself if you click on the Help icon on the Facebook App and select Privacy Checkup.

This is also the place where users can now clear history just like they can for their internet browser. When the news of this first broke, advertisers were in a panic. In our opinion, this is nothing to be concerned about. First, the option isn't very easy to find. Secondly, the number of users who care about this and will do this on a regular basis are minuscule. Most people will continue to use the app as they always have and don't give a thought about what Facebook has tracked about them and shared with advertisers.

## Financial and Health Claims

If you are in these markets, you are already on guard for making claims about financial and health-related products and services.

One of the changes is that Facebook is now employing fact checkers who not only have the ability to get your account banned, but also place a huge disclaimer over your paid *and* organic posts about any claims of financial or health benefits if your claims cannot be verified by the fact checker.

People can report your post as such, and it will essentially get your post removed and risk getting you banned from Facebook.

One specific area that Facebook will not allow any ads for are anything to do with cryptocurrency or other speculative financial instruments.

## Targeting Restrictions

There are three major changes to targeting as a result of the scandals and misdeeds by advertisers:

1. *Third-party data from companies like Acxiom and Epsilon that used to be natively available inside the Ad Set are no longer available.* An example of this was once being able to target someone with over $150,000 in income, who owned a house worth over $500,000, had over $1 million in net worth, was married, and just bought a new BMW. If you didn't realize, this was not data Facebook collected from its users. Rather, it supplemented its data from these firms that had the ability to match it up to every user. This was a dream for advertisers because it allowed micro-level targeting and allowed us to target affluent buyers specifically and eliminate those with lower income. As you can

imagine, this would lead to some extremes for advertisers who were advertising real estate, financial products, credit offers, and employment. Please note, however, that Facebook will still allow you to use highly detailed consumer data from companies like Acxiom by working with them directly and utilizing Custom Audiences that they provide you.

2. *You must declare if an ad will contain offers for housing, credit, or employment.* If you do not do this and Facebook's A.I. detects you are running ads without declaring it, your ads will be disabled and you risk getting your Ad Account banned. Civil rights activists threatened lawsuits against Facebook when they learned about the ability to narrowly target and discriminate with these types of offers. As a result, when you run ads in these categories, you will not be allowed to target by age, gender, ZIP code, cultural affinity, or any interests describing or appearing to relate to characteristics protected by civil rights legislation.

3. *Removal or restriction of other targeting options.* Advertisers have seen a significant decrease in their ability to target smaller, niche interests when building audiences. We've also seen huge changes in our ability to target based on things like job title and function. Some of these things reappear in some form and some go away for good.

Facebook is pushing more and more of their advertisers to move away from Interests and shift toward Lookalike Audiences and Custom Audiences. We've covered these extensively in this book, so rather than complain about what we lost, we're going to show you how to leverage these so that you gain an advantage over other advertisers who are lost without the former abilities.

## PLATFORM AND INTERFACE CHANGES

There have been a few changes to the platform and interface that affect advertisers.

### Campaign Budget Optimization (CBO)

As we discuss in Chapter 9, CBO was set to become a default setting for managing campaign budgets, but as of this printing it is an option. You can set budgets at the campaign level or the ad set level depending on your strategy.

### Facebook Pixel Interface and Integration

Facebook has made integrating their Pixel into your apps and website much less technical. There are many partners like Shopify, Wordpress, and Zapier that allow non-technical advertisers to install and manage their Pixel.

Additionally, the Event Setup Tool helps you visually select events on your website that need to be tracked without having to manually insert code into the page for every event.

### Decommissioning of the Power Editor

Most notable to most advertisers is the decommissioning of the Power Editor, a significant move by Facebook. For those of you who are new Advertisers, Power Editor was a tool that you could use instead of Ads Manager. The current Ads Manager interface is based on a great deal of the Power Editor's functionality.

Fortunately, those who used Power Editor had an easy transition due to the many things Facebook borrowed from that tool to use in the new Ads Manager.

It's impossible to count how many cosmetic and functional changes we have seen in the Ads Manager interface since 2017.

It's most important to realize that it's our job to stay ahead of these changes and maintain a critical advantage over our competitors. For the most part, every change to the interface is for a good reason even if it temporarily throws us off our game for a while.

Personally, we think the interface has gotten significantly more efficient over the years. Things are better organized, and the performance and speed have greatly improved. It has also become far easier to manage your business in the Business Manager function, and it's become more beneficial for social-media agencies that serve several clients at once.

## PLACEMENTS AND MEDIA

The big shifts in placements and media are:

- Shift to mobile
- The rise of Instagram and Facebook Messenger (and other placements)
- Proliferation of video and Video Ads

During my (Bob's) 2016 visit to Facebook Ad Headquarters (which you read about earlier), there were about 100 large brand advertisers surrounding me with $1,000,000+ ad budgets (many of the brands we'd all recognize). In addition, all of the important VPs were there from Facebook and Instagram. I spent about 45 minutes with the lead engineer of the Facebook Ad platform. During that time, I was able to sit with him and show him some unusual quirks of the ad platform I discovered. Would you believe they actually took my feedback and rolled that into an update shortly thereafter?

There were three significant points of emphasis at that meeting which now in 2020 have certainly come to fruition.

### Shift to Mobile

The first emphasis was the shift of Facebook's user base to mobile. We already mentioned it, but it bears repeating that over 93 percent of Facebook's activity is on mobile phones this year.

Facebook owns the mobile phone.

It is mission critical for advertisers to not only design their ads for mobile users, but it's even more important that they check every page of their website to be sure it's mobile-responsive and mobile-friendly.

Nothing will kill a conversion faster than a slow, unoptimized landing page.

Focusing on mobile platforms is also a mindset shift. People's attention on mobile phones is significantly shorter than a desktop. Brevity is rewarded. When you learned about the Deep Funnel concept, you discovered how critical it is you understand not only the device the user is using, but where they are in the buying cycle.

There are ad formats and sizes that significantly outperform on mobile vs. desktop and it's our job as advertisers to know this and leverage it.

### The Rise of Instagram and Facebook Messenger (and Other Placements)

The second big emphasis at that meeting was informing us of how Facebook was running out of space on the News Feed. They couldn't squeeze in any more ads without diminishing the user experience, so the fallout would be greater competition in the ad auction and increased advertising costs.

What they had planned, of course, was to also find new places to push ads, which launched things like the Audience Network, Messenger Ads, Video Insertions, and more. After all, they had to satisfy the demand for space for advertisers because they were waving dollar bills at Facebook asking them to spend it for them!

#### Instagram

Certainly, Instagram was a priority for Facebook since they purchased it in 2012.

What you need to remember as an advertiser is that Instagram is embedded into the ad interface.

It's a significant source of traffic which is in many aspects different from Facebook traffic. Therefore, you need to consider your creative ad approach on Instagram differently from Facebook.

Just like you need to shift your mindset for mobile users, you also have to consider that Instagram is a highly visual medium rather than text, and it's skewed toward a younger demographic that tilts more in favor of women vs. men.

I see far too many advertisers blindly run the same type of ad on Facebook and Instagram and bemoan that one of the platforms significantly underperforms the other.

Ad Manager now provides tools within the interface to customize almost every aspect of your ad for each platform and placement you choose to run on. This is an advantage smart Facebook Advertisers take.

### Facebook and Instagram Stories

In an effort to compete with Snapchat, Facebook introduced Stories into its apps and opened up this space to advertisers as well.

Like Instagram, Stories are unique from the News Feed, and you should be using different creative and strategies on Stories Ads vs. other types of placements.

### Facebook Messenger and WhatsApp

Messenger apps were all the rage in 2019.

Facebook became a major force in the messaging space and placed significant emphasis on growing the use of these apps on their platform.

Per their custom, Facebook opened up spaces on these apps to advertisers and launched a whole new rage called Messenger Bots.

### *Video and Video Ads*

The third emphasis, and by far the most impactful to me, was that all of the Facebook VP presentations included strong statements about their emphasis on video. If you look at the News Feed today, and you look at Instagram and Stories, it's all driven by video.

As Facebook matures even more over the next three years, we can expect to see even more proliferation of video and video tools to help people communicate their story more effectively.

## CONCLUSION

Change is inevitable. Change in the technology and marketing space is rapid and unsettling. However, those who embrace this and keep their knowledge and skills in sync with the changes will win.

Your job is *not* to keep up with every small change made by Facebook (in fact, trying to do so will hurt you more than help you), but rather to understand and have the discernment to understand which changes benefit small advertisers like us and which changes simply allow the big brands to spend more money.

This book is about giving you an advantage over your competitors and succeeding where others stay stagnant. Embracing changes to Facebook will make you a better and more competitive advertiser.

# Acknowledgments

'd like to thank Perry Marshall for trusting me with the honorable task of writing this fourth edition. Perry is a true friend and mentor. I love him like a brother.

A big thank you to Mark Ingles, who was my key contributor for this book. Mark and I spent months of time together over Zoom and worked long days and nights to produce this product. We are very proud of this edition and I am forever indebted to my dear friend Mark for his selfless act of service to this work.

I want to thank my brother and partner in crime, Brandon Boyd, for his loyal friendship and encouragement through the highs and lows of running a business.

Thank you to Matt Gillogly and Mark Imperial, who partnered with me on many projects over the years.

Thank you to my mentors over the years Bill Glazer, Dan Kennedy, Rob Berkley (rest in peace, my brother), and Vivian Hearn.

Many clients and business friends have encouraged me over the years: Bill Bodri, Ali Brown, Ari Galper, Robert Skrob, Nate Hagerty, Victor Cheng, Stuart Jordan, Gary Wilson, Jeff Walker, Ryan Deiss, Josh Long, Brian Kurtz, Adam McCarthur, Justin Sterenberg, Melissa Brummerstedt, Dawn Lyle, Brian Regnerus, Shannon McCaffrey, Carla Garter, and David Nadler.

Thank you to many loyal clients who have trusted my skills for many years such as: Dan Dunne, JD and Amy Crouse, Sander Cohen, Les Cseh, Mike Cohen, Shanyn Stewart, Mark McShurley, Brady Roberts, Steven Shuel, Debbie Phillips, and Elvira Lang.

I want to thank my parents, Bob and Ruth, for always encouraging me to do my best and always valuing family and experiences over possessions.

Finally, I want to thank my lovely daughters, Bethany and Anna, who are going to conquer the world. And much love and thanks to my best friend and lifetime partner, Arlene, who has stood by me for 33 years and counting. I love you and look forward to many more amazing experiences in life with you!

—Bob Regnerus

# About the Authors

## PERRY MARSHALL

Perry Marshall is one of the most expensive business advisors in the world.

His book *Ultimate Guide to Google Ads* is the world's bestselling book on internet advertising. It laid the foundations for the $100 billion pay-per-click industry.

His reinvention of the Pareto Principle is published in *Harvard Business Review*. NASA's Jet Propulsion Labs uses his 80/20 Curve as a productivity tool. He has a degree in Electrical Engineering and lives with his family in Chicago.

Marketing maverick Dan Kennedy says, "If you don't know who Perry Marshall is, unforgivable. Perry's an honest man in a field rife with charlatans."

## BOB REGNERUS

Bob Regnerus is the cofounder of Feedstories, a video sales and marketing agency that turns stories into sales. Since 1998, he has been successfully helping his clients achieve more impact, traffic, and sales through digital media and storytelling. Over time, he developed Deep Funnel Marketing™

strategies to maximize his clients' impact in their marketplace even as new media comes online and tactics have evolved.

Bob has personally served hundreds of clients. He has spoken in 27 states, hosted a radio show on AM560-WIND in Chicago, written six books, and trained tens of thousands. Ninety-nine percent of his clients come to him via referral or after seeing one of his presentations.

Bob has had the opportunity to work with a number of remarkable individuals and companies over the years, including companies like Transunion, Miracle-Ear, Ali Brown, Dan Kennedy, Bill Glazer, Perry Marshall, Golf Academies of America, Weiss Research, HealthSource, Agora Publishing, Bolder Band Headbands, and Dartmouth College. There are hundreds more he has worked with in some capacity to help grow their businesses.

In his personal life, Bob is a husband to his high school sweetheart and a dad to two amazing daughters. He is currently a sophomore boys high school basketball coach and has been coaching boys and girls from ages 6 to 18 for 35 years. He is also a passionate Chicago Blackhawks and White Sox fan.

You can contact Bob for speaking opportunities or media inquiries at Feedstories.com.

## THOMAS MELOCHE

Thomas Meloche was a cofounder of Menlo Innovations LLC, a company made world famous in the bestselling book *Joy Inc., How We Built a Workplace People Love* (Portfolio, 2013). A graduate of the University of Michigan with a degree in electrical and computer engineering, Thomas focused early in his career on people and methodology.

Now running the consulting firm A2Agile, Thomas has assisted many of the world's largest firms, bringing to them four-fold productivity growth and happier employees. You can learn more about how at TomMeloche.com.

## MARK INGLES

Mark Ingles was a key contributor to this book. Like Perry, Mark has an engineering degree and then discovered direct response marketing. Mark has spent his own money on direct response marketing since his introduction to it from Perry in 2003. He ran a printing business for 16 years where he used online marketing (Google Ads) to sell offline marketing (direct mail) and became a master of both. Mark currently works with a select few clients to dramatically increase their sales and fix operational systems that break with the added stress to their business. You can reach Mark at DirectlyResponsible.com.

## KEITH KRANCE

Keith Krance is the primary coauthor of the second and third editions of this book. He is the CEO and founder of Dominate Web Media, which provides Facebook Ads education courses, certifications, coaching, and full-agency ads management services to small businesses and large companies all over the world.

# Index

CPSIA information can be obtained
at www.ICGtesting.com
Printed in the USA
JSHW021457010921
18307JS00004B/4